Journalism Administration

Journalism Administration

Hari Mohan Agarwal
(M.A., Ph.D.)

Reference Press

4831/24, Ansari Road
Darya Ganj
New Delhi-110 002
Phone: 51563444
Fax: 51563334
E-mail: info@essessreference.com
url: http://www.essessreference.com

First Published 2005

ISBN: 81-88583-94-4

Rs.725/-

Published by:
Reference Press
4831/24, Ansari Road, Darya Ganj,
New Delhi-110 002.
Phone: 51563444
Fax: 51563334
E-mail: info@essessreference.com
url: http://www.essessreference.com

Printed in India at:
Mehra Offset Press, New Delhi

CONTENTS

Preface *vii*

1. **The Organisation** **1**
Framework of Newspapers • Real Picture Presentation • Points in Favour • Newspapers Abroad • Issues of Controversy • As an Industry • Competition in the Market

2. **Structural Setup** **65**
Setup of Management • News Collection Sources • Contribution from Outside • Functions in a Process • Opposite Powers • Advertisement, a Necessity • Paper Pioneers • Page Design • Paper Arrangeent • Technical Aspects • Liability of the State • Working System

3. **Management for Development** **143**
Diverse Thoughts • Situation in India • Past Experiences • Different Kinds of Matters • Importance of Newspaper • Aims and Objectives • Success Story • The Instances • Positive Approach • Cardinal Norms • Local Periodicals • Diverse Steps

4. **Process and Devices** **189**
General Devices • Recording Process • Mechanical Trick • The Division • Various Modes • Goals and Objectives • Necessary Factors • Speech

Communication • Effective Means • Some Basic Issues • Various Methods • The Directions • Issue Discussion • Telephonic Consultation • Prior Meetings • Radio's Role • Public Message • Informal Manners • Discussion in a Mess • Audio News

5. **Magazine Setup** 249
Media, as a Force • The Impact • Different Aspects • Soap Opera • Strategy for Competition • Recent Wave • Technology's Role • Computer's Role • Writer's Role • Editor 's Role • Comparative Study

6. **Role of Press** 291
New Approach • The Effect • Practical Side

Bibliography 337

PREFACE

Journalism has become a significant aspect of life and society in contemporary world. Its various sides and wide reaches make it compulsory to administer, properly at a better level. The book in your hands deals with all the administrative aspects regarding the profession of journalism. Although journalism as a profession is part and parcel of private sector, yet, its administration is not free to exploit people. State liability and coordination with government bodies have still to contribute a lot. Therefore administration of journalism lies in dual hands.

Every press and media institution has its own administrative setup. It may be termed as managerial administration. It is responsible to law for all its acts. On the other hand media is under the control of state also. Press activities are controlled by various Acts, rules, codes and norms. It is called controlling the administration.

This book named 'Journalism Administration' deals with each aspect of Journalistic setup and management for development of administrative measures. Process and devices are important points of our discussion.

Language of the book creates no problem to go through it. Subject matter is explained in easy and concise manner. Point wise discussions are in stylistic presentation. All these characteristics make this book reader-friendly and valuable.

Author

1

THE ORGANISATION

Framework of Newspapers

Editor : (a) relations with owner, individual proprietor; partners; private or public limited company or charitable trusts; relations with publishers, printers and public; (b) need for clear line of authority and division of responsibility for policy and production process, relations with staff of Editorial Department and with the Business Section (advertisement, circulation and accounts); Promotion (public relation); Circulation (readers' preferences) and Printing Department (for flow of copy, etc.);

Structure Depends on Nature of Organization : (a) single edition; (b) multiple edition (printing only), multiple edition (chains); multiple-language editions—Joint Editor, Managing Editor, Associate Editor, Executive Editor, Guest Editor — (for book page, arts, fashion, etc.);

Editorial Conference : Editor and Assistant Editors (News, Views, News-Views, Magazine, Art, etc.); News Editor;

News Editor : Deputy, Chief Sub, Senior Sub, Sub-Editor, Sports, Conference Editor — managerial function (flow of copy to press, make-up etc.); editorial function; liaison with reporting section; selection and distribution of copy to sub-editor with instructions on length, headline, etc., coordination; and

Sub-Editor : main tasks—qualifications (general, technical), need for alert mind, quick decisions, cool temper — relations with other colleagues, with superiors and the printing department; rights —Working Journalists Act; professional training; efficient discharge of his tasks, whatever his position in the hierarchy, decides his progress—individual and professional.

Editing General Principles

News Editing : Process by which information is presented to readers in entertaining way for their enlightenment on current affairs—rush of modern life newsflow varied and of complex implications —extraction of relevant material from this vast newsflow.

Reader's Requirements : News is what man is interested in as an individual and as member of a society — food, shelter, clothing, transport, religious and social differences, national and international problems, differences of publication owing to differences in locale, complexion of population, etc., variety of publications — for laymen and experts, etc., — Form Follows Function.

Fourth Estate : Fourth Estate is the press of England. What are the other three estates ? Lords, Temporal and Spiritual and Commons — modern newspapers not mere chroniclers of news but interpreters as democracy requires well informed and enlightened public opinion —catering to popular interest not enough, public interest must be considered.

Basic Responsibilities : Salesmanship aspect — reader as customer — financial viability — advertisement and circulation — warning on threat to freedom of press and hazards of journalistic profession for advertiser's pressures and public lobbying—responsibility to reader —reliable information, entertaining presentation, and enlightenment.

Code of Ethics

Reporter vs. Editor : Why editing ? Reporter gathers news and is primarily responsible for selection and bright and brisk presentation — but editor makes sure the account is well stressed, organized, uses aids like headlines, pictures, charts, sketches etc. to draw the reader's attention — reporter not infallible, rush in getting news makes report defective — editor acts as second mind.

Five W's and one H : Main Factors—what, who, when, where, why and how—editor rearranges details to dramatise value — meticulous examination of details—eliminates editorial expression from news—news is sacred but comment is free — check-up on details —simplicity of language and style deletes trivia, absurdities, irrelevancies, emotionalism, propaganda —care to avoid identification of the speaker and reporter. Coordination with other news of the day.

Warning : In rearranging and rewriting reporter's copy.

Editor should preserve the spirit and personality of the reporter and as far as possible, the words of the reporter—no change for mere changes sake — change only to make the news element a unity, cohesive and emphatic, for greater impact on the reader.

Copy Matter

Copy Received by : 1. post; 2. telephone; 3. telegram; 4. cable and wireless; 5. teleprinter circuit — news agencies; 6. monitoring of radio and television programmes; 7. lift journals.

Types of Copy : 1. City — local news from own reporter or news agencies; 2. District and mofussil correspondents; 3. State and Union capitals; 4. Foreign news from abroad; 5. News, Views, News plus Views:— special articles from own correspondents — Letters to Editors, official information, crime, education, etc.

Copy Content : 1. political, economic and social developments; 2. statements and speeches — press conferences and interviews; legislature proceedings; 3. arts, film, drama, etc.; 4. sports; 5. commerce; 6. gossip — personal column; 7. births and deaths-accidents-sickness-morgue; 8. weddings — birth anniversaries, etc.; 9. human stories from occasional correspondents.

Sources of Copy : 1. Government, the biggest source in India — Secretariat and other offices, Collectorates; 2. Public sector and private sector firms — industries; trade unions; 3. Political parties and politicians; 4. Economic and social organisations; 5. Universities, College managements and students, teacher bodies; 6. Syndicated copy articles, comic strips, etc.; 7. Public utility services; 8. Embassies of foreign countries.

"Tasting" copy for "Slant", Colour and Advertisement passing off as "News"

Distinction between News and Propaganda : Difficult to draw a line, while suppression as well as overmuch publicity will hamper the journalist's service to his readers, total withdrawal is bad; essence of propaganda is selection and spread of ideas or news to induce a desired belief or action — transmission or opinion to influence people — the selectiveness pertains not only to content but also to the decision in what page, in what proportion and in which position and with what typographical emphasis the news should appear.

Propaganda Devices : They are *Amoral* like any other tool of knowledge — either for or against particular cause, person or event —1. Name Call, 2. Glitter, 3. Transfer or usurpation of ideas, functions like fast, Crusades; 4. Testimonial from VIPs—Tyranny of minority opinion, 5. Band Wagon — use of religious symbols, colours, music and slogans — tyranny of majority; 6. Card-stacking giving selective stimuli; and 7. Conspiracy of silence.

If these devices do not accord with the responsibilities of the journalists, they should not be adopted. If the propaganda is harmless, or helpful and does not affect professional standards and is subversive of the above responsibilities, then they may be considered innocuous and used.

Distinguish between colourful and coloured reports.

What was mentioned above is what the journalist should avoid. What follows is what he should guard against, that is, in the above, he should avoid making the readers victims of his propaganda; and in what follows, he should avoid becoming a victim of propaganda by others.

1. Handouts — picked news; 2. Made News — circumstances are created to give publicity to an idea, to a prominent person or organisation etc.; 3. Hoax; 4. Camouflaged public service; 5. Polluted news; 6. Free publicity, professional publicity-mongers— problem of inclusion of who gave the news and why — the inclusion will remove the poisonous effect of such propaganda.

Buying space for advertisement should not be confused with

the pressure to invade news columns — difficulties in drawing a strict line — should hotel names be used in accidents or receptions, so also hospitals, lawyers, doctors, etc. — police reports require mention of police personnel if they are news sources.

Change from region to region, state to state readership differences even within the family, influence of edition time, place of occurrence, developing news, essential and non-essential aspects, advt. and dummy.

Gatekeeper's Function : (a) What item should go into the publication; (b) in what detail and length; (c) where it should go on page; (d) with what typographical emphasis; (e) role of aids like pictures, cartoons, sketches, tables etc. How to make the reader concentrate on what the editor thinks is important and should be read immediately.

For selection of news relates to the specific aims of the publication, maintenance of standards of the profession and catering to the tastes and interests of the readership — popular versus public interest.

Criteria for Selection of News : Immediacy or timeliness, immediate import of interest, writing about strikes etc., preparing the reader to meet an eventuality, background information about what has happened or is about to happen — Cauvery waters and famines etc.

Proximity : (a) geographical news from one's own birthplace of where one studies or works: familiarity; (b) ideological: one's interests, ideological affiliation ; specialists etc.

Prominence : Activities of prominent people, ministers, actors, etc., events in prominent localities: overshadowing nature in Indian Press.

Physical conflicts like communal and caste clashes, wars among nations, war against diseases, inventions and discoveries produce changes, beneficial or harmful — fibre replaces cotton, automation renders people jobless, reservation, dissatisfaction.

Removal of slums, new slums for old, pangs of progress, new problems.

Events for which the reader is least prepared— if Smt. Indira

Gandhi announces retirement from public life etc. — suspense over actor's condition — snags in spacecraft will be concern to people till the snags are removed.

Sex : Issues like sex education, sexual jealousy, murder, etc.— discoveries about sex motivation — use of sex hormones.

Oddity : Odd behaviour of prominent persons — millionaire willing away his fortune for gods; ear-boring ceremony for cat etc.

Role of emotions, issues of universal interest —suffering elicits sympathy, but false sympathy is dangerous — a man sacrificing his life for another, animals in distress, prevention of cruelty to animals in drug industry, should it be done or not. News of value may not always be apparent. It has to be sought after.

Creation of News Interest : Editorial campaign for the benefit of the community.

How much and what kind of crime news should be printed ?

Newspapers probably are reproached more for reporting crime news than for any other reason. The critics say that newspapers make crime by reporting crime.

The factors which make crime news may be summarised as follows :

Prominence of Persons : Wealth and position count in any kind of story, but especially when there is proof of wrong doing.

Prominence of Place : The same test applied to familiar things and places whenever they serve as background.

Property Loss : If all other factors balance, the property loss gauges the news value.

Mystery and Suspense : As long as the police are baffled, news interest thrives and expands. The moment the case is solved, interest dies.

Unique Circumstances : Anything startling, novel, or peculiar especially if it relates to the motive that promoted the act, strengthens the news bond.

Emotional Pull : Police reporters probably unearth more human interest stories than any members of the staff, with the possible exception of reporters.

Gruesomeness and Melodrama : The first lesson a crime reporter learns is that he must eliminate repellent details from his copy. If he fails to do so, the sub-editors will do it for him. This means little colour.

News Desk : There are two kinds of news editors. There is the passive news editor who reacts like a chief clerk in a government office through whom everything must pass, but who does not initiate or inspire any action. Then there is the active news editor who initiates and directs the operation of news gathering. The active news editor's work produces the news on which the paper exists; the page for topical features; the inspiration for dramatic pictures, cartoons and illustrations; and the occasion and theme for the commentaries, columns and leaders.

An active news editor's job is to sell his readers what his fellow beings have been doing since the last issue of his newspaper appeared. How can a news desk be made active ? Mainly in checking the stock sources of news :

1. Government and official news; News about the head of the State, Cabinet, the Legislature and the Administration.
2. Meeting of the legislature, local bodies and subsidiary agencies of Government such as State, Corporation, etc.
3. Functions attended by Ministers, Officials, V.I.Ps.
4. Activities, movements and statements of people already known to the public or interesting to the public such as businessmen, entrepreneurs, scientists, educators, sportsmen, filmstars, cultural and religious leaders, etc.
5. Accidents, crimes, litigation, police.
6. Health and hospitals.
7. Births, marriages and deaths.
8. Money and business.
9. Cultural and religious events.
10. Science and economic news.

These ten themes span a wide range of human activity and interest and should be rigorously exploited to develop news possibilities.

A fundamental general rule for active news editors to remember. It is not enough for a newspaper to report what the Government and the public does. It must report what the public feels, thinks, hopes and fears.

Our newspapers make nothing like enough use of illustrations. This makes them weak in two fundamental ways. They are not telling the news as effectively as they could. And they are failing to use one of the fundamental means of bringing colour and variety: the forbidding greyness of their newspapers.

The old Chinese proverb is still true today : One picture is equal to a thousand words. Not all photographers are genius but an ordinary run-of-the-mill photographer will respond and can produce good news pictures if he is told what to look for. But to begin with, he must, of course, have sufficient technical knowledge to take good pictures.

The newspaperman has to bear two things in mind when he considers photographs for publication. He has to consider the photograph's technical value and also its editorial value. Since you will almost inevitably lose some of the detail in your photographs in reproduction, what you want, technically, is a picture with sharp detail and large pattern. Look for a picture that shows crisply the various gradations of grey —the halftone — that bring out the contents on a face or a building. This sharp detail is called "contrast".

With a mediocre picture, "crop" for the most interesting part and enlarge that for reproduction. The best motto here is one used by the staff of the *Vancouver Sun :*

"If a picture is great it deserves to be played big." If it's an ordinary picture it needs to be played big.

It is far easier to get a photograph technically suitable for reproduction than to find one worth printing on strict editorial values. Judgement comes into this of course but there are a number of useful tests you can bear in mind.

Does the Picture Live ? Every news picture must tell a story at a glance. The best pictures show life happening. They show suspended animation, you might say. They capture something that is there one minute, gone the next.

Is it posed ? In the very best news pictures the subject is not conscious at all of the camera. Then the people in your pictures must be active. Not the "line up" or "firing squad" pictures. You know the sort of thing a group of people lined up like condemned men facing a firing squad. They look straight into the camera. They do nothing else. What kind of story does the picture tell ?

Can you see anything ? Another reason why you should avoid the ordinarily squad group pictures is that most times you cannot even see who the people are in them. If you must use a group picture (say, of a football team) you must make it big or otherwise the individual faces will not reproduce in the newspaper.

Edit pictures for size, shape and detail. A strong vertical stress is an effective shape of picture for a newspaper.

A strong horizontal stress is also striking. Almost invariably you should make the picture bigger than you first thought.

Most newspaper photographs are improved by "cropping" — cutting out unnecessary background detail.

Crop pictures for two reasons: First, you will be getting rid of a good deal of fussy clutter.

Secondly, crop because it will give you more space to display the main points of interest.

Captions : All the rules of news writing apply to writing captions. Captions should be written in short, pithy sentences. They must tell who is in the picture, what they are doing, where they are doing it, when were they doing it, why were they doing it. Give full names to identify everyone in the picture; and be accurate.

Captions should supplement what we can see with our eyes. A caption of a picture showing Mrs. Gandhi speaking should not just say "Mrs. Gandhi speaking." We can see that. The caption should say, even in a sentence, what she addressed the people about.

Overlines or Titles : The caption supplements what we can see with our eyes. The overline never does that. It merely sums up what we can see in an arresting fashion.

News in our Time : Mass communication has given us a

window on the world, and we often might not like what we see through it. But without the news, we would be without the means to correct the ills and injustices of modern-day life.

In his recent book *Eyewitness to History,* the distinguished English professor John Carey tells of how a correspondent from *The Times* of London was sent to France to cover the Franco-Prussian War of 1870. After the decisive battle of Sedan, he rushed back to England by train and ferry boat, staying up all right to write his account of the German victory. He arrived only to find that competing newspapers had published reports of the event sent by electric telegraph two days earlier. *The Times* had literally blundered into a new era in western society — an era in which the news from almost everywhere is available to almost everyone every hour of every day.

The improvement in the transmission of the news coincided with improvements in printing and paper making technology which made possible the speedy production of huge quantities of daily newspapers that could be sold at minimal prices. Meanwhile the spread of literacy owing to compulsory education was opening up a mass market for the "peny press". Soon the ordinary people of the United States, Britain and Western Europe had a ready means of learning what was going on in the world, a privilege once reserved for a relatively small literate minority. Public access to the news had been established : from there on it was merely a series of technological steps to today's 24-hour television news by satellite.

"Arguably the advent of mass communications represents the greatest change in human consciousness that has taken place in recorded history," Carey wrote. "The development, within a few short decades, from a situation where most of the inhabitants of the globe would have no day-to-day knowledge of or curiosity about how most of the others were faring, to a situation where the ordinary person's mental space is filled (and must be refilled daily or hourly unless a feeling of disorientation is to ensue) with accurate reports about the doings of complete strangers represents a revolution in mental activity which is incalculable in its effects."

Public access to national and international news has deeply influenced popular culture, politics, and even philosophy. It has given ordinary men and women a more humanistic and tolerant outlook on life by making them empathize with all of humanity. New reports force us to look human suffering in the face, and make us want to do something about it, whether to donate money to aid disaster victims or call on our governments to put pressure on other governments to stop committing injustices. In the age of the news, no man is an island. We cannot help but be, as John Donne put it, “involved in mankind”.

So pervasive is the news in western countries that it has become one of life’s necessities. There are, of course, times when it is absolutely necessary to know what is happening for our own well-being, as when a hurricane is heading in the direction of where we live. But beyond immediate practical information, we need the news to help us cope with the pace and complexity of modern living. As the Canadian journalism professor Wilfred Eggleston wrote: “Survival of all living creatures requires an awareness of the changing environment .... Speedy and accurate information is required for people to react.”

Out of our need for news has evolved a principle which would never have been thought of in the days before the telegraph: that the public has a right to news that can be trusted. The Canadian Royal Commission on Newspapers broached this concept in 1981 by declaring that people have a “to inform themselves” which is inseparable from their right to express themselves. Canada is one country where the right to the news is enshrined in legislation. To hold a broadcast licence, every Canadian radio station must carry news reports.

The ability to keep track of what is happening and of what is being said is central of our system of government. “A people without reliable news is, sooner or later, a people without the basis of freedom,” political scientist Harold Laski wrote.

Wherever there is no political freedom, the news is always controlled — not only internal news, but news from abroad which invites comparisons with conditions elsewhere and exposes the repressed populace to “alien” ideas. No less a tyrant than Adolf Hitler objected fiercely to free reporting. “Our law concerning the press is such that divergences of opinion between members of the government are no longer an occasion for public exhibitions,” he said at the height of his power.

A man of an opposite cast of mind, the American statesman Thomas Jefferson, once declared that if he had to decide between government without newspapers and newspapers without government, he would choose the latter. At the same time Jefferson was the first to admit that the freedom of the press which he so eloquently upheld could be abused.

This freedom (which today covers the electronic media as well) is by no means unbridled. News organizations are not free, for instance, to ruin a person's reputation, to invade a person's privacy, or to subject a person to 'trial by publicity'. They are prohibited from doing such things by various laws.

Despite these legal constraints, news organizations remain very much responsible to themselves, and there is plenty of room for breaches of that responsibility. Newspapers, radio and television stations carry not only accounts of events, but commentary on those events. Writers and broadcasters of opinion do not need an array of indisputable facts to blacken a reputation or throw suspicion on the motives of an organization; sufficient to mix a few suggestive facts in with a lot of innuendo. A clever writer or editor with an axe to grind can paint a biased picture even in an apparently impartial report.

At one time it was left almost entirely up to newspaper proprietors and their sycophants to decide how much restraint would be applied on their ability to play with the facts, or to publish absolute falsehoods. Their papers frequently distorted the "news" to suit their own political objectives. Sensationalism ran rampant among hotly-competitive big city dailies. The truth was often slaughtered in the crossfire of their circulation wars.

For better or for worse (some say worse) the new generation of newspaper proprietors in North America are for the most part detached from day-to-day operations of papers they own, running large chains from corporate head offices. News organizations have become big businesses, whether their outlet is in print or by electronic means.

The decline of the old-time imperious press barons coincided with the rise of professional journalists who insist that their first duty is not to the boss but to the reader. Sensational dailies still exist, but beneath their splashy lay-out, they will usually be found to be quite scrupulous about getting their facts straight, at least in their news columns.

Today, any news organization worthy of the name pledges itself to ensure as far as possible that the news it presents is accurate, fair and balanced. While this has always been an informal understanding among ethical journalists, many organizations have adopted formal codes of ethics, and some employ ombudsmen to protect the public interest.

By adopting such self-restraint, the media have acknowledged that the dissemination of the news is not just another business. It is a form of public trust, not only because people need information to live out their everyday lives, but because the media have so much latent power. Power must be counterbalanced by responsibility, and news organizations have chosen to exercise that responsibility themselves, rather than risk the threat to democratic practice posed by having governments do it for them.

The greatest power of the media to influence public opinion lies not so much in their commentary on the news but in their selection and presentation of it. "Of course the people won't always vote the way the editorial-writers tell them on next week's sewer by law," observed the 1970 Canadian Senate Report on Mass Media; "but who decides when they'll start thinking and talking about sewers — or whether they'll worry about pollution at all ?"

Back in the comparatively simple world of 1920, the great American columnist Walter Lippmann wrote : "The news of the day as it reaches the newspaper office is an incredible medley of fact, propaganda, rumour, suspicion, clues, hopes, and fears, and the task of selecting and ordering the news is one of the truly sacred and priestly offices in a democracy."

All sorts of judgements come into play when a newspaper or new program is being produced: How long should a story be ? Should it come first, last, or in between ? Within the story itself, which points should be emphasized over others ? In a controversy, which spokesmen for which side should be quoted more prominently ? The answers to all these questions have a strong influence on what people think about issues and events.

How do editors and news directors choose what you will or will not hear about ? According to George Kennedy in his textbook *News Reporting and Writing,* there are five usual criteria: impact (what everybody will be talking about); proximity (all things being equal, something that happens a few streets away is bigger news than something that happens 1,000 miles away); timeliness (news has a short shelf life); prominence ("names make news"); conflict (as in strikes, politics, crime, sports competition); and novelty ("if a dog bites a man, that's not news; if a man bites a dog, that's news").

The yardsticks used by professionals to judge what makes news frequently come in for criticism from the public and its spokesmen. "Trouble : that's (what's) wrong with journalism's current definition of the news," complained the Senate Report on Mass Media. "There is more to life than hassle and strife, but the media's entertainment in drama, conflict and disruption prevents them from reporting it."

The trouble is that people like to hear about trouble as long as it is not happening to them, and the news is to a large extent "market driven". A perhaps apocryphal story is told in the business about a man who started a wire service which carried only good news, and promptly went broke.

It is an open question whether it is the consumers or processors of news who demand that it be delivered at great speed, but certainly any news organisation that is consistently beaten to the punch on stories would fear losing the market share to more alert competitors. Many of the failings of the media can be traced to the haste with which reports are prepared.

The scope for error is enormous when reporting is done in a rush, which is why newspapers and agencies obligate themselves to publish corrections when the inevitable mistakes occur. Speed breeds superficiality; when something is reported in a hurry, important details may be overlooked or misunderstood.

Real Picture Presentation

Even when the time to prepare a report is not unduly short, there is a constant danger of getting events or issues out of perspective. At a time when life is growing even more complicated, salient facts may be lost in the shuffle of all the considerations that come into play. Also, news people see things through their own pre-conditioned perceptions, and "the observers," as communications scholar P. W. Bridgman put it. They must deal with words, and words can be slippery. They sometimes pass on their biases to readers or listeners through their choice of language.

Reporters, as opposed to opinion journalists, traditionally have tried to keep their personal feelings and opinions out of their reports, but objectivity is not without its pitfalls. There is a decided difference between the facts and the truth. It might be a fact that a person involved in a newsworthy situation says something, but what he says might not be true. Still, his words must be reported objectively in the absence of evidence that they are lies.

The school of "new journalism" that grew up in the 1960s contended that true objectivity was a psychological impossibility and should, therefore, be dispensed with. In any case, the new journalists insisted, objectivity was merely an excuse for the established media to support the status quo on questions of justice that cried out for reform.

Though it was practised in the name of democracy, subjective reporting proved to be distinctly undemocratic, which perhaps explains why it is now discredited among most mainstream journalists. Its practitioners felt free to ignore the precept that there are two sides to every story when one side did not agree with their point of view.

Worse, the freedom from the discipline of objectivity blurred the distinction between personal interpretation of the facts and pure fiction: It became just too tempting for some writers not to invent convenient "facts" when a story was (so they thought) written from such a personal point of view that no one could check up on it. In several cases, someone did check up, and found that stories had been falsified.

Although members of every profession will occasionally bring it into disgrace, the cases of fabrication seemed to confirm the views of those who regard the entire media with unwavering suspicion Such derelictions are, in fact, very uncommon. The great majority of writers and editors strive intently to ensure the integrity of the news.

People who excoriate the sins of the media frequently fail to differentiate between reportage and commentary. The media themselves sometimes contribute to the confusion by mixing the two in the form of "interpretative reporting" and not clearly identifying the line between the verifiable facts and what the writer speculates those facts might mean.

Mostly, though, people who rail against the media are indulging in the time-honoured sport of shooting the messenger. They are upset by the endless chronicle of folly and evil which journalists deliver—"the usual depravities and businesses and hypocrisies and cruelties" which Mark Twain said could be found in any morning's news. It is natural enough to want to ascribe blame for all the tumult and grief that seems to surround us. And so journalists are blamed for going out of their way to make the world look worse than it is.

This is particularly so in the case of "investigative reporting," which digs out news rather than waiting for it to happen. The public sometimes seems to have more sympathy with the subjects of revelations of misbehaviour than with the journalists who have uncovered them. "There they go again," people will say. "Why do they have to tell us these things ? Why not let sleeping dogs lie?"

The answer is that our society would be a lot worse off if media did not play such a role; the fear of being exposed is a strong deterrent to corruption. Granted, the media sometimes go too far in their pursuit of real or supposed villains. That is one reason why there are now press councils in many parts of North America. The councils are there to see that, in their lust for justice, the media do not commit injustices themselves.

The most commonly-heard complaint against the purveyors of news is that they "blow things out of proportion". In the most general terms, they certainly do. The bad news which comprises the bulk of national and international reports is out of proportion to the great mass of "good news" that is never reported. At any given hour, nine-tenths of human affairs around the world are proceeding peacefully, smoothly and safely. The stuff of headlines is the other aberrant one-tenth, or less.

Walter Lippmann said that the task of news people is to provide a picture of reality upon which men can act, but the news does not and cannot reflect the whole of reality. Still, it does give us grounds for action to build a better world. There are times when we would prefer not to know just how stupid and bad human beings can be, but if we did not know about it, we would never be able to correct the stupidity and badness. The news is a necessary evil in the advancement of civilization. It might even be said that there can be no civilization without the news.

Open to all parties, but influenced by none.

Only a courageous publisher supported by an inspired, intelligent, and dynamic editorial staff ably augmented by knowledgeable, efficient and dedicated "reporters" can find his greatest fulfilment as a newspaper man.

A newspaper cannot please everyone every day. The newspaperman must know his public : it will help if the reader knows something of the problems of the reporter and the editors, and how they go about solving them.

The newspaper is produced for commercial gain, sold under highly competitive conditions, and must have careful business management. If it is not issued for sale so as to make a profit, it is not a distinct individual, but a part or adjunct of something else. If published to advance any cause, it is an organ, not a newspaper. It cannot be independent unless it earns its living.

The perfect newspaper will be the voice of the lowly and oppressed and forgotten people, champions of the underdog. If in discharge of its responsibility especially in the present "restless world" — it occasionally troubles the public conscience, that is not to its credit. If it is a defender of civil liberty and a friend of righteous causes it is performing a worthy service. Its chief function is to hold up a mirror to the happenings of the day. If it is careful to keep the mirror clean and as flawless as possible, the reflections will be honest, clear and interesting.

Newspaper writing and newspaper reading are not jobs for people who cannot, when necessary, look at a subject objectively. The reader needs to distinguish between knowledge and guessing, between trained and casual observation, between verification and credulousness.

The urge to play up conflict in print and in conversation is widespread, and newspapers might improve their image by curbing it.

News is accurate information about any event of public or human interest, of the record of significant acts or opinions. It tells about something that is different from daily routine.

Two attributes of the good newspaper reporter today are selection and sincerity. He knows what incident to include to give his canvas the image of life, and he cannot be induced to omit an iota of what he believes to be essential. He is neither too dainty to face facts as they are, nor too blind to discern their full significance, but he will not revel in the unhealthy or set down anything in malice. He is true to the facts whether he is writing an account of a college concert or a report of the clash of events in world politics.

The press is not free if those who operate it behave as though their position conferred upon them the privilege of being deaf to ideas which the processes of free speech have brought to public attention.

Just as the citizen tries to order his life so as to live decently, effectively and fruitfully, so a newspaper can contribute to its generation by telling the news in accord with the principles of honesty, impartiality, integrity, accuracy and fairness.

The editorial writer with a sense of responsibility will try to give his readers a balanced presentation of basic facts, tell the purpose of proposed action suggest alternatives, and illuminate the whole matter by his soulful thought.

The word press signifies newspapers, magazines, journals or dailies or periodicals in general. Subject matters to publicise or as reported in the press. Press release signifies to make news known publicly or to allow news to be made known publicly. An advertisement, for instance, is released of a product recently introduced in the market. Press release is a statement given to newspapers, reporters etc. Government corporations, institutions issue press releases to inform the public. Press and news media are powerful, and generally influential to project an image to the public. Indian Press is free press and the people have much faith in the press. The press can effectively communicate to the public.

The press transmits facts, figures, symbols to the readers. It is an objective announcement about a particular matter or event issued to the press for publication to inform the public in time. The press has every right to publish any news item intact or in condensed form. It all depends on its news-worthiness and importance. A press release is not confined only to news items of Government, politics, national and international events. Press releases include advertisements, appointments, legal notices, growth of industry, government notifications, guidelines, achievements, activities, marriages, entertainment, rentals, seminars etc.

A press release is effective only when it satisfies qualities like information, which is concise, clear, and devoid of hackneyed publicity materials. Selection of a newspaper or newspapers for the subject matter and the circle of readers for whom it is meant are the deciding factors for the effectiveness of any press release. They are closely related with each other.

Evidently the wrong selection of newspaper(s) for the publication of any fact is a matter of great significance to achieve the objectives of release. Therefore, in any press release the right selection of newspapers and its significance cannot be overemphasised.

A few illustrations of recent press releases are as under :

Illustration 1

Office of the Andhra Pradesh

Housing Board

'Gruhakalpa' Mukarramjahi Road,

Hyderabad

Press Note : In the Notification No. 13/92 issued calling for applications for allotment of houses at Ongole, the cost of application is mentioned as Rs. 35/- and by post Rs. 25/- by oversight instead of Rs. 25/- and Rs. 35/- respectively. Therefore, it is informed that the applications can be had in person by paying Rs. 25/- and Rs. 35/- by post from the office of the Regional Housing Engineer, A.P. Housing Board, Vijaywada.

For Vice Chairman & Housing Commissioner.

Illustration 2

Wanted Distributors

A company manufacturing PCs and State-of-art new generation Fax machines wishes to appoint area-wise distributors who are : Financially sound. Professionally managed. Having good track record in the field.

Apply within 10 days with full details along with bank references.

To

The Chief Executive,

XYZ Company Limited 15,

Anandha Road Alwarpet,

Madras 600018.

Illustration 3

X.Y. GROUP Requires

Two

Company

Secretaries

For Their New Delhi Offices

The candidates must be members of the Institute of Company Secretaries of India. Past experience is not necessary. Please apply with salary expected within 10 days to :

The Managing Director

X. Y. Group Limited

12, New Colony,

Model Basti

New Delhi-110005.

Illustration 4

Steel Authority of India Limited

(A Government of India Enterprise)

Rourkela Steel Plant

Rourkela-769 011 Orissa Office of the Additional General Manager (MM)

Purchase Department Sub : Second Corrigendum

To Tender Notice No : P/Proj/Modn/4011899124 for signalling and Truck Inter Connection Package under Phase-II Modernisation of Rourkela Steel Plant.

Sl.No.2.0 First line for existing entry please read as the Tender documents will be available for sale from 30-6-1990 to 21-7-1992.

Sl.No.2.1 First line in place of 10-7-1992 please read as "31-8-1992." All other conditions of the tender notice shall remain unaltered.

Registered Office :

Ispat Bhavan,

Lodhi Road,

New Delhi-110 003.

Illustration 5

Notice inviting Tender

Sealed tenders are invited for design, manufacture, supply, erection, testing, commissioning of FEED systems for the Banbury Mixer at our Kankinara Works, West Bengal.

Tender documents can be obtained from Materials Manager (Project), at the address given below on all working days between 10.00 a.m. and 2.00 p.m. up to 21-6-90. Last date of submission of bid completed in all respects is 21-7-90.

Type Corporation of India Ltd.

(A Government of India Enterprise). 19, Jawaharlal Nehru Road, Calcutta - 700 087.

Mass Media Guidelines

1. The sacredness of human personality has to be the vital content of any mass media reporting.
2. Must ever be alive to responsible reporting in this restless world.
3. Newspapers must be open to all parties but influenced by none.

4. Only a courageous publisher supported by an inspired, intelligent and dynamic editorial staff ably supported by knowledgeable. Efficient and dedicated "reporters" can find his greatest fulfilment as a newspaper man.
5. In this imperfect world of "Man, the unknowns," people practising different professions tend to forget the Code of Ethics. Though "Journalism" is a profession, it has to be considered as a mission. Only a sincere "opposition" and an aggressive press could be the guardians of democracy.
6. From being a "reporter" he should endeavour to combine velocity and facility and become a "social scientist".
7. The perfect newspaper will be the voice of the lowly and oppressed and forgotten people, champion of the underdog. Its chief function is to hold up a mirror to the happenings of the day. If it is careful to keep the mirror clean and as flawless as possible, the reflections will be honest, clear and interesting.
8. The urge to play up conflict in print and in conversation is widespread, newspapers might improve their image by curbing it.
9. News is accurate information about any event of public or human interest, or the record of significant acts of opinions. It tells about something that is different from daily routine.
10. The press is not free if those who operate it behave as though their position conferred upon them the privilege of being deaf to ideas which the processes of free speech have brought to public attention.
11. Just as the citizen tries to order his life so as to live decently, 'effectively and fruitfully, so a newspaper can contribute to its generation by reporting the news in accord with the principles of honesty, impartiality, integrity, accuracy and fairness.

Points in Favour

Not only does the newspaper have greater merit than the radio because it is the older of the two media, but also because of the special advantages and conveniences offered by it. The radio listener has to adjust himself to the timings and place of the station, while the reader can take his paper wherever he likes, go through it at leisure and re-read a part which he likes. Even the appearance of the "Radio-Newspaper" and its possible development does not alter the position because the newspaper can give much, much greater variety.

In this era when prompt supply of news is of paramount importance, the radio sometimes beats the newspaper in the game. But even this occasional beating only whets public appetite to read more and at greater leisure about important developments in the reader's favourite newspaper. The ghost that the radio and the press are rivals has been laid to rest long ago.

Illiteracy which is a large chink in our armour, is no obstacle in the case of the radio as it is in the case of the newspaper. The vast areas of the countryside can be opened up and brought under the educative influence of the radio by installing more community sets. The regional radio stations lay more and more emphasis to rural programmes.

Radio-mindedness is limited mainly by one's paying capacity. If the radio sets could be made and sold at cheaper rates and the Central, State and other local taxes on them are brought down, it will be a boon to the lower and middle classes and to people living in the villages.

Despite competition from the radio and the TV the newspaper is undergoing a tremendous revolution not only in respect of new ideas and new methods in editing but also in the introduction of new printing procedures and machines. The major consideration of the print media today is how to catch the interest and attention of the reader so that he continues as ever to wait anxiously for the morning newspaper. There is an attempt to put greater variety in coverage, more human value stories and the lighter type of matter which may inform, instruct and provide entertainment at the same time. Newspapers are becoming more and more humanized.

With the printing revolution already going fast, newspapers, especially weeklies, fortnightlies and monthlies, are using modern methods of offset printing in which many colours are combined to give a better visual effect.

A country's political system (stemming from the political ideology) is obviously related to the direction and speed of a country's total national development. If this assumption be true, then media and national development join in a kind of symbiotic relationship of a complex nature. It is this symbiotic relationship that has been consuming more and more time and effort of researchers and theorists in the related fields of journalism, sociology and political science since about the middle of this century.

Editors and writers are a highly individualistic group who maintain fairly high standards of competence and integrity in evaluating information they pass on to their readers. Newspapers are as much a public utility as water, electricity, gas or transportation. Because they are essential to the smooth functioning of a political democracy and a free enterprise economic system, newspapers keep the public interest foremost in their day-to-day judgement of news.

Newspapers Abroad

The legislature, the judiciary, the executive and the press are the four pivotal pillars on which modern democracy is built. The press, as the Fourth Estate, it should safeguard the principles of democracy by effective dissemination of information. The press plays a paramount role in a democracy, it is not known as the Fourth Estate for nothing. Secularism, socialism, democracy, self-reliance and constitutional values are the important factors to move towards liberalisation of Indian newspaper industry. There should not be any discrimination on the grounds of religion, race, caste or creed.

"The approach to foreign media has been governed by considerations of larger national interest and has ever been and ought not to be treated merely as an issue of economic policy". (N.Ravi, The Hindu).

Issues of Controversy

There is a great deal of controversy and views on the concept of foreign print media. It is nothing but liberalisation of newspaper industry like other economic sectors liberalised and globalised. In other words it is the presence of foreign press on Indian soil. Allowing foreign print media is giving permission to the big foreign newspaper business concerns to commence publishing in India it is a step towards globalisation with liberalisation. The free entry of newspaper and periodicals permits foreign print media to print and publish news and views from India. As a result foreigners directly print and distribute their news. Free foreign print media is possible only with the Government policy of liberalisation to the newspaper industry. The trend in media ownership in recent global village is towards large and free foreign newspapers. The concept of going global has become most popular in recent years in media industries as print, film, broadcast, cable, satellite, marketing and advertising organisations have been expanding their activities across frontiers. Globalisation of newspaper industry with liberalisation policy represents nothing more than trans nationalisation which affects substantially domestic activities.

Communication is the heart of all social interactions. Our worlds in its communication dimension consists of nations affiliated to United Nations. The basis for globalisation is that people cannot live in isolation and human solidarity.

In the year 1955 the Government withheld permission to foreign nationals to own newspapers in India. In the year 1956 the Government laid down that foreign news agencies have to operate in the country by collaborating with Indian news agencies and not directly. The entry of foreign print media also had been thoroughly examined by the first press commission. The ban on foreign nationals running newspapers in the country was imposed during the period of Jawaharlal Nehru. According to Mr. Justice Sarkaria,' 'the ban was imposed in the national interest when the nation's integrity and security was endangered by fissiparous forces operating from within and outside the country".

The major problems of newspaper industry in this country are:

1. Declining sales.
2. Increasing competition.
3. High price.
4. Uneconomic rates.
5. Time and language.

6. Lack of direct servicing wires to all newspapers.
7. Liberalisation policy helping electronic media to huge sums by way of advertisement revenues.
8. Multiple channel.
9. Foreign satellite.
10. Video and cable TV.
11. The advertisement rates of the Government advertisements are uneconomic and lowest commercial rates.
12. Introduction of colour pages by some newspapers, which small newspapers cannot afford.

The recent trend is that the advertisement revenue which other wise would have gone to the print media is now being diverted to the electronic media. The advertisements rates fixed for Government advertisements through Directorate of Advertising x and Visual Publicity (DAVP) are not reasonable. Print media have been facing the problem and challenges from radio, television and is now computing with the electronic media in the form of internet, cyberspace.

There has been a wide debate over the open door proposal for foreign media and its possible threat to the Indian free press. There are different opinions and wide spectrum of views. Editors, and media barons, politicians and intellectuals, and even readers form a part of the wide spectrum of views, divided down the line.

There are supportive of the entry of foreign print media and some objected the same. While some people say the entry of foreign media is not a harmful, while others perceive a threat to Indian free press. On the other hand some people adopts middle path, in view of globalisation, opening the doors to foreign publishing houses may not pose much of a problem provided adequate steps are taken to ensure that their operations are regulated and controlled to safeguard national interest.

No unanimity may emerge on controversial and sensitive issue like this, because it is a question of defending sovereignty, upholding national tradition in a multi-cultural and multilingual country like India. Allowing free entry of foreign print media may, however, require an amount of national consensus.

The ideas and opinions are so sharply divided over whether or not to allow the entry of foreign print media in India. There is no consensus of unanimity on the matter. Opinions widely differ between journalists, politicians, lawyers, academicians and social activities. Interestingly enough the trend is against the entry of foreign media.

It is all above theoretical proposition and it is difficult to see how the Netty of foreign media would work and help Indian press with highest level of professional conduct, standards, latest technology.

However, under the following paragraphs, the merits and demerits of foreign print media are presented.

The Merits

1. Foreign print media would help to get huge investment, new technology and varied expertise and experience. For improving the printing technology and publishing technique and for giving boost to Indian journalism, foreign media are partly recommended, it brings in capital, technology and professional advise.
2. Foreign and Indian press working together would help expand the perception of Indians on multifarious issues of global nature. The open door policy permits a wholesome view of cultural cross currents taking place, in a global village.
3. Allowing foreign print media promotes a healthy competitive spirit and entrepreneur ship in Indian newspaper industry.
4. In a free global village foreign entry into newspaper industry, anybody can own a paper .
5. Allowing the foreign print media in the country in the name of liberalisation would help expanding knowledge.
6. The advent of foreigners into a newspaper industry would bring about an improvement in professional standards of journalism and communication by way of stiff competition. The entry of foreign media would help in widening the perception of the Indians in the matters of both national and international.

7. Foreign newspapers offer higher salaries, perks, and better working conditions, better prospects, career opportunities, greater mobility, better working environment. Thus foreign media will snatch the cream of the Indian journalist by offering better monetary benefits.
8. Foreign print media promote fast declining cultural values. The presence of foreign media reflects credible global cultural revolution brought about by sophisticated printing, phototype and electronic technology.
9. Be global and by global is the order in these days of information revolution and communication age.
10. The target readership of the foreign news papers would mainly be the english reading urbanites.
11. There is no fear of professional competition. Indian journalists are professionally competent with anyone in the world. In respect of standards and professional code the Indian journalists are not lagging behind.
12. Some of the newspapers in India are tied up with some business houses which filter the news and fair views. While some newspapers are bias of political parties and religious sects. The foreign media eliminates this environment in view of competition, standards and other commercial considerations. The problem of politically biased and editorials tailored to sub-serve the politico-business interest may exit from Indian newspaper industry.

The inflow of well known foreign newspapers will not only destabilise the english language Indian newspaper, but also the regional and small language propers through advertisement revenue diversion and readership. It is not advantageous to the vernacular press which may vehemently oppose the idea of entry of foreign media which would be a total disaster as it would irreversibly damage the pluralistick and relatively independent national press.

The Demerits

Be Indian and by Indian is the Indian slogan. The father of the Nation Mahatma Gandhi advocated Swadeshi in all fields.

1. The foreign press would definitely pose a direct danger to

the Indian language newspapers. In fact Indian language newspapers are the real moulders of the public opinion.

2. The concept of liberalisation and globalisation by no means have any relevance to the newspaper industry liberalisation, globalisation of newspaper cannot be equated in the same category of other economic sectors, it is a sensitive media of information and sensitive political matter. This sector is not an economic commodity.
3. The entry of foreign media would affect integrity, and security endangers by fissiparous forces operating from within and outside the country.
4. Giving foothold in the country to the outside newspaper, would endanger the free flow of information by Indian media holding different views.
5. As a powerful outside foreign may not show concern for Indias interest.
6. Editorial policy of foreign newspapers a cannot be controlled, as a result poses a greater danger of national security.
7. Presently small newspapers have been grapple a host of operating problems. The entry of foreign print media may very much affect adversely the small newspaper industry. So the entry of foreign news agencies is a real threat to the small papers. These papers already have been facing problems like competition, low circulation, paltry advertisement revenue and TV and radio drained the newspaper industry's advertisement revenues.
8. Allowing the entry of foreign media implies foreigners claiming right of freedom of expression which is fundamental right guaranteed by the constitution of India to the Indian citizens only but not to the foreigners. Every country has its own laws and constitutions to protect their respective print media and right of freedom of expression, thus provisions of Article 19 would be thrown open to non-citizens. Thus entry of foreign media into India may have some legal implications. Article 19 of the Constitution stipulates that all citizens shall have the right to freedom

of speech and expression. The provision of restriction of ownership of the press to citizens alone is correct one. Foreign corporations are not Indian citizens and hence have no fundamental right to force into our territory.

9. There is also an evident danger of foreign element taking advantage of a free entry to propagate terrorism, separatism, casteism and create social bitterness through publications. The anti-national element would exploit the advantages of press liberalisation to endanger the country.
10. Foreign print media are threat and would pose to nation's security and culture, national integrity, interest, tradition and native way of life. It amounts to cultural invasion.
11. Open door proposal allowing print media would adversely affect country's political and social through resulting foreign rule over Indian minds.
12. Foreign agencies publishing newspaper involves distribution of their news, only through the Indian means.
13. Foreign print media would definitely influence electorate and may endanger democracy.
14. Views are also there that foreign newspapers may lead to serious dent in the circulation and readership.
15. Indian newspaper and magazines are getting government advertisements, hence foreign media is a threat of the advertisement word.
16. It is quote possible to impose a restriction by foreign print media that the employees of the foreign-owned media should be foreigners.
17. The All India Newspaper Employees Federation, PTI Employees Union, National Union of Journalists, UNI Employees Federation and Media Watch Group, in the year 1994 express their opposition to the entry of foreign media on several grounds. There was a "Campaign against Entry of Foreign Media" (CARFORM) in 1994.

To Sum Up :

To summarise is foreign print media globalisation inevitable?

Is it necessary to globalise print media ?

Is global village homogenised ?

Are hybridised, synthesised and urbanised culture promote national interest ?

Globalisation of press or foreign media is not the same category as other economic sectors. Newspapers, through a part of national economic aspect, should not be considered like economic commodity, capital, technology etc. Because it is not an extension of economic policy, the press has social, cultural, national traditional values and commitments.

The conscious of social responsibility of the newspapers of a particular country should not be ignored. The media of the country ideally reflect the social and cultural values of the country, but foreign media do not. There is no doubt about the fact that the so called global society permits to know other cultures and civilization.

Foreign print media may be permitted to a very limited extent and in a restricted way to ventilate fair views under close monitoring. Parameters should be prescribed not causing harm to national integrity and friendly foreign relations.

The overwhelming majority of minus points submitted above indicate creation of an unfavourable environment that may likely be created with the foreign print media. But still it is not a conclusive opinion.

The entry on scientific, technical, educational and informative newspapers and journals can restrictively be permitted. Foreign publications should not be given blanket permission. Strict guidelines, code and standards can be prescribed. The screening procedure promotes quality publication and undesirable publications should be removed. Lower price and greater control over publications, ensuring majority Indian ownership by holding shares holding positions in the Board of Management and editors are some of the safeguarding measures.

Thus the issue is a sensitive. But invasion of foreign media poses a serious danger to the country's independence, sovereignty friendly relations, communal harmony.

As an Industry

Electronic communications were killing print. That judgement has proved wrong or at least premature. True, the antenna of the media picked up tremors in the mid-1970s indicating that Americans' reading and writing skills were declining, and by concentrating public attention on alarming statistics and assertions of decline, the media moved the tremors up the Richter scale. Popular and expert opinion quickly blamed television as a major villain. Particularly as the apparent decline coincided with a drop in newspaper circulation. The analysts so explained the statistics as to raise doubts that the decline was real; experts disagreed about whether or not a problem in fact existed, and if it did, just how serious it was; and historians pointed out that concern about declining literacy had surfaced before and seemed cyclical in nature. Nevertheless, the message through the media was that indeed Johnny could not read or write, and schools and universities were put on notice to do something. Then the media picked up other tremors in society and moved on. Because it lacked dramatic visual appeal, the "story" of declining literacy lent itself more to examination by the print than the electronic media, so illustrating an important point. Although the media all perform the same functions, they cannot in every instance perform them equally well. To some extent their competition for audiences and advertisers is at one another's expense, but each possesses sufficiently unique attributes for supplementary and complementary roles to survive. This chapter, discusses a dynamic not a dying communications technology.

Large Market Area : The creation of mass markets, which only large and costly units could service efficiently, has led inevitably to a contraction of ownership in many cities and towns and thus to the development of newspaper chains. The high point in the number of newspapers published in the United States came in 1909, when there were 2600 daily publications. On this situation, magazine publisher Frank Munsey commented, "There is no business that cries out so loud for organization and combination as that of newspaper publishing. For one thing, the number of newspapers is at least 60 percent greater than we need."

Munsey dreamed of a national chain of 500 newspapers and tried to start it by buying newspapers in New York, Washington, Boston, Baltimore, and Philadelphia. Although his chain failed, he pioneered an accelerating trend in twentieth-century publishing.

In the first half of the twentieth century, more than 2000 new daily newspapers (including those changing from weekly to daily) were started. But, during the same period, 1947 daily newspapers suspended publication to become weeklies, 547 disappeared through merger or consolidation, and at least 302 local combinations took place. At the same time the number of newspaper chains increased from three, publishing 62 newspapers, to 70 publishing 386, with more than two-fifths of the daily and one-half of the Sunday circulation. In the 1950s there were scarcely more than 100 cities with competing daily newspapers. Of the 1500 cities with daily newspapers in 1977, only 2.5 percent-fewer than 40-had competing newspapers. By then the nation's 168 chains owned three-fifths of the nation's 1756 daily newspapers and controlled 71 percent of the circulation.

According to journalist historian Frank Mott, consolidation of newspapers is not a strictly recent tendency, it can be found in all periods. But since World War I, the skyrocketing cost of newspaper publication has been a strong influence in accelerating the tendency to consolidate.

Melville E. Stone established the Chicago Daily News in 1876 with a few thousand dollars capital; in 1925 it sold for $13 million. In 1963 two Omaha dailies were sold for $43 million, and in 1967 Newhouse Newspapers bought the Cleveland Plain Dealer for $53.4 million, Knight Newspapers paid $55 million for two Philadelphia papers in 1969. In 1976 Rupert Murdoch, the Australian press baron, paid, according to Folio magazine's estimate, $30 million for the New York Post at a time when all three New York dailies were losing circulation (between March 1974 and September 1976, the Times dropped from approximately 910,000 daily to 802,000, the Daily News from 2.12 million to 1.93 million, and the Post from 650,000 to 489,000).

In the typical American town in earlier days, more newspaper publishing ventures were attempted than the economy could support. Some newspapers-for example, those founded solely as voices of political parties or other interest groups-went out of business simply because they could not win general community support. Others were founded by people who went into the business apparently on the assumption that to make money it was only necessary to "buy newsprint white and sell it black." They soon discovered that, aside from the problems of editing a mass medium, such factors as rigid advertising and circulation rates made newspaper publishing a dubious enterprise at best. For the new entrant today the problems are even more formidable, particularly in metropolitan areas. Not only has population shifted increasingly to the suburbs, with businesses and service industries in pursuit, but inflation in the 1970s was forcing more and more families to stop subscribing to more than one newspaper.

Both in procuring their raw material and in marketing their products. Newspaper publishers exhibit the familiar behaviour of monopoly and oligopoly. As buyers they use the customary pressures for keeping down costs; as sellers they maintain rigid advertising and circulation rates, discriminate by rate differentials, and practice block selling of space in morning and evening newspapers in combination. The typical newspaper pays out for newsprint roughly one-third of its revenues, which is just about what it receives in circulation revenue. Practically all newsprint is sold in carload lots under long-term contracts, mostly to large publishers. Those who cannot afford carload lots get their newsprint from jobbers, brokers, and paper merchants at open market prices, which are sometimes higher by 10 percent or more than the carload rates.

Procuring syndicated features and wire services is no less difficult for the new entrant. The syndicated feature business is dominated by four major companies: AP news features, King Features, NEA Service, and United Features. Most franchises provide for exclusive territories. Furthermore, package selling enables large publishers to buy up rights to more features than they print. Oligopoly is similarly a chief trait of the two wire services.

The new newspaper is confronted in many markets by chain organization. Chains, especially of large newspapers, have certain special advantages: Notably, they make wider use of editorial and feature writers: it is easier for them to obtain new funds from the capital market; they engage in block merchandising of space to national advertisers, in centralized and large-scale research, and in bulk purchases of newsprint, ink, and equipment; they are better able to make maximum use of specialized technical and managerial services, and of electronic automation-central computers can serve all papers in the chain.

Despite these centralizing tendencies, American news institutions, and newspapers in particular, have been local rather than national because of "a peculiarity in American political organization and the prevailing pattern of family money spending." Ben Bagdikian has written:

More governmental functions are left to the local level in the United States than in other developed countries. Schools, property taxes, land use, public health, large areas of business regulation, and many other political and social activities are controlled by locally elected and locally controlled bodies... These locally controlled policies have maximum immediate impact on family life, such as schooling for children, design and location of homes, routes of local highways, and rates of personal property taxes. Such decisions are made by a complicated but highly localized set of political bodies.

The United States has no national newspapers. The closest approximations are the Wall Street Journal, which in 1977 reached across the nation to 1.46 million people interested mainly in financial news, and the New York Times, one quarter of whose 854,000 daily subscribers in 1977 lived more than 100 miles from New York City. To a much lesser extent, the Washington Post also reached beyond the capital, but it did not compete seriously in national and international circulation with the times. In the late 1970s the Times was spending $35 million a year (the Post was spending $19 million) to support the world's largest full-time news staff-641 journalists (550 in New York, 40 in Washington, 19 scattered throughout the United States, and 32 abroad). There are fatter American newspapers than the Times (the average news hole-the space devoted to editorial words-of the Times in 1977 was 160 columns a day; the Washington Star printed 185 and the Chicago Tribune 218 columns a day), but they rely typically on wire service and syndicated material for much of their content. Almost everything in the Times is staff written.

These huge newspapers with an impact beyond their cities of publication form a tiny minority of American daily newspapers; only half a percent of all dailies have more than 500,000 circulation. Seventy percent of U.S. dailies have circulations of 25,000 or less; 53 percent are published in cities with populations less than 25,000. Although the New York Times has an influence in the United States and abroad out of all proportion to its size, the statistics in the tables below present a clearer perspective on the newspaper industry as a whole and vividly make Bagdikian's point about the localism of newspapers.

As Americans' disposable income has risen, retail stores and service enterprises have kept pace at the local level in competing for this income, typically by advertising through the local newspaper. In 1976 advertisers spent $33.6 billion in all media. Newspapers got $10.2 billion or 30 percent of that, 25.6 percent local, only 4.4 percent national. Because of family spending patterns, the population shift to the suburbs, and the mushrooming suburban shopping centers, a relatively new newspaper category has emerged: the shopper's guide or shopper or throwaway. A typical daily newspaper has a ratio of about 65 percent advertising content to 35 percent news and feature content. Shoppers, by contrast, contain 75 percent or more advertising content, and many are distributed free. And their numbers are growing. The U.S. Suburban Press, Inc., had 850 of these shoppers with a total circulation of 11.3 million in early 1976.

To curb shoppers' eating into their advertising revenues, established newspapers were supporting efforts by some states to exclude shoppers from the tax privileges enjoyed by "traditional" newspapers. In New Jersey state tax officials were struggling to come up with a satisfactory definition of "newspaper." The rise of the suburban press, whether as traditional newspaper or shopper, challenged the domination of major metropolitan newspapers, many of which began developing their own suburban or zone editions in the 1970s to compete for readers and advertisers.

The localism of newspapers and their efforts to attract and hold readers in a competitive market have made the newspaper in many respects a more direct descendant of the early magazine of the nineteenth century than is the contemporary magazine. The word "magazine" is derived from the French word magazine, 'meaning "storehouse," and early magazines were miscellanies of information and amusement. In its growing consumer orientation and emphasis on "news you can use," today's local newspaper is very similar. Readers of all ages can usually find something to interest them in the paper's coverage of local events and activities, in its local and syndicated features, comics, and games, and in its local retail ads and listing of local entertainment. Even the large metropolitan newspapers that concentrate on public affairs and appeal to a readership far beyond their cities of publication-the new York times, Washington Post, the Wall Street Journal, and the Christian Science Monitor-publish a miscellany of serious and entertaining content more diverse than that of a general-interest magazine.

In fact, it seemed in the late 1970s that newspapers had to publish more of such "soft" new and feature material to stave off circulation declines. By adding a section three days a week in 1976 and 1977—Living, a section on food and wine, on Wednesdays Home, on furniture, interior decorating, and gardening, on Thursdays, and Weekend, a guide to entertainment and the arts, on Fridays- the New York Times reversed its circulation decline, increasing circulation from a daily average of 821,000 in 1976 to 854,000 in 1977. Not only did more people buy the Times on the days with added sections-35,000 more than on unsupplemented days-more advertisers bought space. The Times sold more advertising in May 1977 than in any previous month in its history.

To some their local orientation offsets the standardization of American newspapers. Yet whatever character a publisher or editor or the community itself confers on a local newspaper, economy dictates a heavy reliance by almost all on wire and news services for national and international news and on syndicates for features, columns, and comics. Studies have long shown that the comics sections, and particularly the Sunday comics, are among the best-read sections in the paper. A study reported by N.W. Ayer and Company in 1976 found that more than 50 million copies of Sunday comics are distributed to American homes every week, where they are read by over 100 million people. And two organizations, Metro Sunday Comics and the Puck Group, supply over 76 percent of those copies.

Not only do these centralised sources of news and

entertainment make for an essential similarity in newspaper content from place to place, but the newswriting techniques and formulas of the wire services-typically a summary lead paragraph followed by the facts in order or decreasing importance-have influenced reportorial style in such a way that even local stories read alike. The chemistry of the city council members and the nature of the issues they discuss may differ dramatically between Lompoc, California, and Brunswick, Maine, but the way in which the Lompoc Record and the Brunswick Times Record report them is unlikely to differ much. Researchers have argued, in fact, that because of professional norms concerning definitions of news and the inverted pyramid style of reporting, reporters ignore the colour, flavour, and very human disorder and tedium of city council discussion in favour of a concise, objective account of the decisions taken. The effect of this approach, the researchers argue, is to shore up the authority of local government by creating the impression that it is consistently acting decisively and rationally.

Even though the great majority of daily newspapers-approximately 85 percent-have circulations under 50,000, and may therefore appear small enough to serve as personal vehicles for strong-minded, colourful publishers who can stamp the newspaper with their own personalities, the forces of industrialization and urbanization accelerating after the Civil War virtually killed the dominance of flamboyant publishers like Bennett, Pulitzer, and Hearst whose paper were personal, idiosyncratic extensions of themselves. Most newspapers today are corporate and impersonal enterprises.

Examples of the colourful breed of the nineteenth century survive, of course. In New Hampshire, William Loeb, the publisher of the Manchester Union Leader, uses his statewide newspaper with vigorous partisanship against political candidates of whom he disapproves. Rupert Murdoch, the Australian publisher of the New York Post, seems a reincarnation of much of the best and worst of Pulitzer and hearst.

In Las Vegas, Herman M. Greenspun, publisher of the Las Vegas Sun, has carried an adventurous life into his paper. Editor & Publisher gives this account of the extraordinary derring-do of his fight for Israel's survival in 1948. He plundered a naval depot in Hawaii, and, posing as an agent for Generalissimo Chiang Kai-Shek, seized a yacht at gunpoint. He then filled a ship at Tampico Bay with 6000 tons of contraband rifles, machine guns, howitzers, cannons, and tons of ammunition, and sailed to Israel. He was convicted in 1950 of violating the U.S. Neutrality Act and stripped of his civil rights. President John Kennedy pardoned him in 1961. Before becoming publisher of the Sun, Greenspun worked as publicity director for the Flamingo Casino, owned by hoodlum Bugsy Siegel, who was later gunned down. Since then Greenspun has campaigned against gangsters in Las Vegas, and as a result of his investigative journalism and his trenchant front-page column, "Where I Stand," has been hit with more than 100 lawsuits, so becoming the most sued publisher in the nation. He was one of the first publishers to attack Joseph McCarthy, the anti-Communist senator from Wisconsin in the early 1950s; he was the only newsman to testify before the Senate Watergate committee-he said he knew of a $100,000 campaign contribution to Richard Nixon from billionaire recluse Howard Hughes.

Newspaper publishing has other characters, but the generalization holds: Most newspapers are impersonal, corporate enterprises that reflect the middle-class values of their mainly middle-class owners. Not only does the scale of their enterprise distance many publishers from the daily operation of the newspaper, but the professionalization of journalists also sets publisher and reporter apart. The rise of journalism education and of organizations such as the newspaper Guild and the Society of Professional Journalists, Sigma Delta Chi, has to some extent institutionalized journalists' ethics and reinforced conventions such as objective reporting, adherence to which has given reporters a measure of independence from publishers' whims. The Underground Press Largely to protest middle-class values and accepted journalistic responsibilities and conventions and to express their protest in vivid, unrestrained language, an "underground" press flowered in the late 1960s and early 1970s, giving the lie fleetingly to the generalization that newspapers are impersonal, middle-class businesses. There were only four in 1965, but Robert Glessing counted approximately 3000 underground papers that had published at one time or another between 1965 and 1972.

Some underground papers built circulations in the tens of thousands, among them the highly successful Berkeley Barb. In 1969 wrangling between the owner.

Max Scherr, and his staff became public, revealing just how lucrative such an operation can be. It also revealed that, like the capitalists of the commercial press; some underground journalists are money-conscious. A large group of Scherr's helpers broke away and began to publish the Berkeley Tribe, but not before their negotiations to buy the Barb had reached figures in the hundreds of thousands.

It will not do to assign sweeping significance to the underground press. Ray Mungo, one of the founders of the Liberation News Service, which provided material for underground newspapers, has written:

Lots of radicals will give you a very precise line about why their little newspaper or organization was formed and what needs it fulfills and most of that stuff is bullshit, you see-the point is they've got nothing to do, and the prospect of holding a straight job is so dreary that they join the "movement" and start hitting up people for money to live, on the premise that they're involved in critical social change blah blah blah. And it's really better that way, at least for some people, than finishing college and working at dump jobs for constipated corporations: at least it's not always boring... that's why we decided to start a news service-not because the proliferating underground and radical college press really needed a central information-gathering agency staffed by people they could trust (that was our hype), but because we had nothing else to do.

At the same time, it is important to recognize the real strengths of this new journalism. It provided a forum for ideas that were not considered, or not considered adequately, in conventional media. The undergrounders also provided a view of a different life style and afforded different and valuable perspectives.

What this new journalism proved was that a vast distance stretched between the conventional media and important segments of the public. There was a time when a newspaper or magazine served its own small public. The circulation was relatively slender, but editors spoke directly to the central interests of their readers, and they could usually count on reader loyalty. Anyone who cherished another point of view might attack, and a publication that posed a threat might be destroyed-the abolitionist papers, for example-but most people simply subscribed to publications that squared with their own prejudices and idiosyncrasies.

When the conventional media became large and few, however, and editors we're trying to attract mass audiences, separate voices could no longer be raised so readily in a free marketplace of ideas.

Many underground papers succeeded in building close relationships with their readers, at least in part because they revived the art of speaking to a relatively homogeneous audience. One important technique was to present news in heavily subjective prose: "A growing revolt against the selfish and reactionary American Medical Association came to a head here," began an article on Open City a Los a Angeles paper. "Objectivity is a farce" said Thorne Dreyer of Liberation news Service, Jeff Shero, former editor of The Rat, said, "We make our biases clear. That frees our writers to talk about their guts."

Perhaps the strongest challenge to conventional journalism was this "gut reporting." The underground press had a marked distaste for the roots of journalism: the search for verifiable facts.

The underground press, like the revolutionary press of the eighteenth century, was a phenomenon of a period of protest and discontent. It faded for a variety of reasons: because the Vietnam War eventually ended; because the issues diminished in intensity, were resolved, or forgotten; because money and energy ran out; because the journalists turned 30. By contrast, the black press in the United States has struggled and survived by keeping one foot in conventional newspaper publishing and another in militancy and protest.

In 1976 the 325 black newspapers listed in Editor & Publisher International Year Book published mainly in metropolitan areas where black population concentrates, and competed with white metropolitan newspapers for readership and advertising. Only two of these black newspapers were dailies, the Atlanta Daily World and the Chicago Defender; a few published twice a week; most published weekly.

Their need for the advertising support of white-owned businesses and industries forced upon them a conservatism in editorial approach at a time when blacks and become increasingly militant, so creating a tension between publisher and readers. For example, John Sengstacke, publisher of the Chicago Defender, was delighted when Marshall Field and Company agreed to advertise in the defender. But marshall Field is not a store that many blacks can afford to patronize. Nor can Sengstacke afford to take too militant a stance on issues of concern to blacks if he wishes to retain the support of advertisers like Marshall Field. Sengstacke not only confronts this dilemma but must also compete for middle-class black readers, and also for black reporters, with the Chicago Sun-times and the Chicago Tribune. And he must compete for more militant black readers with Muhammad Speaks, published in Chicago by the Black Muslims, and with such other militant organs in Chicago as Black Truth, the Observer, and the Black Liberator.

The militant black organs fit comfortably into the tradition of the black press in this country. Historically it has been a press of protest, ever since John B. Russwurm and the Rev. Samuel Cornish started the nation's first black newspaper. Freedom's Journal, in 1827, to fight slavery. But today major black newspapers, such as the Defender, the Baltimore Afro-American, and the Pittsburgh Courier, which seek to survive in the commercial world by reflecting the interests mainly of middle-class blacks, tend to be more informational organs than organs of protest. And they have had to face the rising costs of the industry as a whole with little of the advertising support on which white newspapers have been able to count. Typically, therefore, these papers have had to scale down their enterprises. In 1945, the Pittsburgh Courier, with a circulation of 257,000, the Chicago Defender, with a circulation of 202,000, and the Baltimore Afro-American, with a circulation of 137, 000, were national weeklies. In the 1970s all three were local newspapers with much reduced circulations. In 1976 the Courier was circulating about 20,800 copies a week; the Afro-American, which published biweekly, was circulating 26,000 on Tuesdays and 28,000 on Saturdays; and the Defender, which became a daily in 1956, was circulating 20,000. Some consolidation and concentration in ownership has also occurred. For example, John Sengstacke bought the Courier chain in 1967, so acquiring 10 newspapers in nine states. By 1976 his chain had been reduced to five papers publishing in four states.

Although the number of black newspapers has expanded, the number of white newspapers has been remarkably constant for decades despite the consolidation and mergers and decline in competition. The rise in educational and economic opportunities for blacks and their increasing militancy in securing those opportunities, often by starting newspapers to express their grievances, explains the expansion of the black press. But the black press in the mid-1970s was showing the same characteristic that explains the stability in numbers of the white press: an emphasis on localism. The major black national papers of the 1970s, Muhammad Speaks and the Black Panther, differed from the early national weeklies-they are organs of religious or political movements rather than of news and information. Most black newspapers, like most white papers, were directed at local communities. As white populations left the metropolitan areas, so contributing to the decline in competing dailies, suburban dailies replaced them to respond to the needs of suburban readers and advertisers.

Coverage of their immediate localities and in-depth, interpretive journalism became the major functions of newspapers after radio and television took over the function of reporting up-to-the-minute spot news. As newspapers lost advertising to radio in the 1930s, newspapers tried briefly to contain broadcast news competition. In 1933 the American Newspaper Publishers Association (ANPA) persuaded the press associations to suspend service to broadcasters. With the support of the radio networks, the Press Radio Bureau was formed in 1937 to edit the files of the press associations and to release news twice daily for no more than five minutes each. The news broadcasts could not be sponsored. But some radio stations refused to abide by the bureau's rules and a new press service, the Trans-Radio Service, was started to sell news directly to radio. By 1940 the ANPA capitulated; allowing the major wire services to sell news to radio and allowing radio to seek sponsors for news. Radio and television can get breaking news to their audiences almost instantly, and the time-consuming background, in-depth interpretive journalism of newspapers is heir adjustment to broadcasting's technological strengths. Because broadcast news is constrained by FCC regulations such as the fairness doctrine and because broadcasters are vulnerable to the government's licensing procedures, broadcast news is typically not as penetrating and controversial as print news. Broadcasters simply do not enjoy protection of the First Amendment equal to that enjoyed by newspapers. This is partly why newspapers rather than broadcasters tackled such controversial, complex, and largely non-visual stories as the Pentagon Papers and Watergate. In the American system of media economics, space is more elastic and less expensive than time. And because of the new electronic technologies in print journalism, particularly the integration of computer technologies into the editing process, newspapers in the 1970s were saving time in a way that enabled them to make more flexible and intelligent use of their space.

Newspapers, then, have survived the formidable competition of broadcasting and, to a much lesser extent, of magazines, by adjusting their functions and by retaining an independence from government and from direct advertising influence. Because many newspapers are local monopolies, advertisers tend to need newspapers more than newspapers need particular advertisers, although their mutual need is obviously great. How intensely readers feel they need newspapers is not really know, although the decline in daily circulation in the mid-1970s suggests that the sense of need was diminishing. Years of readership surveys have produced a profile of newspaper buyers that Ben Bagdikian summarized in 1971 as follows: "...the best educated; those in skilled professional, technical, managerial white-collar jobs; the wealthiest those who live in urban areas; those who are married; and people between the ages of thirty and fifty-four." But in a speech at the Allied Daily newspapers annual meeting in Seattle on May 15, 1975. Robert G. Marbut, president of Harte-Hanks Newspapers, Inc., reflected on these item's: daily newspaper circulation was declining; the ratio of daily newspaper circulation to the number of households had declined steadily over the past decade; and the dependence on newspapers by younger people-the ones 20-35 who are among the prime targets of advertisers-appeared to be declining. Marbut asked:

How are these trends possible? Just the opposite should be true. As people become better educated and more affluent, they should be more prone to be loyal newspaper readers. And, since current trends indicate that we do have a larger number of better educated and more affluent people, why isn't the number of newspapers sold per household increasing rather than declining?

He warned the industry that unless each publisher produced "that unique package of news, opinion and other information designed for the specific needs of a particular market," someone else would do so. And he pointed to the growing number of hungry competitors:

Just look at the number of other media chipping away at what newspapers used to consider safely within their franchise. Whether it be the television sales staff going after local advertisers like never before, or he blanket coverage shopper, or the direct mail penny sayer, or the preprint being delivered by a private delivery service, or the Government's setting up regional computerized job data banks, or in the future a computerized data bank connected to the home by bidirectional cable-all of these vehicles are supplying information to our markets-in what used to be our domain.

No profile of the typical newspaper buyer, then, no generalization about the newspaper's typical functions seems to fit precisely in the flux of the 1970s.

The modern magazine succeeded as a mass medium chiefly because of its original role as an adjunct of the marketing system. Like the newspaper, it was able, over the years, to appeal to an expanding range of tastes and interests. But, unlike other media, most magazines were designed for homogeneous audiences or special-interest groups. And, in contrast to the newspaper, their circulation was nationwide. Thus, although many magazines were directed to specialized audiences, magazines in general developed as a mass medium in the sense that they appealed to large numbers in a national market that cut across social, economic, and educational class lines.

Early in the twentieth century, some magazine publishers, notably those of pulps and digests, derived their income from a small unit profit on a high turnover of copies instead of from advertising. Still others relied on trade associations, fraternal organizations, and professional groups to make up any deficit. But with the rise of national advertising, the great majority-both in numbers and circulation-were bound closely to the marketing system. In effect, magazine publishing became fundamentally a matter of the publisher's deciding on a consumer group that advertisers wanted to reach, devising an editorial formula to attract and hold that group, and then selling advertisers access to it.

In terms of originating a market for the advertiser, the relationship of magazines generally to their audiences is quite different from that of other media. Some magazine publishers have first developed a publication and then let both readers and advertisers seek out the magazine. But the typical magazine follows a less risky strategy. It devises an editorial formula that can be counted on to attract a homogeneous and relatively small special-interest group; then it assembles advertisers who want to address that audience.

In Magazines of the Twentieth Century, Theodore Peterson notes four threats to magazine sin the first half of the twentieth century: the automobile, radio, movies, and television. Yet magazines have enjoyed virtually uninterrupted growth in numbers, circulation, and revenue since 1900. There were well over a thousand more magazines in the United States in the mid-1970s than in 1900; per-issue circulation rose over 98 million between 1950 and 1970, a gain of 44 percent; and advertising revenue tripled between 1950 and 1974, from $458.5 million to $1.5 billion. Peterson ascribes most of magazines' prosperity to population increase, more particularly to rising income levels and the expansion of the middle class, to the spread of popular education, and to the increase in leisure time. Typically magazines, like other print media, have been read by richer, better-educated Americans whose increase has sustained print against the competition of radio and television.

In the 1950s and 1960s, however, some of the major magazines did not merely rely on this group but challenged television on its own ground. They went for the mass audience, by direct mail campaigns and subscription offers at bargain rates. The massive circulations of such magazines as The Reader's Digest, the Saturday Evening Post, Life, and Look resulted Stung by television, these magazines lost sight of their real source of strength, the selective market. Now only the Digest survives in its original form, ranking second after TV Guide in total circulation in the United States.

Try as they might, the mass magazines could not adapt to change, could find no identity for themselves as other media displaced them. How Life, far and away the biggest revenue producer of all magazines before it died, tried tells us much about the structure and functions of the media in general and of the magazine industry in particular. Life's struggle shows that, despite opinion to the contrary, media structure and functions are not fixed but bend to the needs and wants of their constituencies.

Thirty-six years after its founding, Life, the last great mass-circulation, general-interest picture magazine, died in December 1972, because of its status as something of a national institution, Life's passing was mourned with more emotion then sense.

Loyal readers and some staffers accused management of murder; Life could and should have been saved. So presumably could other mass magazines, such as Collier's, which died in 1956, the Saturday Evening Post, which died in 1969, and Look, which died in 1971. Chris Welles, a Life editor from 1965 to 1968, is more persuasive. He studied Life in its death throes in 1971, then conducted a postmortem in 1973, concluding: "The collapse of Life's profit-oriented *raison d'etre* derived from its increasing inability to fill the needs of its two essential constituencies-advertisers and readers."

Increasing affluence, education, and leisure time had fragmented the mass audience and enabled people to pursue a variety of interests to which hundreds of specialized magazines responded. Television satisfied mass tastes. And advertisers followed the audiences they wanted wherever they could be reached most effectively.

Henry Luce created Life in 1936 in the middle of the depression, "to see life: to see the world: to eyewitness great events," and to see them positively. Life was to combat the national gloom and to correct what Luce considered journalism's distorted priorities: "That evil makes big news and good makes little or no news." What particularly annoyed him was the press' interest in scandal. In a speech in September 1937, he said: if there is one fact about our society which is shouted daily to the people of America it is that rich folk get into trouble with chorines and gigolos, steal each other's wives and husbands, indulge in orgies, and are otherwise licentious.

On the relevant issue of whether the press has presented a fair picture to the public of an aspect of American life, the criticism should be turned around. For if there are a number of rich or solvent people who live reasonably decent lives, never get more than moderately drunk and are not sexual monsters-then that is the fact which the capitalist-controlled press has failed to establish.

With something of the awe of discovery, Luce argued that "the photograph ... turns out to be an extraordinary instrument for correcting that really inherent evil in journalism which is its unbalance between the good news and the bad." He explained how Life was using the camera as corrective:

A few weeks ago Life published a picture essay on wheat-I mean wheat, growing and being happily harvested. The article had nothing to do with any frantic row in Congress over a farm bill, nothing to do with the horrors of drought and dying cattle. And it was the lead article and ran for nine pages. Now can you imagine and non-photographic magazine, intended to interest millions of readers, daring to devote its first nine pages to a descriptive contemplation of the fruitful and normal and quiet labours of farms and horses and harvesters and the wheat itself ripening beneath the sun? And yet it is precisely the kind of thing which Life is doing."

But no power of positive thinking could blind Life to the ugly realities of the 1960s and early 1970s. Its magnificent photographers produced some of the most searing and moving pictures of the Vietnam War, around which the discontent of the decade had gathered. Its reporters investigated the troubles prominent people get into. William Lambert reported on Supreme Court Justice Abe Fortas' agreement to accept a fee of $20,000 yearly for life from the Wolfson Foundation (Louis Wolfson was twice indicted for stock fraud). Fortas resigned in May 1969, the only justice ever to resign from the Supreme Court under pressure.

Curiously for a picture magazine, *Life* was in the vanguard of aggressive investigative reporting when it died. But Life's change in editorial formula did not impress advertisers, who in the 1970s could pursue the audience they wanted through the massive, undifferentiated reach of television and the concentrated, selective reach of specialized magazines. Because of this competition, Life's huge audience-it was said that in its prime 70 million adults read each issue of *Life-began* to fade away.

Life's mass circulation survived longer than that of its deceased rivals partly because it acquired a million and a half subscribers from the dying Saturday Evening Post. Circulation was sustained mainly by cheap subscription and low newsstand prices. A study not long before Life died estimated that the average Life reader paid only 12 cents for a magazine costing 41 cents to edit and print. Advertisers had to make up the remaining 70 percent of publishing costs at ad rates as high as $64,000 a colour page: Advertisers found that they could reach more people more cheaply on prime time television. In 1971 the advertising cost per thousand persons reached by Life was about $7.71; by television, about $3.60.

Advertisers questioned Life's identity and argued that people no longer cared enough for Life to pay a reasonable share of the costs. Advertisers withdrew. Between 1966 and 1972 Life's advertising revenues dropped from $170-to $91-million. Its only consistently dependable advertisers were cigarette and liquor manufacturers, who were banned from advertising on television. Publishing costs meanwhile were soaring. Paper prices were expected to double within five years, and postal rates were expected to rise 142 percent within the same period. Life tried for a more affluent, educated audience by allowing its circulation to drop by attrition from 81/2 to 51/2 million between 1970 and 1972, by charging higher subscription rates, and by experimenting with different editorial formulas such as an emphasis on investigative reporting. Readers still drifted away. News-stand sales averaged only 184,000 an issue for the first six months of 1972, a 20 percent drop from 1971 and lower than the sales of Weight Watchers. In its last five years life lost $35 million: another $30 million loss was projected for 1973 and 1974. Confronting that, and fading reader and advertiser interest. *Life* elected euthanasia. Perhaps more imaginative and sharply focused editorial formulas could have saved Life, but it is doubtful that *Life* could have survived as a mass magazine. As advertisers were quick to see, the times were out of joint for that medium.

Today American magazines reflect virtually every shade of thought and opinion, virtually every interest, of their readers. They cover everything from hot rodding, coin collecting, yachting, hunting and fishing, and preparing to be a bride to gourmet dining and calorie counting. Despite the fierce competition and the uncertainties, magazine publishing on a small scale is perhaps the communication most accessible to the new investor. What counts most is the idea. If the entrepreneur has a fresh idea for a magazine, there are likely to be persons willing to finance it. If the magazine can be sustained while it seeks acceptance by readers and advertisers, there is always some change that it will achieve a modest success. And there is a remote change that it will wind up in the company of giants.

The ease of entry into the magazine industry, in contrast to the formidable obstacles encountered in newspaper publishing, broadcasting, and motion pictures, explains why the industry today is dotted with relatively small units, small staffs, and modest offices with little equipment. Magazine publishers ordinarily do not invest in presses and equipment, but instead let out their printing on contract. A publisher who does not wish to compete out their printing on contract. A publisher who does not wish to compete with large-circulation leaders can still launch a successful magazine on a million dollars or so-a comparatively small sum for starting a national medium. Some that began as regional publications started with far less. Jann Wenner began as regional publications started with far less. Jann Wenner began Rolling Stone as a rock music magazine with less than $20,000 and aimed it at San Francisco. Bay Area readers. Then he expanded to national distribution, diversifying content to include top New York writers Truman Capote, Tom Wolfe, and Norman Mailer. In 1977 Wenner, then only 30 years old, moved Rolling Stone to New York. Its circulation was up to 450,000; Wenner wanted it up to a million by 1980.

Factors that make it easy for one publisher to enter the industry also make it easy for competitors to enter. Successful magazines invariably breed imitators, for publishers cannot hide their formulas for success, forced as they are by the nature of publishing to exhibit their best ideas in public.

What Hugh Hefner chose to exhibit in public in Playboy soon stimulated imitators, most formidably Bob Guccione's Penthouse. Hefner had attracted readers with his centerfolds of nude women, the blemishes and too intimate parts of their voluptuous bodies discreetly air brushed. Guccione disdained touching up his photographs and successfully challenged Playboy with candid frontal nudity. For decades DeWitt Wallace had been trying through his Reader's Digest to keep America at moral attention: Hefner and Guccione claimed to be liberating America from its sexual taboos. Whatever the validity of their claim, their magazines reflected the sexual permissiveness of the 1970s.

Both their contents and their distributional methods violated normal publishing conventions. Most magazines rely heavily on advertising: typically about 60 percent of a magazine's contents is advertising, 40 percent is editorial. Playboy and Penthouse virtually reversed the ratio, charging the reader the entire cost of the magazine. Advertising, therefore, was almost pure profit. Their distributional costs were lower than those of most major magazines because they relied more on news-stand sales than on subscriptions, which involve solicitations and distribution of sales through the increasingly expensive postal system.

In the mid-1970s Penthouse, which claimed a worldwide circulation of 5.3 million, was selling over 90 percent of its copies at news-stands. Note that the vast bulk of Time's circulation sells via subscription, although occasional striking covers may well increase sales dramatically. Playboy took malicious pleasure in July 1976 in pointing out that Time was not above using nudity (Playboy mentioned Time's putting the entertainer Chain in a see-through dress on the cover of a best-selling issue) to sell magazines even though in a cover story. "The Porno Plague," in April 1976. Time had criticized Playboy "and its far crasser imitators" for the practice. In a period of escalating postal rates. Time's reliance on subscriptions for approximately 95 percent of its circulation was a crippling expense. In October 1975, therefore, Time began an experiment in three cities whereby subscribers received their Time from a newspaper carrier rather than a mail carrier. Delivery by carriers of cooperating newspapers was expected to be considerably cheaper than postal delivery.

Competition in the Market

Competition by imitation is usually a Darwinian process. The fittest survive. Black publisher John H. Johnson has made a success of limitation because he has not competed with his models. He modeled Black World, titled Negro digest until 1970, on The Reader's Digest Jet, a news weekly, copied the format of the Cowles magazine Quick. Tan copied the true confession magazines. In 1945 Johnson launched Ebony as a monthly and sensational version of Life. He toned down the sensationalism in the 1950s, and Ebony became a magazine for middle class blacks. In the militant 1960s Ebony abandoned its earlier cautiousness and tackled black grievances. An entire issue in 1965, for example, was devoted to "The White Problem in America." Johnson explains that "Ebony's goal is to reflect the attitudes and opinions of our readership as well as to lead. We don't go too far ahead, but we're always pushing for more."

Because newspapers cater mainly to a heterogeneous local community and television mainly to the national undifferentiated mass, the magazine has become the vehicle of the aspirations or ideologies of special-interest groups, one of the means by which they push for more. For decades men dominated the publishing of women's magazines, so reinforcing, it was charged, stereotypes of women as mothers and homemakers. In 1973 journalist Pamela Howard described the professional goals this way: "Ten years ago, I dreamed about becoming editor-in-chief of a woman's magazine. Accordingly, I went to work at one of the largest in the country, only to find that all the Katharine Hepburn roles were filled by short men."

A man, Cyrun Curtis, founded the Ladies' Home Journal in 1883. Although his wife, Louisa Knapp, edited it for six years, it was editor Edward Bok who took the magazine's circulation over a million in 1903. Bok, it was said, had no affection for women, but succeeded with his readers by emphasizing the concept of service for women. And not only for women, apparently. During World War I the Journal ranked third among magazines most demanded by soldiers. Despite their emphasis on serving women, however, magazines like the Journal and McCall's have not led the women's movement as they have led women's magazines in circulation, Helen Gurley Brown gave new direction to women's magazines when she became editor of the Hearst Corporation's Cosmopolitan and dealt candidly with the non-housewifely aspirations and sexuality of women, particularly young single women.

Essence, founded for black women in May 1970, was torn in its first two years by internal strife, caused, some said, by the fact that it was run by men. Initially intended strictly as a fashion and beauty magazine, it had to convince potential advertisers that black women had sufficient buying power to make them a worthwhile market. Advertisers had also to be educated to Essence's requirement that ads in no way demean black women. Moreover, Essence requires that all ads show a black woman, Marcia Gillespie, who started as managing editor in November 1970, became Essence's fourth editor-in-chief in May 1971 and began to change the magazine. "I had wanted to combat the negative imagery which for centuries had been foisted on Blacks," she said. "Forever, it seems, we Blacks have heard how we are stupid, lazy shiftless, unable to build family units.... I didn't want little Black girls growing up as I had thinking only white women were beautiful. I wanted then, through Essence to see and to feel what Black women really are-incredibly vital people who have been boxed intellectually, creatively and emotionally." Marcia Gillespie's approach has been immensely successful. Circulation has grown from 75.000 in 1970 to 550.000 in 1977; between 1970 and 1976 advertising revenue rose from $208,000 to $3.8 million.

When Gloria Steinem and Elizabeth Forsling Harris decided in 1971 to publish his magazine, they were determined to keep women in control. Steinem was to be editor and president. Harris publisher and chairwoman of the board. His was a deliberate protest against the conventional women's magazines (while working at the Ladies' home Journal, Steinem was handed a story by an editor and told, "Pretend you're a women and read this"). For too long, Steinem declared, women have been "sanitized, deodorized, slicked up, and fixed up" in magazines. According to Harris, the purpose was to "communicate the commonality of feeling among women around the country." Pamela Howard described the magazine as "a forum for women who are exploring new ways of living."

Women sports, founded by tennis star Billie Jean King, promoted and celebrated one of these new ways, a career as a female athlete. In the great variety of women's magazines, a shared purpose has united them, symbolized in July 1976 by a meeting of 30 women's magazines to discuss how best to ensure passage of the Equal Rights Amendment to the Constitution.

These women's magazines are comparatively new special-interest magazines of narrow focus. Many of their individual concerns have been forthrightly discussed, advocated, or condemned for years in such journals of opinion, comment, and controversy as Ramparts, The Nation, national Review, new Leader, The New Republic, and Progressive. Their emphasis is on ideas rather than on reportage, and their positions are rarely neutral.

Most of the journals since the turn of the century have been organs of liberal thought, although a few, such as the National Review, founded in 1955, have spoken for conservatism. In their agitation for political reform and social justice, the magazines have often been far ahead of popular thinking. For that reason and others, their way has always been difficult; their circulations have been counted in the thousands instead of in the millions of the general interest magazines, their advertising volume has been lean or non-existent, and their financial position has ever been precarious. Yet they seem to have wielded an influence all out of proportion to their circulations, for they have aimed at opinion leaders instead of the great mass audience. Frank P. Walsh once remarked that he had written an article about railroads for the Nation in the days when its circulation was about 27,000 and a series on the same subject for the Hearst newspapers when their total circulation was around 10 million. No one ever commented on the newspaper series, he said, but as soon as the Nation article appeared, his phone jangled with calls from persons of importance. Charles Beard has credited the journals of opinion with contributing to such reforms as women's suffrage, old-age pensions, social security legislation, wages-and-hours laws, public housing, and public ownership of hydroelectric sites.

Despite the magazine industry's response via specialized magazines to the political beliefs, social concerns, and leisure activities and hobbies of an audience with increasingly diverse interests, a role for the general interest magazine survived in the mid-1970s. One bold test of this notion was Time Inc.'s launching of People magazine in February 1974. Conventional wisdom was that Life died in 1972 partly because television had killed the relevance and appeal of the still photograph, at least in news.

The *National Geographic* was still a haven for lovers and practitioners of photography, but it was not concerned with the timeliness of its contents. Rather it captured in magnificent colour what relatively unexplored and exotic peoples and places remained in the world, or it glamorized the familiar. Somewhat like The Reader's Digest, the geographic contrived a timelessness for each issue. It was not a publication read on the run and discarded. Bookshelves around the world groan under the weight of back issues of the Geographic.

Photojournalism, in fact, has struggled for its less than a century of existence to overcome journalism's bias toward print. It was not until the 1880s that the halftone photoengraving process was perfected, not until the 1890s that the halftone photoengraving process was perfected, not until the 1890s that a way was developed to run off photographs on a rotary press, making it possible to print photographs in newspapers and mass magazines. Unfortunately, these developments coincided with the yellow journalism of Pulitzer and Hearst, who used photographs unscrupulously and sensationally. Then in the 1920s the tabloids outdid Pulitzer and Hearst, selecting, retouching, and faking pictures for maximum sensational impact. Long after it was technologically possible to use photographs, therefore, many newspapers shield away from them or used them sparingly. When the Associated Press managing.

Editors Association decided in 1935 to devote its next session to photography, many editors protested, arguing that photography would lower the dignity of the American press, that photography should not encroach on print.

The damage that yellow journalism inflicted from the 1890's through the 1920s on the respectability and perceived value of photojournalism and graphics cannot be overestimated. By reinforcing the arrogance of print, yellow journalism set back intelligent analysis of what information is best communicated verbally, what visually, and of how words and pictures can be used most effectively to enhance each other's shared purpose-to communicate. In this respect, the advertising industry, typically scorned by journalists, has been light years ahead in its imaginative use of photography, graphics, colour, and design to communicate its messages. Magazines have long had to compete for readers' attention with the colour and allure of advertisements beside their articles and have been much more visually innovative than newspapers. It was about the time that newspaper editors in the APME were deciding to dignify photojournalism by assigning a session to the topic that Henry Luce discovered the positive power of the camera and Life was born. And Life's photography did much to make photojournalism respectable for newspapers. So when Life died and television was seen as an accessory before the fact, many concluded that the day of the general-interest picture magazine was dead.

Yet People is basically a picture magazine; some have described it as television in print. It runs about 15,000 words an issue; Time runs three times/that many. Despite requiems for the picture magazine, People was paying its way within 20 months of its launching in 1974, a remarkable achievement in contemporary publishing. Photojournalists have criticized the magazine as a prostitution of Life, as an exploitation of the form rather than an extension of it, and some have sought their professional future in newspapers rather than in magazines. People offered a flashy, quick look and read into the lives of celebrities. Gossip? No more than a high-class fan magazine? "We do not urn gossip," says Managing Editor Richard B. Stolley. "Everything is checked for accuracy. Instead of concentrating on the issue, we look at the personalities behind them. Our policy is to tell you new things about personalities you already know. We also include unknown people doing things we think are exceptional." People's Washington correspondent Clare Crawford reported in late 1975: "The Fords love this magazine. The President has told me that he hopes we don't mess it up' with pictures of blood vessels and hearts, the way they did with Life. And that's the key to People's success. Nobody from Presidents on down can resist reading about other people."

Superficially this marriage of people and pictures has characterized New York magazine, launched by Clay Felker in 1968. In fact, New York is a mix of serious journalism and lively, imaginative graphics which has had considerably more than local impact on publishing. Early on it became a vehicle for the "new journalism" of writers like Tom Wolfe, Jimmy Breslin, and Gail Sheehy, who were applying the literary techniques of the short story and novel-dramatic scene, dialogue, interior monologue-to the presentation of thoroughly researched journalism. Their writing styles, which reflected much greater sensitivity to the visual sense, to all the senses, than just-the-facts-ma'am objective reporting, and the magazine's bright, provocative graphics gave a pace and excitement to new York that other magazines soon imitated. Milton Glaser, New York's design director, said, "the magazine is not designed to look beautiful, but to convey a sense of energy, compression, density, information. We want it to be fast-paced like the city, easily accessible, underr.anding. We want people to get in and out of it very easily."

In almost every respect, then, it was the antithesis of the staid, dignified New Yorker, which has never been concerned to hurry its readers through the magazine. Rather. The New Yorker communicates an aura of decorous quiet, of leather upholstery and muted paneling, of civilized, reflective conversation by the elegantly styled and cuffed people in the ads it carries. Tradition weighs heavily on The New Yorker, which cherishes the character given it by its founder Harold Ross and by writers James Thurber and E. B. White.

New York, by contrast, has been as mercurial as its founder Clay Felker and as the times it has reflected. In the early 1970s critics condemned its articles as poorly researched, sensational, vulgar, superficial, and trendy. Newsweek dismissed the magazine as "a tedious collection of pop trivia." As Watergate spread gloom in the nation and New York City's bankruptcy depressed the inhabitants, the magazine's breeziness was almost unseemly. Investigative journalism was in vogue, and, although still graphically colorful and irreverent, New York became a more conservative, solidly researched magazine-until the Australian, Rupert Murdoch, bought it in January 1977. Murdoch, who then owned 88 newspapers, 11 magazines, and some television properties in Australia, England, and the United States, is known for a "blood, guts, and girls" formula, and New York admirers were concerned that the magazine would succumb to Murdoch's earthy sensationalism.

Before Murdoch's takeover, New York seemed to be going through a process Clay Felker had described soon after he started New York:

There appears to be an almost inexorable life-cycle of American magazines that follows the patterns of humans: a clamorous youth eager to be noticed; vigorous, productive middle-age marked by an easy-to-define editorial line; and a long slow decline, in which efforts at revival are sporadic and tragically doomed."

In the post-Vietnam and-Watergate trauma of the mid-1970s, national nostalgia had revived a pale version of the Saturday Evening Post. Life was publishing special issues such as "the Year in Pictures" and was talking of a comeback. Some magazines came and went with the public's whims and fads. Many kept pace with society's elemental concerns, and, despite the inexorable life-cycle Felker describes, survived.

We have glanced at only a selection of the diverse range whose covers blaze from news-stands and supermarket racks. As a whole, magazines more than any other medium reflect the pluralism of American society and the multifarious interests, serious and trivial, perennial and passing, that affluence and leisure enable it to indulge.

Like other communications industries, book publishing is a business seeking profit. Like the news media, however, it acknowledges certain responsibilities to the cultural life of the nation: to support and promote scholarship and literature, to influence and elevate taste, to teach and delight. And these responsibilities may transcend, perhaps limit, profit. To some extent, it is easier for the book publishing industry than for the news media to meet its responsibilities. Unlike newspapers, magazines, and broadcast programs, books are not subsidized by advertisers. The news media must please two constituencies-audiences and advertisers. Book publishers must please only one-readers.

In the United States, however, books are not as popular with the mass of Americans as the products of the other media of communication. In 1975 book publishing industry sales amounted to $3.8 billion, $1.5 billion of which, or 40 percent, was spent on educational materials for schools and colleges. But the buying of educational materials is not usually discretionary. In fact, such a minority of Americans chooses to buy books that, strictly speaking, book publishing is not a mass industry. A national best seller may sell between 2 and 3 million copies, which may be read by twice that number of persons. The New York Daily News sells almost 2 million copies daily to New Yorkers; Time magazine sells more than 4 million copies a week; Family Circle sells more than 9 million a month; The Reader's Digest more than 18 million a month; and readership for each of these publications is probably three times circulation. A reasonably popular network television show can expect an audience of between 20 and 30 million on a single night. Even the exception, a best seller, then, cannot rival the reach of the other media. The average hardbound trade book may sell no more than 10,000 copies, the average mass market paperback no more than 100,000.

"Mass market" is a misnomer. Although literacy is almost universal in the United States, the American masses do not yet read books. It was the implication of Marshall McLuhan's pronouncements in the mid-1960s that they never would because the advent of the electronic media had signaled the death of print. In fact, the 1960s were boom years for book publishing. From 1963 to 1969, industry sales rose 59 percent. So far from killing print, the electronic media seem instead to have stimulated reading. Book sales slowed in the 1970s, but retained solid growth. Between 1971 and 1975, years of recession and retrenchment in the American economy, book sales rose 30.8 percent. Hard times particularly affected education, the source of much of the demand for books. Enrollments in schools and colleges declined or leveled off, and taxpayers and their elected representatives at the local, state, and federal levels cut school and college appropriations.

Moreover book publishing was especially vulnerable to the increasing use in schools, colleges, and libraries of the Xerox and other copying machines. Until 1976 U.S. copyright law had been virtually unchanged since 1909, long before the invention of the automatic copier. For years copyright bills to protect the rights of authors were mired in complexity and controversy in Congress. The bill that finally passed in 1976 still permitted some copying for educational purposes without compensation to authors.

Book publishing managed the recession of the 1970s relatively well largely because the industry was a part during the boom years of the 1960s of the multimedia merger and consolidation. RCA bought Alfred Knopf, Pantheon Books, and Random House. CBS bought W.B. Saunders and Holt. Rinehart and Winston, itself created by mergers. Time Inc., bought Little, brown; ITT bought Bobbs-Merrill and Howard Sams; and the Times Mirror Company, publisher of the Los Angeles times, bought a number of book publishing enterprises.

John P. Dessauer comments that these mergers and consolidations ... made resources available without which the industry could probably not have capitalized on its opportunities and fulfilled its obligations to educational and consumer audience alike. They brought new management and new business acumen to the field which had been seriously lacking and which, in many instances resulted for the first time in orderly budgeting, forecasting, planning, and fiscal arrangements.

But, Dessauer adds, the mergers and consolidations "also placed the power of ultimate decision and policy making in the hands of people unfamiliar with books, their peculiarities, and their markets."

The R. R. Bowker Company, which keeps statistic son the book publishing industry, lists 12,000 book outlets of all kinds in the united States. Of these ...6700... handle new books; 900 are department store book departments: 2900 are college bookstores: 7300 handle paperbacks: 1700 carry law, medical, technical, and scientific titles; 4000 sell religious books: 3000 handle juveniles: 1300 are rare book dealers; and 1000 are secondhand dealers.

The book industry refers to these retail outlets as "traditional trade stores," some of which sell books exclusively, others of which sell them only as a sideline. In addition, there are more than 90,000 mass market outlets-news-stands, drugstores, and supermarkets. From early in this century, books have also been sold directly to the reader, by mail order and by book clubs. The first book clubs, the Book-of-the-Month Club and the Literary Guild, founded in the 1920s, appealed to people who could not easily get to a bookstore or who wanted advice on the latest books, and offered them free books and considerable savings on those the club selected. With the increase in affluence and leisure, the book clubs-like the magazine industry-have become increasingly specialized, catering now to the special interests of readership groups: the American Garden Guild Book Club, Antiques Book Club, Detective Book Club, the Movie Book Club, and the Nostalgia Book Club, among others.

Magazine publishers have been the leaders in mail order publishing, an enterprise they began in the 1950s. Time Inc., The Reader's Digest, Newsweek, and Playboy, which are some of the largest organizations involved, prepare and publish their own books and try to sell them, for the most part, to the subscribers to their magazines. From this variety of publishing sources and through this variety of distribution methods, an ever-larger number of books are published each year competing for the attention of a comparatively small number of Americans interested in buying books.

Typically the direct forms of advertising in which publishers engage-in polishers' catalogues and in ads in the important trade publications of the industry, Publishers Weekly and Library Journal-have nothing like the impact on potential readers as the "free" advertising that books receive in the review columns of newspapers and magazines. The most influential of these include the New York Review of Books, Saturday Review. Time, Newsweek, Harper's, and the Atlantic Monthly. The most influential of these include the New York Review of Books, Saturday Review. Time, Newsweek, Harper's, and the Atlantic Monthly. The most important review medium is unquestionably the New York Times Book Review. But all of these combined, and the other newspapers and magazines that review books, cannot review more than a fraction of the books published each year. With all the space it tries to give book reviews, the New York Times Book Review criticizes and comments on less than 3000 books a year. Moreover, the reach of these publications is limited to a relatively small number of people, who tend to be wealthier and better educated than the average. None of these review media is as effective, therefore, as the brief appearance an author may be lucky enough to secure on a network talk show such as Johnny Carson's "Tonight" show on NBC.

Book publishing has "used" the other media of communication to secure sales in more dramatic ways. The growth of the paperback industry has enabled publishers to rush to press with the news in book form. Bantam was one of the first to experiment with "instant publishing" when it published the Report of the Warren Commission on the Assassination of President Kennedy in book form 80 hours after the official government commission report was released to the public in September 1964. (Normally a book takes about six months from completion of the manuscript to publication date.) So successful was its first attempt-the book was an instant best seller, selling over a million copies within weeks-that Bantam published 56 "instant books," or 'extras" as the company calls them, in the next 10 years.

In the 1970s, then, the oldest of the American media, like the other print media, had adjusted to the popularity of the electronic media. It has yielded much of its earlier concentration on fictional entertainment to the movies and television. During the first the first paperback revolution in publishing, in the 1840s and 1850s, and on through the enormous success of the sensational "dime novel' of the 1870s and 1880s to the romantic historical and family novels of the early 1900s, fiction dominated book publishing. The trend toward nonfiction, began after World War I and has accelerated since. In 1960, 16 percent of the new books or new editions published were fiction; in 1974, less than 9 percent were fiction.

Much of the non-fiction exploited sensation and trivia in the news, but the public's taste for these ephemera subsidized the book industry's commitment to the less profitable or unprofitable publication of what the 19th century poet and critic Matthew Arnold called "the best that is known and thought in the world."

Newspaper circulation was recovering in the late 1970s; by proliferating ever more specialized publications, the magazine industry sustained overall circulation; and although the boom in book sales of the 1960s leveled off in the 1970s, the book industry managed modest growth. Print survived the doom prophesied for it partly because owners of print media were alarmed enough to invest heavily in audience research, partly because new technologies enabled quicker, more flexible responses to what the public wanted. Print survived mainly, one suspects, because the written word gives information and ideas, fact and fiction, a life that the electronic media with all their dazzling visual appeal cannot supplant. Significantly, the passion and energy of the generation of the 1960s, the first generation to be dominated since birth by television and one excited by McLuhan's probes, took concrete though not always coherent form in print, in the underground press.

2

STRUCTURAL SETUP

The Federation of Working Journalists (IFWJ) had takes the initiative in asking for an enquiry into certain aspects of newspaper production. It passed a resolution on the subject at its plenary session in Calcutta in April, 1952. It has since expressed satisfaction with the Press Commission's terms of reference. These cover the ground indicated in the Federation's Calcutta resolution, except in one or two particulars.

- Public opinion has for some time been concerned with certain developments in the Indian newspaper world, which have weakened the reader's faith in what the newspaper published. The working journalist is vitally interested in measures designed to regain the reader's confidence. The working journalist seeks the opportunity and the freedom to re-establish the newspaper as a faithful and trustworthy record of history in the making.
- In this era of planning, he is anxious that the status and function of the press be defined with some precision. He is anxious also to understand his own position in the new policy dominated by the ideal of the Cooperative Commonwealth, the Welfare State and the Working Class Democracy. He would like to know what is to be his share in the plans for a better order of society.

- Journalism in India is an unplanned growth. It is a by-product of the political movement, inspired in the early stages by the social and religious reform movements dating back to the time of Raja Ram Mohan Roy. It has radically changed since then, but largely without a steady sense of direction. To remove this deficiency should be one of the objectives of any plan for the future development of journalism in India.
- That is the basic governing purpose of the survey made and the suggestion put forward in this memorandum. The approach is intended to be severely factual. Superficially, much of what is stated in these pages might seem excessively critical of newspaper ownership and control and might be mistaken for morbid pre-occupation with grievances. That would be a misreading of the memorandum. It is not intended to be a document of denigration. It aims at a faithful portrayal of conditions as they are and as they affect the working journalist.
- The Federation feels that it can help the Commission best by presenting facts with fidelity, even with a certain harsh fidelity, where necessary. That does not mean a denial of credit where credit is due. The working journalist readily acknowledges that there are newspapers in this country which strive to maintain professional and economic standards at as high a level as can be found in any comparable country.
- In adopting a predominantly critical tone, the memorandum seeks to reflect the general attitude of the public at large not merely the attitude of the professional journalist.
- The scope of the present enquiry is wider than that of the British Royal Commission. This is a welcome enlargement.
- The Federation's constitution includes proof readers and press photographers among working journalists, and, accordingly all that is stated in the memorandum applies generally to them. No specific reference is made to the press worker, the clerk, and other employees of the newspaper. They will no doubt speak for themselves. Their importance in the newspaper world is accepted. So is the

need for better conditions for them as much as for others. It will be for the Commission to visit the various newspaper offices, meet these and other classes of employees and generally observe the conditions in which newspapers are produced.

- An attempt is made in the memorandum to deal with all the subjects raised in the terms of reference. A certain amount of overlapping has become unavoidable in this process. The same set of facts and suggestions appear in more than one part of the memorandum, but, it is hoped that their relevance to the context would be obvious.
- This is a preliminary memorandum, prepared on the understanding that in reply to the questionnaire, to be issued by the Commission, the Federation and bodies affiliated to will have an opportunity to put their case more fully and with supporting evidence. The Federation and its units are proceeding on the assumption that statements which are made in this proceeding on the assumption that statements which are made in this memorandum and which will hereafter be made by witnesses are fully protected. An authoritative assurance from the Commission to this effect will encourage the production of all the data that can help it in its work.
- Though the central purpose of the memorandum is to describe and explain the existing position and not to suggest reform, reference is made under various heads to certain directions in which remedies may be sought. They are offered as suggestions for exploration. The considered proposals of the Federation will be put forward at the appropriate stage of the enquiry.

Setup of Management

From the point of view of classification according to size and standing, there are, roughly speaking, three classes of newspapers in this country—large, medium and small. From the point of view of types of ownership, there are four— proprietary concerns, limited concerns, private and public, and trusts. From the point of view of periodicity, there are dailies, weeklies, monthlies and very few fortnightlies and bi-weeklies. From the point of view of purpose, all these cover a vast range of activity. It is, therefore, difficult to examine this complicated structure from any one angle. This memorandum will deal with it generally and illustratively and not exhaustively.

- Purely proprietary concerns own many of the small daily newspapers, weeklies and monthlies. There are the single unit papers like the *Hindu* and the *Mail* of Madras, which have no sister papers or editions outside Madras. These are mostly private limited concerns. Some of these grew from small beginnings. A few individuals or the members of a family joined together and started the paper with a small printing press. If income was small, so also was expenditure. With the spread of education, and political consciousness the papers began to build larger circulations, the organisation was modernised, and the financial structure underwent a change. Private limited companies came into being, the shareholders of which were members of the same family. These invested no capital whatsoever in the shape of cash money but had shares assigned to them by mutual adjustment or agreement.
- Next comes the group of papers like the *Bombay Chronicle*, the *Bombay Samachar* and the *Bombay Sentinel* group in Bombay, the *Indian Nation* and *Aryavarta* group in Patna, the *National Herald, Navjivan* and *Quami Awaz* in Lucknow.
- The fourth class is divisible into two parts. *The Amrit Bazar Patrika,* the *Hindustan Standard* and the *Statesman,* all Calcutta papers have duplicate editions in other centres, the first in Allahabad and other two in Delhi. The *Patrika* and the *Standard* have sister Bengali papers in Calcutta. *The Times of India* has two editions, one in Bombay and the other in Delhi, (a third is about to be brought out in Calcutta) and a Hindi paper at all the three places besides a Bengali daily already published in Calcutta. It has also a number of smaller periodicals around it at Bombay, and the Evening News of India, which is an evening paper. The *Vishwamitra,* a Hindi daily, comes out from five places under the same name, while the *Milap,* as Urdu daily,

comes out from three places under the same name and has also a Hindi edition at Jullundur and at Hyderabad. There may be several others in this class.

- The second sub-group in the fourth class are the Goenka group and the Birla group, which have two or more papers at each centre and are linked up with multiple units or groups elsewhere.
- In this part of the memorandum attention is given to the four classes of newspapers. The problem of periodicals are dealt with separately.
- The medium-sized English language papers represented by the *Pioneer* and *National Herald* of Lucknow are six pages on weekdays and eight on Sundays, while the medium class Indian language papers are four pages on week-days and six or eight on Sundays. In this class may be included such newspapers as the *Nagpur Times,* the *Assam Tribune,* the *Deccan Herald* (Bangalore). Their capital is modest, their income sizeable, their staff just adequate. Before the war such of them as were in existence were not doing well; their position improved after the war. The present economic difficulty is hitting this class hard. The main purpose of most of these papers is to serve provincial needs while providing national and international news and comment. They are not free from their geographical limitations. Their circulations are limited, their advertisement revenue is not high.
- The small-size newspapers, daily and weekly, form the majority in this country. The normal size is four pages for a daily and a few small pages for a weekly. Financially they are often in difficulties, the single proprietor or his family or group bear the brunt from month to month. Their equipment is inadequate. Their revenue is poor, their staff is over-worked, their advertisement revenue is precarious, their circulation a few hundreds and they cannot even afford to get the minimum news services. Some papers of this class raise money often by obscure means. The picture of Hindi journalism given in the U.P. Inquiry Committee's report merits study.

- Unlike the average medium-size paper, this class is inclined to be partisan, perhaps because it feels it has no other means of survival. Some of the worst features of Indian journalism, personal and communal, are to be found at this level. The staff is badly paid and untrained. The difficulties of these papers principally arise from the attempt to compete with the big papers in a sphere which is not theirs, instead of devoting greater attention to intensive coverage of local news and local problems.
- There are the trust papers, that is, newspapers or weeklies owned by trusts. *The Tribune* of Ambala, the *Hitavada* of Nagpur, the *Pratap* of Kanpur and the Janmabhoomi group in Bombay fall in this class. Their affairs require deep study.
- Papers like the *Patrika,* the *Hindustan Standard* and the *Vishwamitra,* published simultaneously from more than one centre, are mainly owned by what may be called newspaper families or allies—persons whose main interests are in the newspaper industry. Although the duplicate edition of any such paper depends upon the reputation and efficiency of the home edition, it is the home edition that suffers most. Generally the capital of these subsidiary papers or editions is met from the revenues of the principal papers, with the result that their reserve funds dwindle, their staffs lose bonus and increments, the state loses its share of money by taxation, the office staff, the advertisement personnel, the correspondents and the editorial writers have to do work for two editions or more without any extra remuneration worth mentioning. For example, a correspondent covering the Capital for a Calcutta paper in this class has to be on the lookout for news from the Allahabad or Bombay angle also, as soon as the principal paper starts an edition in these two places.
- We have already pointed out that such a development affects workmen on the principal paper very badly as it absorbs all the available surplus. It provides sinecures and allowances to members of the proprietors' or directors' families. But its effect on the working conditions in areas

where it is simultaneously published is still worse. Such a paper with less expenditure on news services, correspondents, managerial staff and even on magazine sections and leading articles, is an unequal competitor to struggling newspapers in the provinces and ultimately kills them or forces them into the hands of chains. Workers in the duplicating centre have to be dependent on the conditions in home offices and in many cases like *Vishwamitra,* if they are deplorable at home they are more deplorable in the duplicating centres. This has been illustrated in the Kanpur Vishwamitra strike. The management dismissed the entire staff of 32 persons when they demanded some facilities from the management; their place was taken by workmen brought from its other centres of publication. The inside pages and the editorial, in fact everything except the local pages, came printed from Calcutta and were distributed here. We would request the Commission to scrutinise the working of this chain from a variety of angles.

- The effect on healthy traditions of journalism has been bad. On account of centralisation the editor of the edition has lost his status and the proprietor has gained much under cover of coordination. The editorial policy being dictated from one place, the paper wears an alien look at the other places of publication. Sometimes due to failure of one or two editions and the necessity of keeping them going, the principal paper has also suffered. The subsidiary paper needs less staff than an ordinary paper and the scope of employment definitely decreases. Service conditions can be very bad, as is evident from the fact that the conditions in *Vishwamitra* are the worst in the field in which it functions. On top of it, the sudden transfers act as a heavy deterrent on the independence of the journalist who, if found inconvenient, may be removed to a place most unsuitable to him. These transfers also help the management in creating rifts among workmen and utilising patronage to the detriment of *espirit de corps.* It is the experience of working journalists that in practice there is no difference in the working of chains, whether owned by business men or newspapermen. So we would suggest that the evil resides in the system rather than in the personality. Some of the points dealt with above are elaborated in later sections.

- Though they are separately mentioned, big business and chains are not really distinct from each other. They are essentially the same in many respects. The owners have large resources, they introduce a strong and undesirable element of competitive commerce into the newspaper world, own newspapers as one only of many other lines of business activity and use them as instruments of prestige, power and influence. In the interests of prestige, power and influence, they have often overlooked immediate monetary profit.
- Among chains, popularly accepted as such, three are prominent—the Birla, the Dalmia and the Goenka.
- It is well known that the proprietors of two of these three chains are related by marriage; they are knit even more closely by identity of outlook on political, social and economic questions. One of them is now associated with an enterprise for the manufacture of newsprint.
- Chains are of recent origin. The proprietors took over some existing English newspapers and later added Indian language papers and several weeklies. A complete financial picture of them can be obtained only by a thorough scrutiny of their own accounts as well as those of sister concerns. Some of them are reputed to have different sets of accounts. In order to carry out this scrutiny it is necessary that the Commission should engage its own independent auditors and examine the chief accountants and other officials of the concerns.
- The main question for consideration is whether we are witnessing a progressive concentration of ownership of the press in the hands of an oligarchy. The symptoms appear to leave no doubt about the answer. The process at work is somewhat as follows:

  A paper in distress wants to be saved from extinction, A

rich man steps in and takes it over. Another struggling paper feels that it cannot stand competition under the changing conditions and sells out. A third has a proprietor or a set of shareholders, who are tempted by the prospect of ready money and part with their shares. An example of a newspaper changing hands in this way is the *Leader* of Allahabad. The person who was identified with it had at no stage in his lifetime allowed any newspaper magnate to acquire it or exploit it. But within a few months of his death, the newspaper was sold as a purely commercial and political deal with no regard for its special tradition and character. Two millionaires ran neck to neck and one of them succeeded.

- Another example in a different category is the Bharat group of papers. In another part of this memorandum we have dealt with the way in which the staff of the Bharat group have been deprived of their legitimate dues. A close examination of this deal will reveal loopholes in the company law, which are used by financiers to the disadvantage of the public and of the employees.
- The Dalmia chain came into existence in different circumstances. The *Times of India* was sold out by its European proprietors, who felt that a British newspaper of its kind had lost its *raison d'etre* after Britain's transfer of power to India.

  Since then it has branched out from Bombay to Delhi.
- A point to be examined in this context arises from an entirely different attitude adopted by another British concern. The *Statesman* did not share the view that in the new political conditions a British newspaper had no place in India. It continues as the sole journalistic survivor of the old British dispensation. (Incidentally it was the first newspaper in India to initiate the new experiment of simultaneous publication from two cities.) A subject of enquiry would be, we suggest, how far it is in national interest to allow non-nationals to control organs of public opinion in India.
- As regards control we assume that what is meant is the

ultimate control exercised by shareholders. Most Indian newspapers are privately owned. As already stated they are mainly family concerns. They are able to provide finance even without the formality of issuing shares or debentures, and they attract people who have money to invest but who do not want to make their investments openly and do not concern themselves with control or management, so long as dividends are assured.

- In Indian conditions, so far as the newspaper big business is concerned, no precise difference separates management, control and ownership. Members of the same family are employed in various capacities. A good part of what appears in the books as expenditure under the head salaries and allowances returns to the family. The financial resources of these concerns are often siphoned into sister concerns or go to the benefit of relatives in the shape of commission or are shown as high rentals for accommodation or equipment.
- The balance sheets, the profit and loss accounts, the wage bills etc. of newspapers in this class require expert examination by the Press Commission's own accountants. The qualifications of the employees, their relationship to the shareholders and directors and the salaries they draw should also be investigated.
- The case for and against chains and the intrusion of big business into newspaper production may be stated at this stage. In defence of chains and big business, it has been urged that they are legal; that they represent a natural expansion of free private enterprise; they are subject to such indirect checks as are provided by the tradition, the general climate, and the personality of each institution, the general pressure exerted by the susceptibilities of public taste and the instincts of the reader, the power of deep-rooted local loyalties, the presence of several competing non-chain newspapers with the right kind of traditions. Another type of argument advanced is that the chains and the big business interests controlling them have the resources to contribute to the technical advancement of

newspaper production and to the improvement of news services; that they enlarge the field of available employment and so should be welcomed by working journalists.

- The validity of these arguments may be examined both from the point of view of working journalist and from the point of view of the country as a whole. Journalists would not concern themselves with the question whether chains have legal sanction or are theoretically good or bad. Journalists would judge chains by their practical effect on working conditions and on the shaping of newspapers as instruments of social and political progress. Applying this test, it may be observed that chains have not in fact produced better newspapers as compared to non-chain newspapers; nor have they necessarily or invariably provided better conditions of work.
- On the positive side, the following points may be urged:— The whole trend of progressive social and economic thought is against large accretions of productive power in the hands of the few. Decentralisation is an accepted policy. Newspapers in India, as elsewhere, are an industry, and have no claim to freedom from the restrictions and controls which are dictated by social and economic necessity. The only freedom to which they are entitled is freedom of expression. Controls and restrictions are either self-imposed or state-imposed. If newspaper chains are inspired by no higher motives than are other industries, then the case for the application of the same controls and restrictions to the one as to the other is difficult to resist. The State has assumed power, for instance, to control the geographical location of industries. The power rests upon the principle that the State has the right to make sure that industries are established or expanded in the interests of the country as a whole and not in accordance with the individual promoter's convenience or desire.
- Some newspaper chains are acting in a way that raises many disturbing questions. Reference has already been made to the newspaper, which now appears from Bombay and Delhi, and is spreading out to Calcutta? Is it justified

by the promise of better value to the reader in Calcutta than the existing newspaper there provide? By expanding eastwards, is the proprietor diverting profits away from their legitimate use for the betterment of the salaries and working conditions of the existing staff in Bombay and in Delhi?

- The functioning of chains may be examined from the point of view of its effect on the status of the editor. That is a real criterion. Wickham Steed has observed: "The paper's principal purpose is to give the public prompt, adequate, and accurate news, and to reflect and help in the formulation of public opinion. The moment it begins to subordinate that to commercial interest, it begins to deteriorate, to fail in its trust, to surrender the reason for its existence. This is not to ignore the importance of the business side of the paper, but it is to insist that the success of the business side must be the consequence of a thoroughly good editorial side to the public and not the determining factor in the editorial service."
- Scott has said: "The editor and the manager must march hand in hand, the editor one step ahead." In India it is the manager who is one step ahead.
- These quotations set forth the ideal as contrasted with the actual state of things. In actual fact, the *de facto* editor in chains suffers a double deprivation. He does not decide editorial policy nor does he always control the editorial staff, he loses both the status and designation to the proprietor or the managing director, who sets himself up as "managing editor." Such an assumption of title enables the managing editor to suggest that as the *de facto* editor's name does not appear as editor, he would not be publicly associated with any policy that the managing editor may lay down for the paper. This leads to a position in which editorials appear without the *de facto* editor's knowledge. So do news stories and even corrections.
- Some other fundamental objections to chains are: the owner of chains shrinks from risks which the old-time editor or editors or the small proprietor would take in order

to serve a public cause. The proprietor of chains is inclined to buy peace at almost any cost. He does not act fearlessly against the Government and does not challenge its ways even when those ways are felt to be wrong. He has many other interests to safeguard.

- As regards his motives, it is generally the case that he has found newspaper production a fairly safe commercial and political risk. He has tasted the power and prestige that ownership of newspapers brings. He has thus the advantages of a combination of economic and political advantages which few other enterprises provide. Instances are not lacking in which newspaper proprietors have used their position and influence to advance their other trade and commercial enterprises. Some proprietors may be usefully interrogated by the Commission about the licences and permits they and their friends and relatives have obtained during the last few years.
- The *Encyclopaedia Britannica* says: "Multiple ownership of newspapers possesses all the commercial and financial advantages of other big business, but mass production and centralised control destroy individuality. As members of a big combine newspapers lose character, they tend towards a standardised type. They may be between productions than is possible under isolated ownership but the old conception of a newspaper as an institution with a soul of its own, which could not be measured by ordinary commercial standards is gone."
- On the intellectual plane, Wickham Steed observes: "These forces tend to restrict the channels of public information. It stands to reason that when the public of a great city has a choice between only two 'organs of opinion' it is unlikely to be supplied with the same variety and fullness of news and comments as when five or six independent journals are competing for its favour. In this way one aspect of public freedom is curtailed."
- Reference has been made earlier to the possible influence of non-national interests controlling newspaper production in India. Other external influences are those of advertisers

and commercial houses, which are discussed under the relevant head. A recent phenomenon is the importation of foreign journalists by at least one chain, with results which cannot help the progress of journalism. The advent of a non-Indian news editor in the chain mentioned above has meant a certain cheapening and vulgarising of news coverage and presentation in the newspaper concerned. A further type of foreign influence is exerted through the bulk printing of propaganda literature by Indian newspaper presses on terms far above any strictly business considerations would warrant.

- It is argued that if the British Royal Commission has reported against action to end chains, a different conclusion may not be possible in Indian conditions. As against this, it must be pointed out that the Royal Commission's report caused great disappointment to many sections of British public opinion. The feeling against chains is intense in India, where the need to protect infant democratic institutions is much greater.
- Whatever its conclusions might be the British Royal Commission has expressed clear views as to the dangerous character of chains. It says: "The question at what stage of its development either in size or integration, a chain may become a potential danger to public interest does not appear to us to be susceptible of a simple answer. Much depends on the integration of the chain, particularly on the editorial side and on the geographical concentration of its members. While therefore we are of the opinion that the growth of a chain to a size appreciably larger than now in existence would be undesirable, we do not feel able to specify any limit in advance of such a development and we do not recommend that any statutory limit should be put."
- In passing, we would refer to some preventive-cum-curative steps taken in two democracies. In U.S.A. proprietors of newspapers are required, under rules enforced by Government, to submit at intervals details about invested capital and any increases or decreases in such capital that might have taken place. Other restrictions are also imposed under anti-Trust laws.

- In France, a limit is placed on the number of shares one can hold in a newspaper. That limit is ten per cent of the share capital. The law also provides that any person, who has a predominant voice in any industry having a capital. more than ten million francs, shall not own any newspaper.
- In any effort to counter the effects of chains in India, similar restrictions are worthy of examination. It may also be considered whether special powers, analogous to the Reserve Bank's powers of inspection of banks, should be assumed to receive and inspect the accounts of newspaper establishments.
- A suggestion canvassed in this connection is to foster and encourage the present trend towards increasing association of employees with the management and control of newspapers. This is a trend of which the ultimate issue will be cooperative management and control by the staff. Experiments in this field have already been undertaken but whatever degree of success may attend these individual efforts to break new ground, cooperative ownership, management and control constitute the next important stage in the evolution of newspapers as a whole in Indian conditions. It is our claim that cooperative ownership, management and control really mean the production of newspapers, not as a profit-making or prestige-building industry but as instruments of public good. Cooperative control and management may be established either by voluntary action of existing newspaper interests or by legislation.
- As a way of countering the effects of chains, the British Royal Commission in its report has discussed suggestions to peg newspaper circulations. This idea may be investigated by the Commission in relation to Indian conditions.
- In the case of chain as well as non-chain newspapers, it has been pointed out that job printing or publication of journals, magazines and books, undertaken by a newspaper unit, should not be kept apart in the matter of accounts. Such bifurcation of accounts is felt to be a device intended to keep down figures of revenue. This requires investigation.

News Collection Sources

The general set-up and functioning of news agencies may be examined under three broad heads:—

- Distribution of Indian news to Indian newspapers.
- Distribution of Indian news to foreign newspapers.
- Distribution of foreign news to Indian newspapers.
- These are closely related functions in which the major Indian news agencies are engaged in association with foreign agencies. The major Indian news agencies are:

The Press Trust of India, which works in association with Reuters; and

The United Press of India, which works in association with Agence France Presse.

- Foreign agencies functioning in India, without any form of association with any indigenous agency, are:—
    1. The Associated Press of America, which handles Indian news for foreign newspapers;
    2. The United Press of America, which covers both Indian news to foreign newspapers and foreign news to Indian newspapers;
    3. The Near and Far East News Agency, functioning more or less on the same lines as the U.P.A.
    4. Tass, the official Russian agency, covering Indian news to Russian newspapers and distributing Soviet official news to the Indian Press;
    5. A Chinese news agency, working on the same lines as Tass.
    6. Other similar agencies like the A.P. of Pakistan, and Exchange Telegraphs, whose interest is confined to the supply of Indian news to the press of their respective countries.
- Because of its importance, the position of P.T.I. deserves full and close examination. The P.T.I. is the successor to the Associated Press of India in the internal sphere. The A.P.I. was an Indian subsidiary of Reuters. The P.T.I.'s

status is different. As its name implies, it is a trust. It was formed mainly by the bigger newspapers in 1948, as an agency independent of Reuters. But it entered into a form of partnership with Reuters for the supply of Indian news to foreign newspapers and foreign news to Indian newspapers. This change in the relationship between the two agencies was a natural development that followed the change in the political relationship between the two countries.

- The full picture of the negotiations between Reuters and the P.T.I., which resulted in the present arrangement, is not available. It is difficult to judge whether in determining the terms of the partnership, due account was taken of the fact that without the agreement with the P.T.I., at that stage, Reuters could not have continued to operate as the main supplier of foreign news to India. Under the policy laid down by the Government of India then, teleprinter facilities, on which Reuters depended, were to be given in a strict order of priority. They were to be given first to Indian news agencies, second to Indian newspapers, and third to foreign news agencies. The physical and technical equipment of the Posts and Telegraphs Department at that time was so limited that foreign news agencies would have had to wait for a long time before their claim for teleprinter facilities could be considered. Reuters, therefore, was under the pressure of immediate and urgent need to come to an agreement with the P.T.I. This need should have been fully reflected in the conditions of the agreement. Whether it was so reflected requires investigation in view of several disturbing stories that are current.
- As far as information available to the Federation goes, the main features of the P.T.I.'s Articles of Association are:

  Not more than one hundred shares can be held by any one newspaper;

  Maximum voting strength of the newspaper is five irrespective of the number of shares held;

  No profits to be distributed to shareholders; Share capital Rs. 5,00,000;

A number of debentures issued at 4 per cent guaranteed interest;

The present annual income estimated at Rs. 50 lakhs, or ten times the share capital.

- The negotiations with Reuters were carried on without the substantial approval or support of all Indian newspapers. Some of the smaller newspapers in particular kept away. The major part of the share capital came from the bigger newspapers which include what are known as chains. It was open to them to take shares in the name of each of the newspapers owned by them. And their effective voting strength grew in proportion. Thus the restriction on voting strength has no practical effect in their individual cases.
- In the actual financial working of the P.T.I. the distinction between legitimate expenditure out of revenues and legitimate expenditure out of capital is not strictly observed. Instances have been known of capital expenditure being met from revenues. This is an innovation which it may be claimed has been sanctioned and sanctified by the Government of India's new budget practice. But the effect of the P.T.I. adopting a similar practice has inevitable repercussions on the salary of the staff. From this point of view, departures from accepted cannons of financial practice are of vital interests to employees on whom the efficiency, the integrity, and the objectivity of the news service as a whole rests.
- The levy of subscriptions for the service provided by the P.T.I. is an important point which influences the agency's manner of working. The complaint has been heard that some of the bigger newspapers, who are directors of the Trust, allow their monthly subscription to fall into heavy arrears. To that extent the burden of keeping the agency going is shifted to the more conscientious and more regular subscribers, among whom are the smaller newspapers which own no shares or debentures, and whose financial resources severely restrict expenditure on news services.
- Both from the point of view of the staff and in the interest of the general public as a whole, the outstanding point to

consider is how far the P.T.I. in its present form and under its present management has performed its function of providing an efficient, independent, objective news service. An answer is implicit in a number of recent omissions. [Full details will be supplied to the Commission in confidence at a later stage.]

- A new type of influence on the character of the news service is exerted by the extension of the service to commercial houses and speculators. This criticism also applies to the United Press of India. In support of such extension it is argued that it is necessary in order to increase revenue. The service was originally confined to the supply of market rates. It is being gradually enlarged to include fluctuations of rates every few minutes. When legislative efforts to curb stock exchange speculation are being promoted, it should be examined whether any agency could be permitted directly or indirectly to provide information on which speculative transactions are based.
- The P.T.I.'s agreement with Reuters is due to expire early next year. The Board of the P.T.I. is said to be acutely divided both on the question of termination of the agreement and on the question of alternative arrangements to procure foreign news. The ideal alternative would be bulk purchase of news from a number of news agencies including Reuters, pooling the news in Bombay, and providing a properly coordinated, composite service to the Indian newspapers. This is desirable because dependence on Reuters alone for the supply of world news has deprived the Indian reader of a balanced picture of world events. It has meant that in situations such as have developed in Iran or Egypt, where British interests are deeply committed, objectivity and balance are not scrupulously observed. In a system of pooling such as is now suggested what Reuters provides in such situations can be corrected and symmetrised by what other non-British agencies provide. While, as already stated, this is the ideal arrangement, the Federation is not in a position to say whether the cost of it is within the present financial resources of the P.T.I.

- The Federation, however, would suggest that this as well as other difficulties and shortcomings of the P.T.I. are curable by drastic reorganisation of the whole set-up.
- One proposal that has been suggested in this connection is that control of the organisation should be given to an independent public corporation such as has been suggested for All India Radio. It would be a corporation composed of representatives of one or two cultural bodies, organisation of journalists and the Chief Justice of India. The number of members could be kept down to a reasonable limit of nine or ten.
- The corporation might be financially assisted by Government, if necessary. At first sight the idea of financial assistance from Government might be dreaded and dismissed as reactionary, retrograde and undesirable. In actual fact, however, Government assistance is at present being provided in a fairly generous, though indirect, way. The Central Government are buying the P.T.I. service for All India Radio and for the External Affairs Ministry's use. Many State Governments are subscribing to the P.T.I. service. An element of assistance is also present in the terms on which teleprinter channels are leased out to news agencies and newspapers. What is now suggested is in fact an extension of these concessions in the case of the P.T.I. and the U.P.I., the latter when it becomes a public trust. In one form or other concessions are given by every Government to national news agencies the world over. One of the heaviest items of expenditure in the P.T.I.'s budget is the annual rental on teleprinter lines, even at the present concessional rates. This could be reduced in the case of a public corporation taking over the news service. If this service is properly manned and directed, association with Government in the financial sphere need not influence the character of the news provided.
- A public corporation of the kind suggested has positive advantages. It will prevent concentration of power and eliminate the influence of any one group either of proprietors, editors or others. It will remove financial anxiety

which generally leads to a search for revenue in desirable as well as undesirable directions. It will enable the agency to come to an arrangement with more than one foreign agency and so get rid of monopolies such as have been enjoyed by Reuters. It may enable the agency eventually to develop a network of correspondents all over the world. It could deal with big and small subscribers impartially and enforce regular payments of subscriptions without fear or favour.

- The other Indian news agency functioning on a comparable scale in India, the United Press of India, is a joint stock company whose directors include newspaper proprietors, politicians and businessmen. Dr. B.C. Roy, the West Bengal Chief Minister, is its Chairman (on leave). It shares the defects of the P.T.I. and has certain peculiar faults of its own. Its association with Agence France Presse, an avowedly official news agency, must be closely examined.
- A serious defect, common to both the agencies, arises from conditions of work of the staff and particularly the method of recruitment and promotion and the extent to which family and other relationships influence them.
- This has been dealt with more fully under working conditions. Attention may be drawn to the provision in the staff recruitment rules of the United Nations and certain Government of India departments, under which every applicant is required to declare his family relationship with any existing member of the staff. Relationship with directors or proprietors is equally a matter on which full light should be thrown in considering applications for jobs in newspaper offices.
- A development which must cause misgiving, is the grant of teleprinter facilities to the United Press of America. As far as the Federation knows, the technical position has been that foreign agencies would come last and would only get a share in surplus facilities, if any, left over after the needs of Indian news agencies and newspapers are satisfied. But the general policy has been understood to be that the greatest care and vigilance would be exercised

in judging the credentials and record of any foreign agency that asks for teleprinter facilities. Such a policy, strictly applied, would normally discourage any foreign news agency establishing a rival news supply on its own without the intermediary of an indigenous agency. Is the grant of teleprinter facilities to the United Press of America good in national interests? Were newspapers or other interests concerned consulted before the foreign agency was helped in this way?

- The foregoing survey of the position would suggest these lines of enquiry:—
   1. How far is the present position and functions of the P.T.I. helpful to the provision of an efficient, independent, impartial news service to Indian newspapers?
   2. How far does the preponderance of certain big newspaper interests influence the character of the news service of the P.T.I.? Is it desirable at all in principle? Does it lead to suppression or slanting of certain types of news in deference to the express or implied wishes of these interests? How far does the composition of the United Press of India hamper, in a similar manner, its news services?
   3. Is the control of the managerial and editorial functions of the agencies vested in one and the same hands? How far is such a combination responsible for the present situation? How can the editorial side be kept free of the influences of the managerial side in regard to objective coverage of news?
   4. How far does the revenue from commercial service influence the character of the news?
   5. How has the PTI's partnership with Reuters and UPI's association with AFP worked?
   6. In arriving at PTI's partnership with Reuters was full advantage taken of the position of strength the PTI occupied at that time?
   7. Were Reuters assets in India correctly valued? Were the terms of the partnership more advantageous

financially to Reuters than to the P.T.I.? Did any newspaper proprietor or any other negotiator play any part in weighing the scales against the P.T.I.?

8. What alternatives to the present P.T.I. set-up are feasible? How far will a public corporation or a cooperative organisation with Government aid be an acceptable alternative?
9. Financially how have the two agencies been working? What are the defects due to and how can they be cured? Are newspaper subscriptions commensurate with the service rendered? Are the bigger papers paying their due share?
10. What alternative arrangements are possible in place of the expiring partnership with Reuters? How far is bulk purchase of news from more than one foreign agency possible from the financial point of view?
11. What is the policy of the two agencies in regard to recruitment and promotion? How far are they based on merit and on other considerations?
12. How far are adequate communication facilities available for expanding the organisations both internally and externally?
13. In the collection and supply of news, do the agencies pay adequate attention to all regions?
14. Do the agencies give impartial attention to all parties and interests?

Periodicals : Like the daily press, but to a greater extent, the periodical press in India has developed as an adjunct to the Indian political movement. But India has no periodical press in the sense in which it is understood in the U.K. or the U.S.A.

- In the Indian languages especially, it was the weekly that was first established owing to its low cost. The daily followed later. In areas, where the dailies have not developed, the weekly press is still a powerful factor. Where the dailies have become powerful, weeklies, especially those which had been vehicles of political views have become casualties.

- Periodicals can be broadly classified into weeklies and biweeklies and quarterlies.
- They cover mostly the political or commercial fields. A few of them are well off, but the vast majority lead a hand to mouth life, (while a few even resort to doubtful means for continuing their existence). In the fields of science, art, literature and so on, there are few high class periodicals. Some of them are financially well off. Cinema periodicals and such other publications must be mentioned as a separate category. They are mostly mouthpieces of some interested company or producer or some other interest, some of them are nothing more than sheets of scandals about those engaged in the industry. Another new development is the large number of children's magazines. Parents and educationists have been complaining that some of them are of such a standard that they have a very unhealthy influence on the children's minds. The possibility of fixing some standard for such magazines and even qualifications for those conducting them is worth examination.
- From the point of view of ownership there are two types:
  (1) those owned by chains and big newspapers—a recent development, and
  (2) those owned by proprietors or private limited companies.
- Among the types of ownership, should also be mentioned those of political parties or leaders of political parties. Weeklies, which are concentrating on sensationalism, are a new type.
- In the private limited or proprietary concerns the proprietor is most often also the editor and in the case of the smaller periodicals has very little other staff. The monthlies occupied a high position in the thirties but have now fallen on bad days. They were edited and run by men of great eminence, who conducted them, not for financial gain—most of them worked at a loss—but in a missionary spirit or for educative purposes. The periodicals at one time used to get a large

quality of advertisement but these have generally been diverted to daily newspapers now.

- Newsprint and paper account for a large portion of the expenditure of periodicals. Most of the periodicals cannot import directly. During the war and since then newsprint has been in acute shortage and they have had to depend on agents or on the waste from the big papers. Mostly they have been buying in the black market. Even now good printing paper for printing blocks etc. is mostly imported and is costly, and the periodicals find great difficulty in obtaining them. The Commission should devote some attention to the needs of this class.
- When the Press in India began to develop as an industry and commercialism crept in, some of the proprietor-editors entered the periodical field where they felt they would have less competition from more organised big business. For some time their hopes fructified. But recently the big papers and chains have entered this field also. These have an advantage over the ordinary periodicals. They are able to use the waste newsprint from their dailies, utilise the vast printing resources of their presses and thus produce periodicals at rather cheap rates. They are able to print a large number of copies, not all of which are circulated in fact, though they swell circulation figures and advertisement revenue. At no distant date they may be a threat to the periodical press, where some independence now exists.
- In the U.K. the national dailies do not come out on Sundays. This self-restraint on their part has helped the growth of the periodical press there. There are a number of papers coming out on Sundays, giving some minimum news but largely devoted to feature articles and other matters of general interest. Even where a concern bringing out a daily also brings out a Sunday paper, the staff of the Sunday paper is entirely separate. In India, on the other hand, newspapers, which used to observe a weekly holiday before the war, now come out on all days in the week, with a magazine section on Sundays.
- The advent of big business into the periodical field with

its emphasis on large circulations, has also brought with it all the evils of such a development in the dailies—cross-word puzzles with gifts, comic strips and cartoons, lowering of standards to pander to lowest human tastes etc.

Contribution from Outside

Feature Syndicates are yet to develop in the country. There are a few functioning, but the general complaint against most is that they take away a large share of the payment received and some of them do not even give proper accounts.

- One feature syndicate is conducted on a purely personal basis. It "syndicates" the writings of the conductor, and rarely writing of others. This syndicate is nevertheless recognised as a news agency by the Government and even by the Parliament Secretariats, whereas free lancers, to whom journalism is a whole time occupation and means of livelihood, are denied such elementary facilities as access to the press gallery of Parliament and are not put on the press list of the Information Department.
- Inquiries may usefully be made to find out whether some of these so-called feature syndicates really exist, excepting in name, and how they function.

Functions in a Process

Journalism in India is generally looked upon as the product of a missionary, as opposed to a mercenary, inspiration. The old-time journalist's equipment and outlook fitted into that background and tradition. His approach is different now. It corresponds to the transformation of the newspaper into an industry, a large part of which, as stated elsewhere in this memorandum, has passed into the hands of big businessmen. The journalist is feeling the impact of many of the undesirable accompaniments and few of the benefits of industrialisation. His physical and mental strain has greatly increased but the higher living standards which might have helped him to stand that strain have not come his way in any large measure.

[Fairly full details of working conditions of journalists are given in the reports of the Madhya Pradesh and Uttar Pradesh enquiry committees.]

- *Emoluments:* The legacy of the 'missionary age' of Indian journalism is preserved today only in the austerity of the journalist's emoluments. Salaries in the large majority of cases are unrelated to cost of living. The working journalist feels that if it is essential to keep a Government servant or a judge above want in order to enable him to discharge his duties efficiently and independently it is no less essential that the journalist should be treated on the same principle.
- When the old-time newspaper began to give way to the new industrialised product newspaper employees other than the working journalist took the necessary steps to place themselves in a position of bargaining strength and obtained quite a few rights. The working journalist stood on false dignity and was left behind.
- It is necessary for the Commission to look closely into the argument put forward on behalf of the employer class that no detailed enquiry into working conditions is called for and that the industry cannot bear the burden of any increase in wages and emoluments. Facts are set out in this memorandum to demonstrate that both these lines of argument are untenable.
- Disparity in scales of remuneration ranges from Rs. 60 to Rs. 2,000 even in the same office. The proprietor or the manager exercises his right to play off one member of the staff against another by arbitrarily increasing remuneration. Promotions, unaccompanied by increments in salary, are not uncommon.
- Persons performing the same function in the same institution are paid different scales of salary. The difference is not accounted for by seniority. Initial salaries are different. In the Indian language papers, one person is often required to do a variety of jobs, as sub-editor, reporter, leader-writer, and sometimes proof-reader, frequently in the course of one day.
- Such salary as is fixed is not regularly paid. No fixed dates for payment are observed in a majority of newspapers.

- Dearness allowance is paid in some offices but it generally bears little relation to cost of living or its fluctuations. Where any conveyance allowance is paid to reporters, there is no uniformity of principle even in the same office. On one newspaper chain, there is the instance of correspondent who has a car and is paid less by way of conveyance allowance than another who uses only a bicycle. The allowance is obviously not fixed by any recognised standard.
- *Working Hours:* In several newspaper offices there are no regular hours of work for the editorial staff. On the reporting side the position is worse. Even on leading newspapers the maximum number of working hours is not strictly enforced. A basic requirement of the profession is that working hours should be specified and fixed according to international practice, which provides for six hours during the day and five hours during the night. In the News Agencies, particularly in the smaller stations, working hours are anywhere between ten and twelve a day.
- *Night Duty:* There is nothing that a newspaper man dreads more than night duty, and there are few newspapermen who can avoid it. The employee of a newspaper in present conditions runs the risk of sacrificing a few years of his life, corresponding to the hours he spends on night duty.
- In the large majority of cases, journalists on night duty do not get normal rest and relaxation. They are on duty often without a sufficient break. Amenities like tea are not generally provided by the office. Fans in summer and a fire in winter are a luxury. In some offices, sub-editors retire very late, almost at the break of dawn. Not many offices provide retiring rooms. Even newspaper offices which can afford it hardly make any arrangement for conveyance for the weary men after night duty. Public transport is not usually available at the hours at which their duty ends, and so they often walk or cycle long distances. Yet the office may have fleet of cars parked on its premises. It is not unusual on a cold or rainy morning to see newspapermen after night duty spreading themselves on

the tables or on the floor with a newspaper file for a pillow, and later trudging out tired and jaded. Night work is a nightmare in these offices.

- *Overtime:* There is a general demand for overtime work, but in the majority of cases there is nothing like overtime payment for members of the editorial staff on the ground that they are not workers covered by the Factories Act.
- *Weekly Off:* On the bigger papers the "weekly off" is provided. On the smaller ones even this is not available in practice. In many offices the off is not given when the shift changes, but only at the convenience of the employer, and it is not unusual for a person, after doing night duty till past-midnight, being required to work in the following day's shift.
- *Sunday Work:* There is only one day's rest in the week for a newspaperman, though the functions he is called upon to discharge are such as require longer rest and recuperation. It is to be noted that it is not one day in a six-day week as in other countries. In India it is the practice to produce the same paper on Sundays too without a separate staff for the Sunday edition. A Sunday paper functions as an altogether separate entity in other countries and has its own special set up.
- Incidentally in Indian conditions work on Sundays has meant for newspapermen enforced aloofness from active social life and absence of normal contact with the people.
- *Provident Fund, Bonus and Other Benefits:* Barring a few papers, there is no provident fund benefit, especially on the Indian language and the smaller sized papers. Where there is such a scheme, the employer's contribution generally is half of the employees and the employee gets the benefit only after he has put in some years' service. And because of insecurity of service, it is rarely that the employee gets the employer's contribution. Even on some of the bigger paper the employer's contribution is not fixed at a satisfactory level. Many employers excuse themselves from contributing their share on one ground or another. In one Calcutta group the proprietor has excused himself

from contributing to the provident fund scheme on the ground that his net annual income is below Rs. 35,000 after payment of income tax. The books of the company seldom show an income over this figure. The provident fund contribution is also only on salary and not on total emoluments. In some offices, it is not unusual for an employee to get half his emoluments as salary and the other half as dearness allowances. That brings the management's contribution down still further. Though the Act provides for it, in many papers, the provident fund money is not kept separately, and, the amounts are not unoften utilised for running the paper.

- Only a few papers give some sort of bonus. Even those which make huge profits do not as a rule give bonuses, though it is now accepted that bonus is not ex-gratia payment but a sort of deferred wage. Even where bonus is paid, it has no relation to profits made. In some chains, profits are diverted to losing subsidiaries, and the staff get no bonus. Bonus in respect of the past year is paid during the current year only to those who remain on the staff on the day the payment is made, with the result that those who have earned the bonus but have left the paper do not get the bonus.
- Payment of gratuity is largely absent. In one news agency, the management is now actively considering a proposal to retire compulsorily those who have put in 25 years service and over, but it has not indicated that any gratuity is intended to be paid.
- The same is the position with regard to pension. There are also no provisions in regard to compulsory insurance. In certain offices, even when a person is engaged in hazardous work, there is no automatic insurance cover.
- *Leave Rules:* The provision for leave is unsatisfactory. A few papers are generous enough to give casual, privilege and sick leave. Even in major newspaper offices, privilege leave is not easily available, may be because of shortage of staff, nor is it allowed to be accumulated.
- In the language papers conditions are much worse. It is

difficult to obtain even sick leave. Some managements insist that a person should exhaust his privilege leave before he can take sick leave. In the news agencies which have no closed holidays at all, especially at smaller centres, the provisions for casual leave, sick leave and privilege leave are not observed in practice. On many occasions, when a journalist's services are dispensed with, his accumulated leave has been callously forfeited. In some offices discrimination is made among members of the staff in the matter of leave. In some cases extra leave is adjusted, while in other cases salary is cut for the period according to the whims of the management.

- *Holidays:* Absence of closed holidays in the newspaper industry is a serious grievance. Under the exemptions granted to the newspaper printing presses, the list of closed holidays has been gradually curtailed, and some newspapers work even on all-India holidays. The news agencies have no closed holidays at all. Nor is there any provision in such cases for compensatory leave.
- *Accommodation:* Accommodation has become a major problem in most areas. In the towns and cities now, rents are high and take away a good slice of the salary. Many journalists have to live in abnormal conditions. One newspaper built houses out of the company's funds for the staff originally, but the rent that it fixed was so exorbitant that it was not within the reach of the employees. The buildings have since been let out to others.
- *Medical Aid:* This is largely absent. Barring a handful of concerns in the country which have their own doctors, there is no provision for the free medical aid.
- *Amenities:* Amenities like canteens and recreational facilities are largely absent.
- *Recruitment and Training:* Though the work of a newspaperman, especially in the modern newspaper is as much a craft as that of an engineer, a doctor or a lawyer, no regular system or scheme of recruitment and training exist in most offices.

- Modern journalism requires not only large background knowledge but specialisation. There is need in journalism for a high standard of education coupled with vocational training. This need is all the more on the Indian language papers. Till recently there were no facilities for training journalists either on newspapers or at the universities. In the past few years diploma courses in journalism have been introduced in a few universities but even they are not in a position to give the sort of practical training that would enable the trainees to get employment of the right type. In the newspaper offices at present a person can learn only the hard way. Most of the newspapers demand trained and experienced men, but few have cared to take steps for the training of men. Generally, newspapers do not encourage paid apprentices while some like to recruit apprentices under the guise of training them and take free service from them. Even in institutions where diploma courses have been instituted only raw persons are being taught a few rudiments and turned on into an already overcrowded field. The utility of such training and such other factors should be carefully assessed.
- *Contracts:* In most offices no appointment letter is given to the employee on recruitment nor is a contract signed. In several cases dismissal orders are the only written proof of appointment.
- *Security of Service:* There is no security of service in the profession. Services are terminated without any case being shown. In one recent case a senior member of the editorial staff (with twenty-three years' service) of a big chain, was dismissed, and he died soon afterwards. The shock was too great for him.
- A change of management in the newspaper industry has also come to mean termination of employment or at least the threat of it. Another factor is a sudden change in policy.
- *Notice:* Great hardship is caused by termination of services without adequate notice. The root cause is absence of definite or agreed terms of service in the great majority of appointments. Attention is invited to a Bombay decision

given last year, in which the City Civil Court held that, in the case of journalists, termination of service could not be made on a month's notice. The court laid down the dictum that a journalist could not be treated as though he was a domestic servant; that his work was such that alternative employment was not easy to obtain.

- The case of the *Bharat* of Bombay illustrates some of the most serious defects that require quick remedy. A brief reference has been made earlier to this case. It deserves fuller treatment in this section. The facts given here are all that could be obtained by the Federation with its limited resources in matters of this kind. The Commission will no doubt be able to get all the details for arriving at correct decisions.
- "Bharat" and allied publications were started with a distinguished board of directors, including Mr. K. M. Munshi, Mr. S. K. Patil, Mr. R. D. Birla, Mr. Tulsidas Kilachand, and Mr. Dharamse Khatau. Two apparently separate companies were formed for the purpose of publishing the papers. One was Akhil Bharat Printers Limited; the other Hindustan Newspapers Limited. The promoters were the same in both cases and Mr. Dahyabhai Patel was managing director of both, Akhil Bharat Printers owned the press and rented it to Hindustan Newspapers. Almost from the very start, Bharat began to lose heavily. Why it could make no headway despite the powerful auspices under which it began its career, is in itself a matter for investigation. The Hindustan Newspapers fell into arrears of rental to Akhil Bharat Printers. Arrears of staff salaries accumulated. In the case of one of Bharat's correspondent in Delhi, details of which were communicated to the Federation, the arrears amounted to Rs. 25,000/-. The management embarked upon a policy of drastic retrenchment. Editorial staff was cut down. Many were sent out without adequate notice. One of them took the matter to court, which gave an important decision in favour of working journalists. (This is referred to earlier. It held, first, that in the case of a journalist of the status of the complainant, six months'

notice must be accepted as the rule, second, that in consideration of the financial condition of Bharat some concession was called for and therefore compensation in lieu of four months notice should be given). In the meantime, the management of Akhil Bharat changed hands. Hindustan Newspapers Limited gave away the "goodwill" of Bharat and other allied publications and a part of its assets such as newsprint stocks and newsprint quotas to Akhil Bharat Printers. In return the debt owed to Akhil Bharat Printers was written off. Hindustan Newspapers received further assistance in the form of a sum of money. Thereafter Hindustan Newspapers Limited went into liquidation. The employees, including the sub-editor who holds a decree for four months' salary, have still to recover their dues.

- From a study of this case, it should be plain that not only proper conditions of work have to be prescribed, but that machinery should be established to enforce those conditions and give speedy relief to the aggrieved employee. Sufficient legal remedy is not provided by the present Payment of Wages Act, which places a limit upon the amount recoverable under its provisions.
- Suitable amendments to the Companies Act are in our view necessary so that amounts due to the employees as arrears of salary etc. are made the first charge on assets at the time of liquidation. These and other remedies were suggested by us in our memorandum to the Company Law Enquiry Committee of the Government of India. The Committee, we regret to say, has not discussed them.
- The need arises in an acute form for standardisation of jobs and for the fixation of reasonable and regular scales of pay. These may have to vary from place to place or from region to region. The Commission will presumably first obtain information on prevailing conditions. In that task the questionnaire prepared by the Bombay Union of Journalists, will be of great help. It suggests a number of questions to be posed to newspapers. The replies are bound to be revealing.
- *Mofussil Correspondents:* If the conditions of a staff man

are bad, those of the mofussil correspondent are much worse. He is not on the staff; he is paid probably something by way of honorarium and retainer and something extra for what is published. In many cases, however, he is paid nothing; he is expected to be content with the free supply of the newspaper. So most of this class have to find other sources of livelihood. This inevitably has its repercussions on their work. Most of them do not get any conveyance allowance. Thev might incur some expenditure, write out a story and send it to the paper only to have it 'killed' and thus lose even the little money they might have got if it was published. Their status and position are particularly bad.

- Local Politicians and Officials—even Ministers—many times try to bully such correspondents. In one case which came to the knowledge of the Federation, a correspondent in Cuttack had been for years functioning for two papers, belonging to two chains. Both chain proprietors knew this fact. Suddenly one morning, the correspondent, according to his version, found that one of the papers had appointed another, the invalid son of a Minister of that State as its Cuttack Correspondent. A few days earlier, the proprietor of the chain had met the Minister at Puri. When the correspondent asked the management of the paper why he was treated in this fashion, he was told that his coverage was not satisfactory, that he was working for two papers, that the paper's requirements were being met by the agencies and hence his services were being terminated. It is learnt that as soon as the Minister concerned ceased to be a Minister his son's appointment was also terminated. The whole story leaves in one's mind a strong feeling that this was a case of Ministerial interference and pressure so that a correspondent more amenable to the Ministry could be appointed. Perhaps it was a case of a newspaper proprietor putting a Minister under his obligation.
- *The Free Lance Writer:* In the absence of a proper weekly press, the position of the free lance writer is very bad. The rights of this class are not always respected even by the most reputed papers and weeklies. Many times the articles

sent by a free-lance writer were accepted and published but it is months before payment is made to him, if it is ever made. The honorarium is generally poor. Government publicity bureaus and foreign information services are practically tending to throw the free lance writer out of occupation. With the steady stream of handouts, articles, photographs etc. flowing in, newspapers find it easy to fill space without the need to spend money. For one thing it is a wholly one-sided picture that the reader gets, for another journalists are robbed of opportunities to study and make any thoughtful contribution.

- Reference has been made earlier to irregularity in the payment of salaries and allowances in many establishments. Mofussil correspondents, more than other employees, suffer from this form of hardship. The farther away the employee is from headquarters, the less attention does he receive from the management in the matter of payment. A census of correspondents who have not been paid for long periods and of the aggregate amounts due to them has not been made, but it would disclose revealing figures. The total arrears may be roughly estimated at a few lakhs of rupees.
- From the personal knowledge of several members of the Federation, it may be stated that in a large number of cases, correspondents have given up attempts to recover arrears. Even the expense of the labour courts are generally beyond their means and have in many cases to be met by contributions from colleagues or by journalists' organisations. It is also not clear whether correspondents can get relief under the present labour laws. Sometimes decrees have been obtained but not executed.
- *Settlement of Disputes:* The point is worth reiterating at this stage that newspapers are now accepted as an industry, and that the journalist who produces or processes material for publication in newspapers must be included in the definition of "worker" entitled to protection. In view of the peculiar conditions of newspaper work, however, special machinery within the framework of the Industrial Disputes Act would have to be evolved to settle disputes.

- A lacuna in the present Industrial Disputes Act has been pointed out. Its provisions are not applicable to all persons who have the right to organise themselves as trade unions. This requires to be remedied. It has been suggested that the definition of the word "workman" in the Industrial Disputes Act should be coterminous with the definition in the Trade Union Act. The definition of "employee" should be such as to include everyone whose work is intellectual, clerical or manual or a mixture of them, but who has no control over management or direction of the concern.
- *Labour Laws:* The present industrial legislation has grown mainly with the factory worker in view. It is only on our application that the Shops and Commercial Establishment Act, U.P., the Payment of Wages Act, the Industrial Disputes Act have been interpreted to benefit in some cases the working journalists also. The general feeling is in favour of a uniform press workers' law throughout the country.
- The Press Workers' Law should be operated through special Press Benches in various regions. Pressmen working in a particular region irrespective of the fact that their employers happen to exist outside that regional Bench's jurisdiction should be governed by that law on an all-India basis. The employers, too, must be governed likewise. A newspaper having its head office at New Delhi in case its representative works at Lucknow, should not claim exemption on the ground that New Delhi is outside the Uttar Pradesh jurisdiction so far as industrial law is concerned.
- It is desirable that finality should be reached at some stage in decisions of these industrial courts. If High Courts are free to review decisions of the Central Labour Appellate Tribunals by means of writs, the result would be prolonged uncertainty.
- A time limit should be set to the trial and decision of cases in the industrial courts.
- The cost of litigation should be borne by the management in case the delay is caused on account of the management.

- The most important factor is that there must be some competent machinery to enforce the decisions of the industrial courts.
- If possible the Government must maintain a list of journalist assessors to help these industrial courts on important technical issues.

Opposite Powers

Freedom of the Press is a principle on which there is unanimous agreement in theory but sharp difference of opinion in practical application. There is agreement on the thesis that freedom of the press, like other freedoms, is subject to restrictions; but as to the extent and character of restrictions, the press has differed acutely from the Government. The press opposed the amendment of Article 19(2) of the Constitution.

- That opposition was based on grounds, some of which were later upheld by the Supreme Court. In its judgment in the case of *Shailabala Devi* vs. *the State of Bihar,* the Patna High Court had held that the constitutional guarantee about Freedom of Expression protected even incitement to violence. The Government's contention was that this judgment created an impossible situation. The Supreme Court on appeal held that even under the article in its original form, the right of freedom of speech did not protect incitement to violence. There was therefore no need or justification for the amendment of Article 19(2).
- The Press (Objectionable Matters) Act was opposed by the press and very strongly condemned by our. Federation, and it was eventually modified in response to public criticism. But opposition to the Act as a whole stands, though it must be acknowledged that no complaints have been heard of the way in which its provisions have so far been used.
- Journalists generally agree with the conclusions of the Press Laws Enquiry Committee with regard to Sections 124 A and 153 A of the Indian Penal Code, the Cr. P.C. as it is made applicable to the press and in particular with the views expressed by Messrs. S.A. Brelvi and K. Srinivasan. We also agree on the need to amend the

Indian Telegraph Act and the Indian Post Offices Act. On the Official Secrets Act, the general view is that its provisions should be applied only when defence and national security are adversely affected.

- The Preventive Detention Act in its present form contains a provision against action which is prejudicial to foreign relations. At the time it was enacted it was opposed on behalf of working journalists. The general feeling is that any legislation intended to protect the heads of foreign States should at least be on a reciprocal basis. Journalists endorse the Press Laws Enquiry Committee's comments on the Foreign Relations Act.
- Apart from restrictions placed by law, ministerial and administrative attempts at interference are not infrequent. The Federation passed a resolution on this subject at its first session in 1950. The position has not changed since then.
- This is illustrated by the way in which the Cuttack correspondent of a Madras paper was removed and the invalid son of a Minister appointed in his place. The Federation passed a resolution on this subject at its Calcutta session in April, 1952. This is referred to under another head.
- On the question of Defamation, the Madhya Pradesh report says: "Newspaper libel should cease to be a penal offence, and the remedy of the person libelled should be the claiming of damages in civil courts. If it is not thought desirable to implement this suggestion, we would suggest that where a newspaper publishes any matter of a libellous nature *bona fide,* and it also publishes a contradiction when apprised of the facts of the case together with an apology by the Editor and Publisher of the paper, it should be relieved of criminal liability." This would bring our law in the line with the latest law in England.
- We should also deprecate attempts to set up public servants to sue or prosecute for libel, unless the attack made is beyond the bounds of reason.

- We are of the view that where the State has launched the prosecution of a newspaper and has failed, it should be liable to pay damages.
- As regards Contempt of Court, the same report says: "We see no reason for continuing to subject the press to the uncertainties of procedure tender this law, by which the Court becomes party, judge, jury and witness in its own case." The suggestion has been made in England that all cases of this nature should be referred to the Director of Public Prosecutions and tried by a jury in the normal way. This is an alternative procedure, which is already available.
- We would mention here a few other laws, which may not strictly come under this head, but which we consider should also be looked into *Name of Editor:* Under the law as it stands at present the name of the editor is required to be published. This has been misused by the proprietors. In the course of its enquiry, the Commission might canvass the question whether the legal provision compelling the publication of the editor's name is at all necessary under the changed conditions. The removal of the legal obligation would not of course mean that no newspaper will publish the editor's name but an excuse for the proprietor to appear in public as the editor will be removed.
- *Disclosure of Source:* The journalist's right to refuse to reveal the source of his information must be upheld in legal form as there is still some doubt about it. If the right of a priest, who hears the confession of an individual to clear his conscience, is to be upheld, if the lawyer who is defending an individual against society is to be given the legal right, there is no reason why the journalist, who performs equally important functions in a different plane, should not have special protection.
- *International Decisions:* From time to time, we should either by legal enactment or settled usage and convention adopt international decisions bearing on the freedom of the press and the freedom of information.
- *Privileges of Legislatures and the Press:* After January 26, 1950, legislative bodies in India have been increasingly

concerned with their privileges but do not seem to show equal interest in the privileges of the Press. A resolution passed by our general session at Calcutta viewed with grave concern the tendency of legislatures, under the guise of protecting privileges, to assume powers that they do not possess under the Constitution. This was in reference particularly to the case of the Editor of *Swatantra* in Madras and to that of *Biltz* in the Uttar Pradesh Assembly. The position is that though, subject to the other provisions of the Constitution the privileges have been left vague and nebulous, in the Constitution it was intended, and the chairman of the Drafting Committee said, while moving the article in the Constituent Assembly, that at a later stage a clear law may be enacted defining the privileges. This definition has not yet been attempted. The result is that action taken by legislatures to protect their undefined privileges is not subject to scrutiny by the courts unless there is a clear encroachment on fundamental rights, as happened in the case of acting editor of *The Blitz* vs. *The U.P. Legislative Assembly.* This is a subject on which critical examination and positive recommendations are needed.

Advertisement, a Necessity

Advertisement is the source of a large part of newspaper revenue. Advertisement and circulation act and interact on each other. The larger the circulation, the greater the advertisement revenue. And revenue so earned is used to sustain circulation drives.

- The social value of advertisement is undoubted. It puts the buyer of goods and services in touch with the seller of goods and services. Both help the social, commercial and financial life of the country. Some kinds of advertisement have a certain news value and are of public interest.
- The only two well-known journals in India which have tried to be independent of advertisements are the *Indian Social Reformer* and the *Harijan.*
- For the sake of revenue most newspapers accept advertisements irrespective of quality and utility of the

goods advertised. Few would care to reject an advertisement unless it is too bad or unless there are limitations of space.

- As the size of newspapers has been reduced during and after the war advertisement has overflowed to the small papers, but this advantage may disappear when the size increases, as it does now.
- As a rule the smaller papers do not receive the attention they deserve. They are paid poor rates. Indian language papers suffer in a special degree. The case of Hindi papers is explained on page 41 of the U.P. report. This applies to other Indian language newspapers as well.
- The working of the audit bureau of circulation and its usefulness may be enquired into. Government and social agencies can keep a check on advertisements of doubtful value. There is definite need for a code of advertisement ethics.
- *Influence of Advertisements:* Our Federation is interested primarily in the influence of advertisements on the editorial work of a newspaper, and we are stating below some important aspects of the question.
- Advertisements may be classified into three sections: display, classified and financial. The agencies providing advertisements are Government and their allied organisations, municipalities and local authorities, tourist bureaux, company promoters, banks and insurance companies, shipping companies, transport companies, advertisers of manufactured goods of many varieties, film-makers and cinema theatres, astrological and matrimonial agencies, those who want to accept or offer services etc.
- Instances have come to the notice of members of the Federation in which the editorial staff is asked by the advertising department to keep out or soft-pedal news stories that may hurt the feeling of advertisers and so damage the paper's business. Sub-editors have got into trouble for allowing matter to appear which has meant loss of business. Neither are instances uncommon of

advertisements being cancelled because of the policy of a paper.

- The advertisers' influence runs along two lines. "Puff" paragraphs are sent along with an advertisement, and they appear along with the main news, and pass off as news. Some advertisers are refusing to allow the old customary word "Advt" to be put at the end of what really is not reading matter but an advertisement. Not a few of them would have a picture published along with such reading matter. The newspaper supplements issued from time to time do a lot of boosting together with genuine publicity of the industry in whose name they are issued. Most of the matter is supplied by the industry. The finance or city columns are liberally used to promote the interests of companies. Exaggeration is plainly discernible in these columns. Instances are also known of news being manipulated to boost certain interests and ventures. Astrological advertisements are being overdone. It is not altogether unknown for news of labour unrest to be played down or shut out, where such unrest occurs in concerns, who are big advertisers.
- A word may be said about Government advertisement. It carries with it prestige and value. Strictly used, it must be space bought with money. It was not so in the British days when the placing of Government advertisements was a matter of favour shown to Anglo-Indian and pro-Government papers and withheld from papers of the other camp. While things have improved to a certain extent, it would appear that newspapers are still suffering from the hangover of the past, as evidenced by the remark appearing in paragraphs 107 and 108 of the Madhya Pradesh report. Indian language papers still suffer under a handicap in the matter of Government advertisements. A recent reply given by the Information and Broadcasting Minister in the House of the People shows that the bulk of Government's expenditure on advertisements has gone to the benefit of a limited number of English newspapers, while the balance is spread over a much larger number of Indian language papers.

- The Union Public Service Commission does not place its advertisements, even in regard to clerical and lower categories of jobs, with Indian language papers.
- The question also arises how far political considerations weigh in the placing of Government advertisements. The West Bengal Chief Minister stated in the Assembly recently in reply to a question that the Government did not always consider the volume of circulation of a newspaper in the distribution of advertisements. The reference was to the amount of advertisement given to a recently started language paper in preference to papers of longer standing and wider circulation.

Paper Pioneers

The time has come when circulation should be considered not in terms of hundreds but thousands of copies of monthlies, weeklies and dailies in English and the Indian languages. Some cardinal points that are of importance in regulating the future of newspaper production may be stated here.

- It would be the duty of the State to create conditions ensuring equality of opportunity to all people and parties, classes and communities alike. The smaller newspaper must live no less than the big.
- With the passage of time and the diminished importance of English in this country, there will be fewer papers published in the English language while no one can set a limit to the growth of papers in the Indian languages. The limit can only be set by the growth of democracy, and the ambition must be the widest possible dissemination of knowledge.
- Experience has shown that with eight pages, of the standard size, for the bigger newspaper published in English and six pages for newspapers published in the Indian languages the essential news and a sufficient volume of paying advertisements can be carried.
- It is held by people whose views are entitled to respect that a newspaper should depend less on advertisement revenue and more on circulation revenue.

- It is in the interest of public morality and genuine journalism that certain evil practices, which have crept into the profession, are eradicated. The so-called crossword puzzle and square word puzzle competitions are instances. Objections to them are many and decisive. These competitions have many elements of chance and few of real skill and intellectual exercise.
- Out of the total of entrance fees collected, a large part is kept apart as proprietors' profits; out of the balance the special Government tax is paid and the residue is given away as prizes. These prizes are given not only to those who have sent correct solutions, but also to those who have sent the highest number of solutions and also to news agents who sell the highest number of competition coupons. Whether the conduct of such crossword puzzle competitions (not mere publication of crossword puzzles as in the British Journals) is a legitimate part of newspaper production and whether it adds to the prestige and dignity of the Press are vital matters for inquiry.
- It has been proved by British experience that circulation obtained through competitions is of really no value of the advertiser, inasmuch as the extra number of copies bought by solvers are not read. The solvers do not even look at the news, let alone the advertisement.
- Crossword competitions consequently involve waste of newsprint, which might be profitably employed for other purposes.
- The legality or otherwise of these lotteries passing for tests of skill deserves examination. It is almost certain that those who run these competitions are trying to keep themselves within the limits of the law. If that is so the limits of the law require enlargement to reach them.
- The law must be uniform throughout India. Recently a chain newspaper transferred the headquarters of its square words competition to Delhi, because of some difficulties arising under the laws of Bombay. Another chain has expanded to Calcutta, we are told, so that it can avoid the rigours of the Bombay law.

Page Design

We are discussing the subject of presentation of news, even at the risk of repetitions, under a separate head as it has many facets and concerns many sections of people connected with newspapers—the proprietor, the public, the working journalist, the advertiser, the reader and perhaps a few others as well. The picture should be taken as a whole not only for further exploration but for remedial recommendations. We shall here refer to what may be called the tone and tendency in the presentation of news and not to details of presentation.

- To the Commission it is of primary concern to examine how this most important aspect of journalistic work is done in the interests of the public to many of whom it is the only medium of education. The press has to keep before itself the ideal that it is a part of our intellectual life and a maker of our national well-being. That position must be maintained more vigorously than ever, in order to enhance democratic values and to render services faithfully and efficiently.
- To the journalist it is a matter of personal honour and professional integrity to produce not only an attractive but an honest and dependable paper. The guiding principle has been thus laid down for him: "facts are sacred, comment is free".
- The line of enquiry should be as to whether this principle is not in danger because of certain new developments. In recent years, especially in the post-independence period, the comment is often heard that the old standards of objective presentation of news have fallen and that news is being "manipulated" to suit either the interests of individual proprietors or of certain class. Public faith in what appears in the press is so shaken that the tendency is to dismiss as "a mere newspaper story", even reports and articles published on the basis of the most painstaking investigation. To working journalists, interested in the growth of the press on right lines, this is a disturbing development. Working journalists, no less than the proprietary and other interests, who are concerned with the growth of the press on right lines must view this development with concern.

- We would maintain with pardonable pride that the country's hoary traditions of intellectual integrity have been well maintained by journalists and newspapermen for a long time and we have no doubt that they will only be too eager to continue these illustrious traditions. A new situation has however arisen. They were till yesterday free men; entirely free they are not today, then work, being dominated by new motives and forces.
- It must be admitted that the Indian Press is less partisan than in many other foreign countries. There is no such difference here, in the upper reaches of newspapers between a "quality" paper and a "popular" paper, with a vast gap between them. The journalist for his part is old fashioned enough to believe in doing his work as a craftsman and without much of a conscious bias, while the technical excellence of his work was never higher than it is today.
- Standards of news presentation have four aspects—intellectual, moral, political and technical. It is a vast subject. We are here presenting briefly the general defects of news presentation as we want the defects to be cured by attacking the causes thereof at the roots. These defects are inaccuracy, distortion, suppression, sensationalism, angling, partisanship, tendentiousness and splash.
- *Inaccuracy:* This is largely due to working against time, want of knowledge, inadequate facilities of reference, fallibility of sources, the wide range of error inherent in the vast volume of work done. It would be point of honour to reach precision, like a scientist, but a journalist may have everything but time on his side.
- *Distortion:* This denotes an ulterior motive. This was not largely practised in India but the entry of speculative elements into journalism is having its own influence.
- *Suppression:* This can be the result of a deliberate policy like shutting out labour and leftist news in a capitalist-owned paper or the result political partisanship and group rivalries. One way of suppression is to cut down the news or play it down even when it is accepted, or put it in a place inconspicuous and out of all proportion to its importance.

- *Angling:* Selection is an essential part of newspaper work, not only of the matter received but of the points that should be stressed and played up in sub-editing. This clearly reveals the bias of the paper and is permissible to some extent. Otherwise there would be no difference between a labour paper, a conservative paper and a liberal paper. But there are limits beyond which this must not be done. We fear we are exceeding this limit in this country pretty often, though we are nowhere near the practice in some other countries.
- *Sensationalism:* This implies want oneness, irresponsibility, exaggeration, "over presentation" and "over stressing". Part of this may be inescapable in newspaper work where "news" means something out of the way and sensational events are an essential part of news structure. But when big money is sunk in newspapers and the drive is for big circulation and big advertisements, inevitably the main ingredient of the daily concoction must be sensationalism. Here we may go down the slope.
- *Partisanship:* Few regard newspapers to be on oath all the time. It is not possible. But partisanship is the enemy of impartiality. In news columns it generally takes the form of keeping down the opposition to the minimum and playing up one's own causes and friends and thereby presenting a misleading picture of what is happening. It is difficult to tell how long the old Indian traditions of a newspaper published for gentlemen by gentlemen will remain.
- *Tendentiousness:* This is an offspring of the mentality of partisanship. This is generally to be found in "write-ups", "forecasts", "surveys" etc.
- *Splash:* This is the result of the need for the modern style of display, irrespective of the importance of the news item and means overdoing for the sake of appearance. It spoils the sense of value and proportion.

The defects mentioned above may be traced to various factors:

- *Proprietor:* He has interests, political views and prejudices of his own. If he belongs to business his main job is to make money. Besides circulation and advertisement revenue, some newspapers receive contracts for printing periodicals and doing job work for some interests who want to have them on their side. This work is paid for at more than the market rates, which really amounts to subsidising. The proprietor naturally takes the main share, apart from the editorials, in the publication of opinion-forming news, which is only second in importance. If he has other interests besides newspapers, he brings the play of forces into journalism which are alien to it. Pessimism and optimism become saleable commodities. Some newspapers in India have begun to play up the interests of certain wealthy parties, say with regard to the promotion of this industry or that and with regard to tariffs, protection etc.

- *The Public:* The public is full of its own limitations and prejudices. Papers, therefore, begin to play up communal passions, for the purpose of increasing circulations, for the same purpose they also pander to low tastes, "emphasising the novel and the sensational rather than the significant" and giving the reader "exposures and scandals". In this connection the question may be posed: Do these papers get the enormous circulation, they do not otherwise deserve, by probing into matters which the more responsible section of the press seems strangely reluctant to publicise? Possibly between the gross overstatement of one section and the studied understatement of the other, truth gets muzzled.
- *Pressure Croups:* These exercise some influence, particularly at the bottom levels, with their municipal wranglings, personal animosities and political rivalries. This explains why our district or local journalism is often bad. The local papers are instruments in the hands of the contenders for power.
- *Economic Difficulties:* These naturally play their part.
- *Journalists:* Journalists have their own limitations undoubtedly. They are poorly paid. Some of them are not too well educated or trained. They have their own prejudices and passions. The staff is often inadequate and they have to scamper through their work, with the result that they are

victims of high speed thinking and writing. They have little time to check up inaccuracies and have few facilities of reference. They must please the proprietor to keep their jobs and so even their natural subjective bias has to be subordinated.

- On the point of adequacy of staff, a comparison is relevant between the strength of the editorial staff on the average Indian newspaper and on comparable British newspapers. The British newspaper, according to persons with personal knowledge, has on each shift something like twice the number of men one finds on the Indian newspaper. This means that on the British newspaper, each man has correspondingly a smaller quantity of matter to handle and correspondingly more time to handle it in. The result is more careful and tidier presentation. In India the case is not rare of one or two sub-editors shouldering the burden of bringing out an edition.
- *Government:* Under party rule ministers want press support and a man with a paper commands their ears. Some aspects of this are explained in detail in other sections. Governments not unoften use advertisements as a means of patronage. Where the proprietor or his family has political ambitions and the ruling party has something to offer, the newspaper loses its independence and becomes a party sheet.
- *Other External Influences:* Rich persons in trouble are always trying "to keep it out of the newspapers" particularly court cases involving scandals. The police are occasionally interested in shunning publicity, though they are usually helpful to reporters. Some religious authorities frown on radical papers while some religious heads forbid birth control propaganda, for instance. Inter-provincial bickerings are another such influence.
- The various remedies suggested for curing these defects, which are worth examination, are the growth of education, training of journalists, code of ethics, a press council to control those connected with newspapers, improved financial resources of publishers and owners in order to

make them economically independent, reduction in the power and potency of money and adoption of legal remedies wherever called for.

Paper Arrangement

Newsprint is not at present being produced in this country. Efforts, however, are being made to produce it. Controls on consumption were introduced during war time, which worked indifferently and often the stocks were perilously low even for the best of papers. The size of newspapers was reduced to four pages. There was a good deal of black marketing, much of it by bogus newspapers. The controls have been recently lifted, but the smaller newspapers have been at the mercy of the importers, some of whom are big newspaper proprietors. Even with the recently enlarged size there is pressure on space, leading to lower standards of editing, and strenuous work for the editorial department, which today accepts only about one-eighth of the copy that comes to a newspaper office.

- Paragraph 497 of the British Royal Commission's Report on the Press refers to the relation between liberty and adequate supplies of newsprint and the place of newsprint in popular education. This needs no emphasis on our part.
- The need for cutting down foreign supplies of newsprint may be judged from the fact that it would be dangerous to depend on external sources, even as it would be wrong to depend on foreign supplies at the time of war.
- It is suggested that the State should have reserve powers of rationing and controlling the use of newsprint, for it is clear that the old days of ample supplies and cheap prices will not return. The interests of the small newspaper, which is the pillar of democracy, should be particularly protected.
- Whether cooperative control and ownership of imported newsprint among newspapers can be effectively done requires exploration.
- The main thing to secure is uniformity of price for the rich and poor papers alike. Where necessary the size of the big papers may be cut rather than that the small papers be forced to become smaller.

- A newsprint manufacturing mill is set up in Madhya Pradesh but its production date is steadily receding. The Commission, we trust, will go into this project as well as suggestions for the establishment of a mill in the Himalayan region where wood for pulp is stated to be available in plenty.

Technical Aspects

- India does not manufacture printing or composing machinery. If our own nation cannot manufacture for some time, as evidently it cannot, we would suggest that foreign firms may be encouraged to start manufacture in India of machinery suitable to Indian conditions. In our opinion it is necessary that emphasis should be placed on the manufacture of machinery for small papers and small rotaries.
- As regards composing machines they have been slowly coming into the language press, but rather too slowly. We are not oblivious of the difficulties of the big keyboard required for the Indian languages etc., but this is a direction in which research and experiment with the full support of the State are absolutely necessary.

Liability of the State

- The guiding principle in this matter was laid down exactly hundred years ago by Delane, Editor of the *Times,* London, in words which have become famous.
- Replying to a declaration by Lord Derby in the House of Lords that "in these days as the English Press aspires to share the influence of the statesman, so also must it share in the responsibilities of the statesman", the *Times,* under Delane's editorship, wrote:—

"If the first of these principles be established, the second follows as a matter of course, and we of all men are last disposed to lower the proper functions or to deny the responsibilities and the power which may derive from the confidence of the public."

"But be that power more or less, we cannot admit that its

purpose is to share the labours of statesmen, or that it is bound by the same limitation, the same duties, the same liabilities as that of the Ministers of the Crown. The purpose and duties of the two powers are constantly separate, generally independent, and sometimes diametrically opposite. The dignity and the freedom of the press are travelled from the moment it accepts an ancillary position. To perform its duties with entire independence, the press can enter into no close or binding alliances with statesmen of the day, nor can it surrender its permanent interests to the convenience of the ephemeral power of any Government...."

- Relationship between the Press and the Government in the larger sense of the effect of governmental policy and action on the freedom of the press is dealt with in earlier parts of this memorandum. What is attempted here is to examine the relationship in what may be called the administrative sense. The problem is one of machinery best suited for the establishment of channels through which the press could be kept informed of governmental plans and decisions and Government may be kept in touch with trends of thought and opinion among the general mass of the people, as distinguished from special economic, social or political interests.
- Such points of contact between the Government and the Press are provided by correspondents and reporters meeting Ministers or Secretaries both at the Centre and in the States. Press conferences provide the occasion for Ministers or Secretaries to explain official policies and policy decisions. Information bureaux or public relations officers are other agencies intended to supply correspondents and reporters with official releases and explanatory material of the normal kind. Some aspects of this are dealt with later in this section under Special Correspondents. In some states, Press Consultative Committees are in existence. Their functions, however, are not precisely defined. In one State it would appear that the Chief Minister made use of the Committee to urge pressmen to create what he described as enlightened public opinion in support of his Government's taxation measures. This

brings up the question where the line is to be drawn between consultation and appeal for assistance.

- The basic questions for consideration may be posed as follows:

  Should there be liaison between government and the Press at these levels? If there should be, by what method can it be maintained?

  On any liaison machinery that is established, should there be representatives of the profession as a whole or of any class thereof?

  Is the present advisory system suitable? How well has it worked so far?

- The general view of working journalists is that the press advisory system, as it is, has been unsatisfactory. It was essentially a wartime device introduced by a foreign regime, whose interest rarely extended beyond maintenance of peace and order. Its weakness is mainly in its composition. Its members represent either purely proprietary or managerial interests or evenly balanced as to be ineffective in practice. Adequate representation is not provided for practising journalists. The result is that problems are not judged solely with reference to their professional implications. The Federation has demanded that the press advisory system be scrapped and in its place the press consultative system be tried with suitable changes as regards membership, so that working journalists may have adequate representation.

Machineries and Qualities of Printing

- Professional organisations of practising journalists are of recent origin. They first appeared in the 1920's on a regional level. Among them were the Indian Journalists Association, Calcutta, and the Journalists Association of India, Bombay. The membership of both extended beyond Bengal or Bombay. Gradually the need became apparent for a better organised body to deal with definite problems affecting relations between employers and employees. The urge in this direction quickened when newspapers began to pass into the hands of businessmen and industrialists, and familiar pattern of employer-employee relations began to reproduce itself. Organisations grew up in U.P., Punjab, and in South India in the 1940's. These were years of newsprint scarcity, which hit the small newspapers hard. These newspapers, of which publications in the Indian languages formed the largest number, combined to protect their interests.

- Hindi journalists came forward on their own account about this time. They held two successive conferences in Delhi. Their main concern was participation in Press Advisory Committees and such other matters. In 1943 Hindi journalists met in Calcutta and there took up matters of more immediate professional interest. A committee was appointed to recommend measures for the improvement of working conditions. It gathered evidence on the basis of which at the conference held in Kanpur a number of demands, including basic salary and grant of gratuity were put forward. Soon afterwards came the move to organise themselves on trade union lines. A conference of Marathi journalists was also at work at about this time. It adopted a set of demands concerning basic salary and conditions of service.
- The All India Newspaper Editors Conference began as one of the most representative bodies, mainly for taking joint action to meet the situation created by the individual civil disobedience movement of the Congress and the Government's plans to deal with it. Those who took part in or watched the first session in Delhi will recall the glow of collective strength that lighted up the proceedings, and the chilling sense of apprehension with which the Home Member of the day followed the progress of its work. Whether the fine promise of that meeting was fulfilled in the later evolution of the conference is a matter of controversy.
- The membership of the A.I.N.E.C. was in large parts the same as that of the Indian and Eastern Newspaper Society, an earlier body, which had been recognised by the

Government as representing newspaper ownership and management. The A.I.N.E.C. dealt with a number of problems but, to our knowledge, not so much with the main subjects in which working journalists are interested, namely, service conditions and maintenance of professional standards. Even on problems of more general interest, the approach of the A.I.N.E.C. was somewhat restricted. This is illustrated by the suggestion made on its behalf to the Press Laws Enquiry Committee, that "provision should be made for summary and in camera trials of offences under this section (Section 153 A of the Indian Penal Code) in order to avoid the evil effects of publicity".

- In 1941, when repressive laws were enacted including those that place restrictions on the press, the A.I.N.E.C. assumed a new role. It began to work in close association with Government on the Press Advisory Committees at the Centre and in the provinces. Members of the standing committee of the A.I.N.E.C. were mostly also members of the Central Press Advisory Committee. The two committees generally met at about the same time and in the same place. As members of the Central Press Advisory Committee they received travelling allowances from the Government. This was a practical convenience but a psychological handicap.
- August 1942 was testing time. As part of the movement launched by Gandhiji, newspapers were called upon to close down. On this there was a sharp division of opinion, from the effect of which the A.I.N.E.C. as a whole has not yet recovered.
- The need for working journalists to organise themselves separately became apparent about this time. Working journalist organisations grew up in the States first. That gave the impulse for the formation of an all-India organisation. A convention of working journalists met in 1950 in Delhi, and decided to form the present Federation on an all-India basis. The question whether it should be organised on trade union lines was canvassed. A general trend in favour of trade unionism was revealed. The only

dissentinent being the Southern Indian Journalists Federation.

- The Indian Federation of Working Journalists at present has 18 units affiliated to it from most of the States. Two other units are shortly going to be affiliated, one in Assam and the other in Mysore.

Special Correspondent : A vital link that brings the legislature and the executive into direct touch with the press is provided by the Special Correspondent in Delhi and the correspondent or reporter in the State capitals.

- The institution of Special Correspondent is still in its early stages in India, and so it has some of the faults that are inseparable from any new branch of a profession. One fault arises from multiple representation. Some of the senior correspondents in Delhi function as a one-man news syndicate rather than on the salutary principle of one man one newspaper, with the advantage of complete concentration on development of a really "special" coverage for that newspaper. Multiple representation may have served its purpose in conditions in which the general body of newspapers with their limited financial resources could not maintain a correspondent each to serve each of them exclusively. Conditions are now comparatively better, and the trend must therefore be away from concentration and syndication and towards individual representation.
- A parallel development must be the division and specialisation of correspondents in Delhi and elsewhere in the political, diplomatic and parliamentary spheres. Here again the present practice is for one correspondent to function under these various nomenclatures.
- The system of special correspondents is regulated in its dealings with the administration by rules of accreditation. A similar system is coming into existence at the State capitals. The working of the rules of accreditation has disclosed defects to which the Federation has drawn attention. One principal defect is that Indian language papers are placed at a disadvantage and their

representatives have in practice to wait longer for accreditation than those of English newspapers. The complaint has been made that in many instances non-nationals visiting India as representatives of non-Indian newspapers and news agencies obtain ready recognition and accreditation while the cases of Indian journalists are kept pending for weeks or months.

- The most serious defect arises from the character and composition of the Central Press Advisory Committee, the only professional body whose advice is sought before accreditation is given. This Committee, as stated earlier, is nominated by the All India Newspaper Editors Conference, on which a large number of newspapers in India are not represented.
- The rules of accreditation work in a way that encourages the process of multiple representation to which we have referred above. After waiting in vain for accreditation, some newspapers have been compelled in the past to give up the idea of having their own staff men and to enter into "string" arrangements with existing correspondents.
- In the States the system of accreditation is still in the process of evolution and working journalists feel that there is still time for the States to avoid some of the defects noticed at the Centre. There are certain other undesirable developments in this connection to which reference may be made in the courses of oral evidence.
- These and other classes of conduct emphasise the need for a professional code. The Federation has adopted such a code. Its acceptance is no more easy than the voluntary acceptance of any other form of self-restraint.
- Correspondents reporting the proceedings of legislatures and local bodies have a few problems peculiar to themselves. Complaints have been received of municipal and district board authorities treating correspondents with discourtesy. In the House of the People a large number of correspondents at present face a sudden deterioration of status, arising mainly from classification and gradation

of elementary facilities, to which all journalists working in the Press Gallery should normally be entitled.

- An attempt is in progress for Press Gallery correspondents to form a separate association of their own through which to represent their case to the Speaker on this and other matters.

The Future : As an intellectual and social force, journalism in new India has before it a future of expanding influence based on service. Education will spread; the number of newspaper readers will grow; and newspapers will be called upon to meet increasingly exacting cultural and educational demands from the community. Some of the ideals that the journalist must keep before himself in meeting the challenge of the future are freedom of expression, the ideal of service, the ideal of efficiency, equality of opportunity and the ideal of cooperation.

- The maintenance of high standards is inextricably bound up with the question of the new set-up in the field of journalism. The Commission may enquire into several suggestions which have been made.
- These include: Ownership of newspapers by public limited liability companies, cooperatives, or public trusts.
- The party paper should be recognised as inevitable in a democracy. The non-party and non-partisan paper, however, should be the ideal. It should be a medium for providing an impartial record of news and for giving a courageous lead, when required.
- There is a body of opinion favouring the adoption of the model of the *Daily Herald,* London, in which a sympathetic capitalist combine owns a nominal majority of shares but leaves editorial conduct and policy to a progressive party and to professional men of ability and integrity. The establishment of cooperatives and trusts are advocates by many. These with their non-profit ideal have a wide appeal in India.
- The need is for medium-sized newspapers, rather than big ones. Among several recent suggestions is one for the ownership of plants on a. cooperative basis, if necessary

with State aid, but without the shadow of State interference. This would largely help the weekly newspaper, which cannot afford to have a printing plant of its own. In fact, several of them, whatever their difference as regards policy, might be printed off the same plant. This form of cooperation exists in England. In India even daily newspapers might profitably adopt this method of production particularly in the less developed areas.

- The need has been stressed for giving special facilities to women to publish periodicals of their own to press their causes.
- The Indian newspaper of the future must obviously be produced and sold at a price that is suited to the purchasing power of the ordinary citizen with his low income level. The general public might welcome tabloids, giving the maximum possible news and the minimum possible advertisement, and relying more on circulation revenue than on advertisement revenue.
- The Indian language paper, with a wider mass appeal, should be easy to produce with a limited capital, a small plant, teleprinter and radio news services, and trained men to give it a strong local appeal.
- The suggestion has been made for the setting up of a statutory body to hold a decennial enquiry into the working of all public institutions, professions, and industries including journalism. This would be in harmony with the ideal of the Welfare State.
- The proposal for the establishment of a Press Council has been discussed. The model is suggested by the British Royal Commission and is worked out in a private Bill now before the British Parliament. It requires modification to suit Indian conditions. It would meet with ready acceptance if it functions as a central body keeping a watch particularly on professional standards and safeguarding the status.

Working System

The psychology has witnessed an explosion of knowledge about how human beings process information .Much of this new knowledge concerns limitations and biases in perception, memory, and reasoning Research on eyewitness testimony has highlighted the distortions in perception and memory that can plague observers, particularly observers under stress at the moment of observation or recollection. Similarly, studies on the way people make inferences have shown us that people often favour anecdotal information over more reliable base rate statistical information. Even when instructed to be "objective," they often seek and select data according to preexisting expectations or theories.

Other research has documented the difficulties people have evaluating risk. Still more research has shown that people easily ignore sampling biases, fail to understand regression effects, often believe, they "knew something all along" even if they didn't, tend to attribute the causes of people's behaviour to dispositional rather than to situational factors, and often imagine association between events where nose exist. Significantly, many of the errors and biases to which fall prey only get worse under time constraints.

For journalists who pledge allegiance to objectivity and/or fairness as they observe and interpret people and events, such knowledge is potentially of great relevance. Yet only a small percentage of what we know appears to have found its way into journalism classrooms, most of it in upper-level or graduate courses that consider how audiences, as distinct from journalist, process information.

Moreover, hardly any of this knowledge seems to have found its way into courses and text-books that train students to write, edit, and report the news. Even those texts that do devote space to documented distortions in interviewing and observation (of. Rivers & Harrington, 1988) have either ignored more recent findings on cognitive error and bias or drawn upon but a small portion of this research.

Increasing Pressure : Given the growing demands on journalist to report and interpret the activities of an increasingly complex society and the demonstrated importance of the news media for setting public and private agendas, this is a shame. It is also a problem, we may be able to do something about.

In the pages that follow, we will outline some of the more

important errors and biases in thinking that psychologists have documented in recent years. We have little formal knowledge about the existence and operation of such bias as in journalists (as we have noted, and lamented, in Stocking & Gross, 1988). However, we do know they have been found in a variety of professions and across a variety of tasks (cf. Loftus, 1979; Sims, Gioia, & Associates, 1986; and Rogoff & Lave, 1984), leading us to think they probably show up in journalists' work as well. We hope that journalism educators, when altered to these common errors and biases, will be motivated to learn more about them and seek ways, in classrooms and text-books, to bring them to the attention of their students.

As everyone knows, "seeing is believing." When someone says, "I saw it with my own eyes," people listen, believe, and remember.

Indeed, psychologists who have studied the impact of eyewitness testimony in jury trials have found that jurors, when reaching a verdict, given much more weight to eyewitness testimony than they do to other kinds of evidence (Loftus, 1979).

Not surprisingly, journalists seem to understand intuitively the power of eyewitness accounts. Thus, as van Dijk (in press) has pointed out, editors so value first-hand reports that they "may even send a special envoy to places where already dozens of other reporters are present."

The problem is that eyewitness accounts, while more convincing than hearsay accounts, are not always reliable. Research on eyewitness testimony (c. f., Loftus, 1979) is very clear about this fact: Observations can vary and err as a function of variety of factors such as prejudice, temporary expectations, the types of details being observed, and stress. It is very easy, in other words, for one's observations (and one's memories about observations) to be distorted or flat-out wrong.

In one of the most well-known demonstrations of the fallibility of observations, reported in Loftus (1979), Hastorf and Cantrill (1954) examined people's perceptions of a football game between Dartmouth and Princeton. The game, one of the dirtiest and roughest played by either team, was filmed and shown to students on each campus. Students were instructed to note any rule infractions they saw and to rate them as either "flagrant" or "mild."

Inspite of instructions to be completely objective in their observations, students at the two schools perceived the infractions very differently. More precisely, students at Princeton saw the Dartmouth players make 9.8 infractions, more than twice the number of infractions they saw their own team make (4.2). Moreover, they saw the Dartmouth players make more than twice as many infractions as Dartmouth students saw their team make. Princeton students tended to rate the violations by their own team as mild and those committed by the Dartmouth team as flagrant. Dartmouth students were more evenhanded when they saw the film, seeing about the same number of infractions for both teams (4.3 by Dartmouth and 4.4. by Princeton); but they also tended to see the violations of the opposing team as more flagrant than violations by their own team. Obviously, people don't always see what others see; even when instructed to be objective, they often see what they want to see.

Evident Facts : It is perhaps an obvious point that one's personal prejudices can unconsciously affect the accuracy of one's observations; personal prejudice is usually what journalism educators mean when they warn about "bias" in the news. However, research on eyewitness testimony (Loftus, 1979) suggests that other factors besides personal prejudice can lead to unreliable eyewitness reports, among them: temporary expectations, expectations from past experience, and stress.

Eyewitness accounts can also be unreliable when the event has been witnessed infrequently and for a short period of time, when violence has boon involved, when a long time has elapsed between witnessing the event and reporting it, or when the witness is under stress at the time of recollection. Researchers have also found that information introduced after an event has taken place can alter the memory of it; thus, if a reporter witnesses a concert and then reads a competitor's article on the concert, the reporter may alter his own memory of the event to conform to information contained in his competitor's account.

The point in all this (and much more, contained in Loftus, 1979) is simple: People, Journalist included, may put more weight on eyewitness accounts than they do on other kinds of evidence. Unless journalists are aware of the ways that eyewitness accounts can be biassed and erroneous, they, like juries, may fallaciously assume that such accounts offer more truth than they do. Such assumptions could, in turn, influence reports to "count on" such accounts and prematurely limit their reporting efforts.

Related to people's tendency to weight eyewitness accounts more than other types of evidence is a tendency for people to favour anecdotal or case history information over base rate statistical information (information about the percentage of cases in the population).

This tendency to underutilize more reliable base rate information, to focus on specific individuals and make less use of information about the population from which individuals come, has been vividly demonstrated in a study by Hamill, Wilson, and Nisbett (1980). In this study, subjects read a magazine article about a Puerto Rican woman who had a number of unmanageable children by a succession of common-law husbands. When this anecdotal case was presented along with base rate statistics indicating that 90 per cent of welfare recipients "are off the welfare rolls by the end of four years," subjects regarded the case history as more informative than the more reliable base rate statistics. Put another way, the statistical facts had less impact on people's views about the laziness and hopelessness of welfare recipients than did the single vivid case.

Just why people favour anecdotal information over base rate information is unclear. It may be because the information contained in anecdotes is usually more vivid (Nisbett & Borgida, 1975; Nisbett & Ross, 1980), or it may be that the information in anecdotes seems more relevant (Tversky & Kahneman, 1978): But regardless of the precise reason, what the Hamill *et al.* study and related research suggests for journalist, who routinely use anecdotes to "personalize" the news, is a need to handle anecdotal information with considerable caution.

Some sources are masters of the anecdote. Intentionally or unintentionally, they may present anecdotal data that do not square with more abstract statistical information. If reporters fall victims to the tendency to favour vivid anecdotal information over pallid but reliable statistics, they, and their audiences in turn, may be misled.'

Intellectually, most of us probably realize that preconceived ideas shape how we view, interpret, and remember information. But what we may not realize is the extent to which such notions bias us.

In recent years, psychologist have conducted research revealing that preconceived ideas can be very powerful indeed in shaping what we see, understand, and remember. In fact, so powerful are their effects that it is hard to imagine they do not affect the work of journalists and journalists-in-training.

Search for Facts : The tendency for people to seek, select, and recall data according to preexisting expectations on theories is called the "confirmation bias". To understand its pervasiveness, it is important to understand how it works.

Two processes seem important here. First, when people seek information with respect to one theory, they are unlikely to seek information with respect to another theory simultaneously. People, in short, test theories one at a time, or sequentially. So, for example, the person who is testing a theory about the negative impact of feminism on women's like is unlikely to test theories about its positive impact as well. Similarly, the individual testing the theory that there is a "crime wave" against the elderly (Fishman, 1980) is unlikely to test the opposite theory that there are no crimes against the elderly.

Secondly, as people seek information with which to test their theories, they show a dramatic tendency to use a theory-confirming strategy. For example, a reporter who has theorized that there is a crime wave against the elderly may unconsciously sock out sources that confirm this theory— the potential and actual elderly victims in a bad part of town, the head of a crime prevention programme for the elderly, etc. Further, the reporter may ask questions of these sources—about increase in reported crimes, efforts to reduce crimes, and the like—that confirm the theory, without asking probing questions that might disconfirm the hypothesis (Snyder & Swann, 1979).

Not only may expectations influence the sources to which reporters turn and the types of questions a reporter may ask, but they also may influence journalists' evaluation and selection of data. One pervasive bias in perceivers' decisions about what information is most relevant or credible is the tendency to regard information that is consistent with one's prior theories as the worthiest pieces of information (Darley & Gross, 1984; Hayden & Mischel, 1976; Snyder & Gangested, 1981). Thus, when one is testing a theory about the nature, causes, or outcome of an event, the information that will be selected as most useful is information that is consistent with and confirming of one's theory.

Information that runs counter to one's theories is discounted a number of ways. For one thing, disconfirming evidence may be regarded as transient or situationally induced. For example, a political figure who is thought to be honest and forthright and who is then caught in lies about events may be regarded as momentarily confused, or without recall, or perhaps induced to perform dishonestly by misguided advisers or the pressure of office (Ross, Lepper & Hubbard, 1975). Even if journalists themselves do not interpret actions in this way, they may regard such interpretations by others as highly credible and so give them prominent play.

Secondly, disconfirming evidence may be regarded as arising from poor or shoddy sources. Thus, one may be particularly critical of the methodology of the disconfirming study, and, in fact, so critical that the study may Be discarded as entirely unreliable. Reporters may similarly discard sources (persons or resources for data) that are disconfirming of their theories by virtue of their judged unrealiability.

Fishmen (1980), in his account of how a series of events in New York City came to be linked together as a "crime wave" noted that once a crime wave was established in journalists' mind it took on a life' of its own, guiding reporters' perceptions of hitherto unconnected crimes and city police officer's as well. "A week and a half after the coverage started, the police wire was steadily supplying the press with fresh incidents almost everyday." Even when a reporter examined police crime statistics and discovered that crimes against the elderly had actually decreased (not increased) compared to the previous year, the crime wave theme remained in place. As Fishman tells it, "The reporter was puzzled and eventually decided to ignore the police figures. He felt they were unreliable and incomplete, and anyway he had to do the story as originally planned because the whole issue was too big to pass up or play down".

If people, including journalists, are unaware of the extent to which they seek to confirm their expectations and theories, it may be in part because the processes-mat allow this to happen operate below the level of consciousness. Reporters may honestly believe they are objectively considering all sides to an issue, while in practice they are processing information in a way that confirms what they expect or believe.

Inherent Dangers : Everyday, on the news, from their friends, in the movies, people hear about risk—the risk of diseases, natural disasters, technological mishaps, nuclear war, author emissions, passive smoke. And, based on what they hear, people perceive some risk as greater than others. But are they right?

Psychologists have done a great of research on people's perceptions of risk in recent years, and their findings include the following:

1. Anything that makes a hazard appear very memorable or imaginable, such as a recent disaster, vivid film, or media coverage, can influence one's perception of risk; thus, someone who has just seen the movie "Jaws" may overestimate the probability of being attacked by sharks on their vacation to the ocean, and someone who has just seen "The Towering Inferno" may overestimate the probability of being killed in a high-rise tire.
2. People overestimate the risk of death from dramatic or sensational causes, such as homicide, accidents, cancer, and natural disasters, and underestimate the risk of death from the undramatic causes such as diabetes, emphysema, and asthma, causes which kill one at a time and are common in nonfatal form.
3. When people lack strong opinions about hazard, they are highly susceptible to the way risk information is presented; thus, the way information is framed (whether, for example,

> one says "only about one per cent of the nation's five million chemical processing units handle hazardous waste materials that could result in runaway reactions," or "as many as 50,000 of the nations' five million chemical processing units handles hazardous waste materials. . .") can have a major effect on perceptions.

In short, researchers have found that people have a great deal of difficulty accurately perceiving risk (Slovic, 1986).

Not surprisingly, some of these same difficulties have revealed themselves in news media coverage of risk (c.f., Combs & Slovic. 1979). Thus, it appears that journalists, like lay perceivers, process risk information poorly.

"Reporters obviously need to be educated in the importance and subtleties of risk stories," psychologist Paul Slovic has written in an article detailing some of difficulties inherent in informing and educating the public about risk (Slovic, 1986). In obvious agreement, a number of psychologists, mass communication researchers, and other groups have produced materials and events, including articles, pamphlets, films and workshops, to help reporters understand and clarify risk issues (c.f. Fischoff, 1985a, 1985b; Risk Reporting Project, 1986; Institute for Health Policy Analysis, 1984).

Preventing Measures : Since the news media are a dominant source of information about risk, it seems incumbent upon journalism educators to alert students to the ways in which they may err (and be influenced by the intentional and unintentional errors and biases of sources) as they process information about risk. It also seems incumbent upon us to alert them to some of the ways they can minimize such errors and biases.

Although journalism educators have recognized for sometime the need for journalists to pay attention to biases in formal poll data (c.f. Wilhoit & Weaver, 1980), they have given relatively little attention to the need for journalists to attend to sampling biases in other realms, though they probably should. Researchers have found, for example, that people can and often do ignore biases in existing samples of information (Fisk & Taylor, 1984).

In one of the few text-book examples of this shortcoming in

journalism, Tankard (1976) points to how journalists covered the Watergate hearings during the 1970s. One reporter, using letters reportedly sent to Senator Ervin's Committee, concluded that televised hearing were appreciated by audiences, while another reporter, judging from call-ins to television stations, concluded just the opposite. Apparently, neither reporters stopped to consider the inherent biases in the samples they drew upon in reaching their conclusions.

People have a poor understanding of regression, the fact that extreme events will, on the average, be less extreme when observed again. As a result, they often use extreme events to predict future extreme events (Jennings, Ambalie & Ross, 1982). In journalism, regression effects are sometimes appreciated, as when a literary critic raves about a first book but at the same time urges readers to wait for the next book because previous experience suggests that second novels often are not as good as the first ones. However, other times they may not be appreciated, as when reporters herald the first very positive results of a study on a new drug. The study may show positive results, even great results, but it is only one study, and chance alone may have accounted for the findings.

The Result : Psychologists have found that once people learn the outcome of an event, they tend to exaggerate their ability to have foreseen it. Thus, in one experiment, students were asked to predict the likelihood of various ,possible outcomes of President Nixon's forthcoming trip to Moscow and Peking. When, in the wake of Nixon's journey, the students were expectedly asked to recall their initial predictions, they remembered them as very close to what they now knew had happened (fiscoff & Beyth, 1975). This tendency to overestimate what could have been foreseen is known as the "hindsight bias" or the "I-knew-it-all-along" phenomenon, and it seems to have been operating in much of the post-hoc moralizing about journalistic coverage of the shuttle disaster (I knew or would have known, so others should have too); it may also have been operating when Sen. William Proxmire bestowed "Golden Fleece" awards on research that documented or explored the "obvious," though many journalists didn't recognize the fact.

Illusory Correlation : Sometimes, psychologists have found, people greatly overestimate the frequency with which two characteristics or events are related), or they even impose a relationship where none exists (c.f. Crocker, 1981; Jennings. Amabile & Ross, 1982). This phenomenon, known as illusory correlation, has been demonstrated in a number of circumstances, but particularly when two things happen to be associated in meaning. Thus, if journalists commonly associate "long hairs" with demonstrations (that is, they expect to see people with long-hair at demonstrations), they may overestimate the frequency with which long-haired people attend such events. Likewise, if reporters associate university-based artists with which such artists (as distinct from community based artists) have been awarded such grants.

Some of the research on illusory correlation (c.f., Chapman & Chapman, 1982) appears to suggest that expectations can also lead people to compose illusory casual (as distinct from simple correlational) relationships between characteristics or events. Consider the journalist who notices that an abnormally high number of children living near a chemical spill have been born with birth defects. In reporters's mind, chemical accidents often causes human health problems; if there is an increase in birth defects, following a chemical accident, it would appear that the increase must be due to the accident. In the face of such strong prior expectations, it may never even occur to the reporter that a simple increase in the birth rate may have caused unusually high number of defects.

Fundamental Attribution Error : In journalism texts and journalism classrooms, we do considerable talking about journalists' role as "interpreters" of behavior and events; we tell students not only to report behaviour and events but also to explain the reasons behind behaviour and events. But for many of us, that is, as far as our training takes us, we provide to real understanding of what goes into making casual inferences and the biases and errors that can, and often do, occur. As a result, We send out students who, in their role as interpreter, are likely commit a number of cognitive errors. Some of these errors are documented in attribution theory research, which concerns how people make inferences about their own and others' behaviour.

Research on one such error, the ubiquitous "fundamental attribution error," suggests that one is more likely to attribute another person's behaviour to his or her own dispositional qualities than to situational factors (Jones & Harris, 1967). Thus, reporters discovering a case of scientific fraud at their local university are more likely to explore the theory that the person was a "bad apple" than to explore the theory that the "barrel itself was rotten." There are documented exceptions to the fundamental attribution error, of course, but the tendency needs to be recognized.

Distinctive Attitudes : There are numerous other documented biases and errors in people's thinking. But our point, we hope, has been made In most skills courses and most journalism texts, we put great stock in observable facts without adequately emphasizing some of the ways observations can vary and err. We warn our students to be wary to their own biases, but we appear to do very little to demonstrate how easily biases and prior expectations can affect their selection of data.

We encourage students to "personalize" the news but fail to warn them adequately of the dangers, often unwittingly reinforcing the cognitive tendency to favour case histories or anecdotal information over important base rate information. In the same vein, we encourage coverage of activities that pose social or environmental risks, yet say little or nothing about the errors people commonly make when assessing risk. In these and many other small ways, we may be unknowingly failing our students and our profession.

The need—to learn more about such errors and biases, and to bring what we know and learn into the educational setting—is great. Admitedly, it may not be easy. Most of us have all we can do in a term to teach students the traditional fundamentals of interviewing, observation, and mining documents. To bring this knowledge into classroom successfully will require us to develop exercises that will provide opportunities for learning about cognitive distortions without sacrificing the basics.

Teacher's manuals for undergraduate texts in social psychology often contain exercises for demonstrating such errors and biases; some of these might be modified for use in writing, reporting, and editing classes, but others will have to be developed from scratch. We must also work to integrate this and related knowledge into traditional journalism text-books. Some materials produced by cognitive social psychologists are accessible enough to use as readings for undergraduate journalism majors (c.f., Loftus, 1979: Stanovich, 1986), but most are not. It is imperative that those capable of translating psychological research be involved in producing and testing classroom-appropriate materials.

Whether journalists and journalists-in-training will be receptive to efforts to meet this need is another matter; another cognitive tendency that psychologists have documented is the "overconfidence phenomenon," or the tendency for people to overestimate the accuracy of their judgments (Fischoff, Slovic & Lichtenstein, 1977). Also uncertain is whether journalists, even if receptive, will be able to inhibit these errors and biases, particularly under time constraints, which have been found to exaggerate such problems (Kruglanski & Freund, 1983).

Still, there is evidence that, at least under some circumstances, people can inhibit some of these biases. Simply telling people to be unbiased won't lessen people's tendency to maintain a theory in the face of disconfirming evidence. However, some research suggests that telling people to consider carefully how they are evaluating evidence and to watch their bias as they go through the process of interpreting data does help (Lord, Lepper & Thompson, 1980). Asking people to explain why the theory might be wrong has also worked in some experiments (Anderson, 1982).

By doing nothing, we can be almost certain that journalists, to the extent that they do make these mistakes, will be condemned to repeat them.

Mindful Thinking : There is a legitimate concern with bias in news reporting. Unfortunately, critical audiences tend to assume that the bias they detect is the personal bias of the reporter whom they see on television or whose byline is at the top of the article. This reduces the issue to one of personal fairness (or ignorance), and the remedy most often suggested is to replace to distract attention from the far more important issue of organizational bias, Indeed, if the organization is "titled" in its preferences in one direction, news will tend to be distorted regardless of the fairness or unfairness—of the individual newsman. Just as a roulette wheel mounted on a tilted table tends to favour some numbers over other numbers no matter how fair the croupier might be, a news organization that is tilted in a certain direction because of the way it is structured, will also tend to favour certain types of stories over others. When confronted with such a biased wheel, it would obviously be unprofitable to attempt to explain its outcome by studying the biases of the croupier. To understand the criteria by which the media decide what is news, it is necessary first to describe the interests and values of the news organizations.

Television news provides perhaps the clearest case of the process by which reality is systematically reconstructed by news organizations. To begin with, network news organizations have, unlike some newspapers and magazines, absolute control over their product. Av Westin, vice-president of ABC News, described the process of control candidly in a memorandum (Epstein 1975):

> The senior editors decide if the story has been adequately covered and they also estimate how long the report "should run. In most cases, correspondents deliberately overwrite their scripts giving the producers at home the opinion of editing it down: selecting which portions of the interviews are to be used and which are to be discarded... In some cases, the senior producer "salvages" a report by assigning the correspondent to redo his narration or by sending a cameraman to refilm a sequence.

Under such a regime, a correspondent has little opportunity to insert in a news story personal values that run counter to the network's objectives. Nor does the description in the West in memorandum quoted above apply only to ABC. During the year I spent observing NBC's and CBS's news operations, I saw even more rigorous controls maintained on news stories—including constant review by network executives.

In controlling the news product, the network organization attempt to satisfy certain basic requirements that will allow them to continue as viable businesses. They must maintain a national audience for their advertisers, a need which, in turn, requires that the news programmes be accepted by the affiliated (but independently owned) stations around the country. They must satisfy the ground rules laid down by the Federal Communications Commission (FCC), which licences and monitors television stations. They also must maintain credibility as news media. And they must confirm to budgetary and time restrictions to maintain profitability.

The Pressure of Time : Out of these basic requisites flow the rules and logic that shape network news. The most obvious constraint is time. The networks allocate only thirty minutes each night for their network news programmes. From this time budget, approximately seven minutes must be deducted for commercials and non-news items. This leaves only twenty three minutes for the presentation of between five to eight filmed news stories and the narration of other news events. Confronted with this reality, the producers of network news programmes have no choice but to limit most of the news stories to a duration of two or four minutes. This enforced brevity leaves little room for presenting complex explanations or multifaceted arguments. In practical terms, two to four minutes is not sufficient for providing the historical context or detailed geographic situations of most events. To make news stories understandable to a national audience in this brief slice of time, producers find that they have to be reported almost entirely in the present/future tense. The focus is on what is happening, not why it is happening or what the root causes are. This time requisite ineluctable leads to a picture of society as unstable. If great events happen without cause or historic context, then it appears—atleast, to constant viewers of network news—that any institution is capable of foundering, collapsing or being overthrown without evident cause.

The Audience and the Advertiser : A second requisite that shapes television news is audience maintenance. It is assumed by network executives that if the stories on a news programme are unclear, confusing or visually uninteresting, a portion of the audience will switch the channel to another network. Such a loss of audience would not only lessen the advertising revenues from the news programme, it would— even more important—lessen the revenues from all the network programmes that follow, since the news programme is regarded as a "lead-in" for the network's evening of entertainment programmes. Network executives therefore insist that news stories have both visual interest and visual clarity. In attempting to satisfy this requisite, news producers have come up with a common formula for audience maintenance.

The Perception : The first assumption made by news executives and producers is that viewers' interest is most likely to be maintained through easily recognizable and palpable images; conversely, it is most likely to be distracted by unfamiliar or confusing images. This has special force in the case of dinner-time news when, according to studies, the audience has fewer years of formal education than the population at large— and when a large proportion of the viewers are children. In practice, therefore, cameramen, correspondents, and editors are instructed to seek and select pictures that have an almost universal meaning. Stories thus tend to fit into a limited repertory of images, which explains why so often shabbily dressed children stand for poverty, why fire—symbolically—stands for destruction, and so forth. Since television is regarded as a medium for the "transmission of experience" rather than for "information," complex issues are represented in terms of human experience ; inflation, for example, is pictured as a man unable to afford dinner in a restaurant. The repertory, of course, changes. But at any given time, images— especially emotional ones, which are presumed to have the broadest possible recognition—are used to illustrate news events.

A second assumption in this logic of audience maintenance is that scenes of potential conflict are more interesting to the audience than scenes of placidity. Virtually all executives and producers share this view. Network news thus seek situations in which there is a high potential for violence but a low potential for audience confusion. News events showing a violent confrontation between two easily recognizable sides in conflict—for example, blacks versus whites, uniformed police versus demonstrators, or military versus civilians—are preferable to those in which the issues are less easily identifiable. Even when the conflict involves confusing elements, however, it usually can be reconstructed in the form of a two-sided conflict. Network news therefore lends to present the news in terms of highly dramatic conflicts between clearly defined sides.

A third, closely related, assumption is that the viewers' span of attention—which is presumed to be limited—is prolonged by action or by subjects in motion, and is sharply reduced by static subjects such as "talking heads". As has been previously discussed, the high value placed on action footage by executives leads to a three-step distillation of news happening by correspondents, cameramen, and editors, all of whom seek the moment of highest action. Through this process, the action in a news event, which in fact may account for only a fraction of the time, is concentrated and becomes the central features of the happening. This helps to explain why news on television tends willy-nilly to focus on activity.

A fourth assumption made by news producers is that stories are more likely to hold viewer's attention if they are cast in the form of the fictive story, with a discernible beginning, middle, and end. One NBC vice-president suggested to news producers that all stories should have rising action, a climax, then a falling action, and a seeming resolution. According to analysis done by NBC's audience research experts this form would "lock" the audience into the news story. Since the film is generally re-edited by the producers, it is relatively simple to cast most happenings in this fictive form. The net effect, however, is that reality is reconstructed into a series of events that never actually happened in the form in which the audience witnesses them. Events do not necessarily begin, build, and resolve themselves in terms of the visual data that are available to a television news team. Yet all the behind-the-scenes oscillations, twist, and contigencies of reality are neatly ironed out.

Networks and the Local Stations : Another basic requisite flows from the demand of affiliated stations that network news be differentiated from their own local news programmes. It must appear to be national news. The problem is, of course, that all news is local in the sense that it occurs in some locality. Network producers resolve this tension by combining a series of local reports into a single national story. For example, the opening of a new subway line in Washington, D.C. may be considered a local story; it can be converted, however, into a national story by commissioning and fusing stories about subway in two or three other cities and then subsuming them all under a nationwide theme such as "Can the Cities Survive?" This process of nationalizing the news yields a constant agenda of national crises in place of local happening.

Finally, governmental regulations of television impose another basic requisite on producers; they must appear to be fair on controversial issues by presenting opposing views. This requisite is satisfied by soliciting views from spokesmen of the two opposing sides in a dispute— and then editing these conflicting views into "a dialogue". To avoid obvious disparities, the producers usually seek the most articulate spokesman for each side. Not only does this treatment tend to reduce complicated issues to a mere debate, point/counterpoint style, but it also gives presumptive legitimacy to both sides.

Organizational requisites cannot by any means explain all the outputs of television news. The personal quirks of producers, editors and reporters contribute to news programmes. There are also indisputable fashions and trends that change the level of consciousness of news reporting, The organizational requisites do explain, however, many of the built in tilts that influence television news.

Distinctive Frame : Print media have a different set of organizational requisites. Most afternoon newspapers, for example, face the problem of delivery:-the news must be reported, written, printed and delivered to newsstands spread over a metropolitan area before commuters have returned home from their jobs. They also must find news that has occurred after the deadlines of the morning newspapers. This severe restriction on time, coupled with union regulations that restrict periods in which the paper can be printed, have led the afternoon newspapers to focus their coverage on sports, horse racing, and stock markets. Morning newspapers, news magazines, and monthly magazines face different sets of organizational problems.

One question finally must be asked: Given these constraints, do the media present a picture of reality upon which rational men may take decisions? In spending over a year watching the three television networks collect, analyze, and present data in the form of news stories, I concluded that these pictures of reality were systematically distorted by organizational requirements. Dealing with such distortions involves the same problem as dealing with systematic distortions in a map. No map presents a perfect picture of reality. However, if one understands that such areas as Australia and Greenland are reduced in size, it is feasible to use a map to understand the geography of the world. Similarly, news itself requires some adjustments to compensate for systematic distortions.

If news media clearly and honestly stated the constraints and limits under which they operate, the adjustment would be far easier to make. Unfortunately, they tend to hide rather than to explain these constraints. News magazines, for example, print a false publishing date on each issue (usually a week after publication). This deception makes it difficult for the reader to ascertain the point when news had to be cut off because of the deadline. The value of news to the public would be greatly enhanced if news organizations revealed, rather than obscured, the methods by which they select and process reality.

3

MANAGEMENT FOR DEVELOPMENT

With the dawn of civilization, communication has become an integral part of human life. Man has used communication which includes symbols or sounds (oral) to link himself with the external world. In the process, he realised its potential or fulfilling his socio-economic needs, and established contacts with others belonging to varied cultural and ethnic backgrounds, cutting across geographical boundaries.

The invention of script which facilitated easy communication among people gave a new dimension. The advent of the printing press extended the reach-out capacity of communication. By the turn of the twentieth century, the advancement of science and technology led to the development of other channels of communication such as radio, film and television, which were put to greater use for dissemination of information, as well as for propaganda. Because information plays a vital role in disseminating various views, it is increasingly used to influence the opinion of the people.

After World War II, many nations in Asia, Africa and Latin America became independent, and started formulating their own policies of development. The view that mass media could play a vital role in national development influenced these policies. Thus, communication used to further development was called "development journalism" or development communication (Lent, 1979; Singhal and Rogers, 1989).

Quebral (1975) defined development communication as the art and science of human communication applied to the speedy transformation of a country from poverty to a dynamic state of economic growth to make possible greater economic and social equality and the larger fulfilment of human potential. The term "development journalism" emerged in Asia, more specifically in the Philippines, through the efforts of journalists such as Juan Mercado and Alan Chalkley (Lent, 1986). Later in 1967, the term gained popularity with the creation of the Press Foundation of Asia, financed by Asian newspapers and the Ford Foundation (Altschull, 1984: 151).

Nevertheless, those who conceived development journalism in the beginning believed that national development depended heavily on economic development and felt that journalists trained in economics could report competently about problems pertaining to a developing country. During the 1970s, development journalism came to be called 'commitment journalism' as some Third World nations realised that journalism could be an effective means to promote the State's ideologies and its campaigns (Forsythe, 1990)

Diverse Thoughts

Scholars have used the three concepts growth, modernisation and development to describe and explain the goals of newly independent nations. These nations, while formulating their strategies of development, after World War II followed the economic development model of western industrialised nations. They believed that industrialisation was the quickest way to development. Consequently, they invested in heavy industries like steel mills, hydro-electric dams, etc./at the expense of the rural and agricultural sectors of economy. Meanwhile, Walt Rostow, David McClelland and other scholars in the 50s and 60s put forth various theories of development for the benefit of the less developed countries. Rostow (1960), an American economist suggested a five-stage model for the development of a nation. Essentially, he constructed a five-stage model of transition from a traditional economy to a modern industrial complex: the industrial society, pre-conditions for take-off, take-off drive to maturity and the age of high mass consumption. He believed that every society would pass through these five stages of economic growth leading finally to the last phase: the age of mass consumption.

While economists interpreted development as economic growth that would bring changes in the social and economic structure of a country, psychologists argued change at the individual level would pave the way for the modernisation of a country. The works of two American scholars in the early 60s David McClelland and Everel Hagan were highly influential in this direction.

McClelland (1961) propounded a theory that focussed on achievement motivation or desire for excellence. He argued that the need for achievement (n. ach.) would propel an individual to meet challenges and take risks to succeed in the face of difficulties. The industrial nations, according to McClelland, comprise individuals with high levels of achievement motivation, which led to high rate of national economic growth. Entrepreneurship is one of the expressions of achievement motivation. He, along with David Winter, conducted experiments in Kakinada town of Andhra Pradesh (India) in the late 60s. They trained small businessmen to have higher achievement motivation and then measured its consequences in their business success (Jhingan 1994: 51).

Hagan (1962) believed that developing societies comprised traditional personalities which the industrial societies had more innovative personalities. He put forth the argument that the individual had to change for development to occur in these countries. Innovative personalities could be fostered by improving literacy, by expanding mass media, by urbanization and by promoting nationalism.

Communication Theories : Communication scholars were also involved in Third World development. In this connection, the two works—Daniel Lerner's *The Passing of Traditional Society* (1958) and Wilbur Schramm's *Mass Media and National Development* (1964) were influential. Modernization, according to Lerner, was essentially transforming traditional societies into modern ones. He identified four indices for modernization—urbanisation, literacy, mass media exposure and political participation. People had to be mobile, empathetic and should participate in development. When people are mobile, they look for something new and empathy would make them search for something new. From his studies of the Middle East, he found that exposing individuals to new people, ideas, attitudes, etc., would accelerate the process of modernization. The increase in physical mobility through transportation could be enhanced by the exposure to mediated experience through mass media. Thus, the mass media were important agents of modernisation and hence he called them 'magic multipliers'. Lerner's model shows that modernization occurs in three phases: increasing urbanisation tends to increase literacy rates; rising literacy tends to increase media exposure; and increasing media exposure accompanies wider economic and political participation. Schramm on the other hand, argued that as information was a vital ingredient in moving a nation towards development, a developing country could facilitate development by expanding the scope of its mass media.

During the 1960s, the dominant paradigm influenced and guided many national development programmes. According to Rogers (1976), the dominant paradigm of development grew out:

(a) the industrial revolution in Europe and the United States;

(b) the colonial experience in Latin America, Africa and Asia;

(c) the success of the Marshall plan in Europe's post - World War II development;

(d) the quantitative empiricism of North American social sciences; and

(e) the capitalistic philosophy of economics and politics.

The dominant paradigm, ideally, concerned itself with what it did to the people to raise their standard of living (Singhal and Rogers; 1989). Thus, it emphasized growth of the economy to alleviate poverty. The essential features of the dominant paradigm were summarized by Hernandes-Ramos and Schramm (1989: 10) as follows:

(a) Industry is the prime mover of the economy. Therefore, a major part of investment must go into industry and what is necessary to fuel it includes raw materials, transportation and training.

(b) Modern society requires more specialists than generalists within each field (e.g. industry, health).

(c) Public education is needed to raise the abilities of the entire workforce and encourage their participation in government. Healthcare and family planning are needed to increase the well-being of the population and curtail demand for jobs, housing and so on.

(d) The profit from centrally owned and managed industry, trade and sale of manufactured goods would be expected 'to trickle down' from the centre of the system to the periphery, from industries and central markets to agricultural sector and from cities to villages.

(e) The situations in which rapid development is desired, necessary information can be diffused and persuasion can occur through the mass media with the aid of an extension service. Adoption of promising innovations should be encouraged along with increases in productivity.

The dominant paradigm saw mass communication as a powerful and direct force to diffuse information and innovations about development issues to the masses (Rogers, 1976). Communication scholars thought that growth of the mass media was essential because communication which was linear and one-way transmission would reach the wider audience. The indicators of national development, such as, per capita income, literacy, urbanisation and industrialisation have also correlated with indicators of a well-developed media infrastructure (Mody, 1991; Melkote, 1991). Thus, UNESCO study suggested a minimum standard for mass media availability in the Third World ten copies of daily newspapers, five radio receivers, two television receivers, and two cinema seats for every 100 of its inhabitants.

In the early 1970s, communication scholars realised that role of mass communication in facilitating development was often indirect rather than direct (Singhal and Rogers, 1989). This realisation led to criticism of the dominant paradigm of development. Moreover, Third World countries did not derive any benefits by imitating the western economic development model because problems in these countries obstructed social development

(Rogers, 1976; Mody, 1991). The internal causes included traditionalism, widespread poverty, illiteracy, growing population and adequate institutional mechanisms to pass on the fruits of economic growth to the general population, especially disadvantaged groups. Added to these problems, red-tapism, inefficiency and corruption acted as contributing factors (Singhal and Rogers, 1989). Industrialisation in the Third World countries caused other problems such as reduction of labour, increased unemployment and large-scale migration from villages to cities. These social changes occurred and the Third World countries were unprepared to face the consequences (Narula, 1994).

The failure of the model paved the way for evolving a new development paradigm (Singhal and Rogers, 1989; Melkote, 1991; Narula, 1994).

The new development paradigm recognised many paths to development suitable to developing countries. Pluralistic in its approach, it encompassed all sections of population. The key elements of the new paradigm, according to Singhal and Rogers (1989) are:

1. greater equality in the distribution of fruits of economic growth, information, and the consequent socio-economic benefits by focussing on such weaker sections of the population as the poor, women, racial and ethnic minorities;
2. people's participation, knowledge sharing and empowerment to facilitate self-help efforts by individuals, groups and communities;
3. self-reliance and independence in development, emphasising the potential of local resources. Self- reliance became a key concept at both national and local levels, implying that every nation, and perhaps every village, could develop in its own way;
4. integration of traditional and modern communication systems and the use of 'little media' along with the 'big media' such as the television and the film, in order to facilitate development.

It is in this context that the role of the Press in national development assumed importance and emerged as development journalism or development communication to facilitate mass participation, mass mobilisation and group efficacy in development planning and execution. In this light, communication scholars such as Rogers and others envisaged the main roles of the press as follows:

1. to provide information about development problems and possibilities and appropriate innovations;
2. to circulate widely information about self- development accomplishments by local groups so that other such groups could profit from their experiences (Singhal and Rogers, 1989, 22-23);
3. to act as a catalyst between policy-makers and beneficiaries at all levels; and
4. to activate bureaucracy on the launching of development programmes required at all levels (Parker and Mahammadi, 1977: 189).

The role of developmental journalism thus came to be seen as crucial in facilitating development in third world countries. Experts have offered various definitions of developmental journalism.

Vilanilam (1975) defined it as 'journalism that deals with the process of developing nations'. The same view was further elaborated by Aggarwal (1978a), according to whom developmental journalism basically reports the development process rather than events. The emphasis in developmental journalism, is, therefore not on what happens at a particular moment or on a given day but on what is happening over time.

Thus, developmental journalism covers the entire gamut of socio-economic and cultural developmental journalism and does not differ drastically from regular news coverage. Rather, its emphasis is more on development aspects keeping in view the context of development; and it examines critically and reports the relevance, enactment and impact of development programmes (Aggarwal, 1978b; Ogan, 1982). The second Press Commission of India (1982: 28) stated that "development reporting should tell the story of what is going well as what is going wrong. The press should investigate the reasons for success as well as failure of various development programmes affecting the lives of common people at different places under different conditions".

However, western scholars like Stevenson (1994: 144), Hachten (1996: 30.35) and Righer (1979) viewed developmental journalism as advocacy journalism or propaganda journalism by the government because journalists mostly depended on government handouts. Righter (1979) said: (Developmental journalism's) Successes alerted governments to the importance of economic and social reporting—and its potential usefulness, if systematically applied to mobilizing mass support behind government policies. Intended to enlarge the areas of free debate, the concept has been taken over by governments, extended to cover all communications and integrated into an official variant of new journalism *(op. cit. p.* 189).

Aggarwal (1978b) criticising the western view, argued that developmental journalism is not synonymous with officially prepared news. According to him, developmental journalism in the developing countries makes the highly urbanised and elitist media relevant to their predominantly rural societies.

Golding (as quoted by Guneratne, 1980) pointed out the origin of developmental journalism in four ways in which it was produced:

First, by stressing the generally educative function of news either about specific pieces of information or by arousal of general awareness of events and their implications.

Second, by producing stories which displayed particular social needs or problems it was hoped that government would be provoked into action.

Third, by giving prominence to local self-help projects news could encourage emulation of such activities in other communities.

Fourth, the news could tackle specific problems, such as elite corruption, often with prudent obliqueness.

Forsythe (1990) outlined the objectives of developmental journalism as follows:

1. developmental journalism has a basic purpose: to inform, to educate and to entertain;
2. its objectives are to investigate, analyse, interpret, and to commit oneself to development;

3. it should give accurate development information, that facilitates the development process itself;
4. it should aim at promoting mutual understanding between the leaders and the people by carrying policy and other messages of the state to the people and relaying people's needs and aspirations to the people;
5. it has to motivate people and policy towards what people need, and to stimulate people for maximum participation in development;
6. it should encourage and inform people about productive attitudes, *i.e.*, cooperation in long-term national efforts, attitudes favourable to work such as agriculture, good health practices, acceptance of new innovations, etc., and
7. it should help build a common fund of knowledge and ideas that favour the cohesion of the social structure and enable people to become actively engaged in national development.

Situation in India

Developmental journalism was practised in India even before the term came into existence. One example is Mahatma Gandhi's writings in his journals, *Young India* and *Harijan.* Gandhi educated the masses on topics that he considered of vital interest to the progress of the nation. He profusely wrote on contemporary topics such as Hindu-Muslim unity, removal of untouchability, prohibition, promotion of Khadi and other village industries, and the popularisation of spinning wheel as a means of supplementing the income of the semi-starving and half-employed village peasants in India (Murty, 1966: 79-80) Gandhi said the newspapers should understand and give expression to people's feelings,.arouse among the people certain desirable sentiments, and fearlessly expose defects in public life.

Prior to Independence, newspapers influenced and moulded the opinion of the people on social issues such as sati, child marriages, bride burning and so on. Journalism in those days functioned as a mission to awaken the masses socially and politically (Murthy, 1966; Yadav, 1985; Parthasarathy, 1991).

Past Experiences

After Independence, researchers as well as newspapers conducted a few experiments in developmental journalism to facilitate rural development. Selden Menefee and Audrey Menefea conducted an interesting study of mimeographed newspaper in Mysore containing some development information. Known as Menefee experiment, a small newspaper called *Gram Samachar* (Village News) was published in Kannada, the local language, for 13 weeks to test the effects of communication on the villages. For the purpose, four villages were chosen near Mysore in Karnataka. The researchers found an increase in the information level of the regular readers because of the newspaper (Menefee and Menefee,. 1967).

B.G. Verghese, the then editor of *The Hindustan Times,* New Delhi conducted another experiment. In 1969, Verghese asked a team of reporters to write periodically about *Chattera,* a small village in Haryana about its people, their problems and the process of development taking place in that Indian village (Yadav, 1991). Aggarwal (1978) reported:'Our Village, *Chattera....*'is a bold attempt to give rural orientation to the predominantly urban based and elite-oriented newspapers in the country. It is the form of journalism that can prove of immense help in bridging the rural-urban communication gap in the Third World".

Another experiment in developmental journalism undertaken during 1981-84 was the 'Identify backward village experiment' (IBVE) by *Udayavani,* a Kannada daily. In 1981, *Udayavani* came up with the idea of identifying and reporting on activities in the ten most backward villages in South Karnataka. It defined 'backwardness' as lack of educational facilities, electricity, post office, telephone, medical facilities, clean water and road network. These villages were identified by the coordinator of the project, Ishwar Daitota, after eliciting opinions from readers through a survey conducted by the newspaper staff. The paper then published 30 stories every month on these villages. During the experiment, the *Udayavani* programme was successful in getting basic amenities to the villages. However, Daitota and Sanjay (1990: 50) noted that the activities among the villagers and government officials dropped sharply once *Udayavani* had withdrawn from the project area.

In another experiment, a researcher started a rural newspaper, *Gramavani* in 1993 in Deulpadi, a village in Ganjam district (Orissa) to give information to the rural people. The fortnightly newspaper reaching eight villages of the panchayat continued for 16 months. A major objective of the experiment was to provide development information to the people. The contents of the newspaper included agriculture, health, forestry and animal husbandry. The newspaper brought awareness among the villagers exposed to the newspaper (Jena, 1995).

Development Reporting: The second press commission of India (1982) in its survey of the state of the press in the country observed that "the extent of development reporting in regional language newspapers had improved considerably in some widely read dailies in Bengali, Kannada, Malayalam and English. These newspapers have reported regularly on development-related topics and major socio-economic issues such as the conditions of tea gardens, labour problems of drought and irrigation, 'dowry death' and the general ill-treatment of women, the plight of under trial prisoners and the living conditions of urban slum-dwellers, etc."

However, developmental journalism has not gained much currency among Indian newspapers. Obviously, the Indian press is known for its wide coverage of political news, gossip and sensationalism (Goswami, 1994; Nandy, 1994a, 1994b; Karlekar, 1994). Hence, vital issues such as primary education, population control, the state of urban decay, power crises, etc., get a backseat (Rai, 1992; Singh, 1994; Shourie, 1995).

Despite these developments, the second Press commission (1887: 30) again observed that "the reporting of non-official initiatives in rural development, educational reforms, leprosy eradication and so on is less extensive than the in-depth reporting of the implementation of official development programmes. It is unfortunate that our newspapers become aware of such non-official activities only after they have been honoured by Jamanalal Bajaj Foundation or Magsaysay Award."

Further, reporting on rural development does not receive much importance in the press although 70 per cent of the population in India live in rural areas. Rural stories rarely get front page coverage unless they were disastrous events such as starvation deaths, flood, famine or a policy pronouncements (Gupta, 1994).

Different Kinds of Matters

The causes of backwardness in development reporting in Indian newspapers, according to Bhattacharjea (1994) are:

(a) Inadequate information and poor understanding of the subject of development among practising journalists;

(b) Absence of training in marshalling and presentation of facts in an attractive format;

(c) Poor interest shown by newspapers in development coverage, and

(d) Lack of funds and support from the newspaper establishments.

Another important reason for the Indian newspapers for not taking up developmental journalism seriously is the entry of businessmen into the profession and the commercialisation of the press. Newspapers came to be increasingly owned and managed by top businessmen in the country (Rao, 1982; Yadav, 1985; Vilanilam, 1989: 65; Joglekar, 1990; Nayar, 1994). The advent of new technology helped the launching of new dailies all over the country. The publication of multiple editions from many places went up as technology facilitated this venture (Chaturvedi, 1992; Saddhar, 1992). The Press Council of India annual report 1991-92 observed that "this factor (new technology) operating in tandem with other forces, is leading to increased concentration of the newspapers in the hands of some big business house or trading interests. As a result, the newspaper business in India is fast becoming a money game."

The growth of newspapers in India since independence substantiates this conclusion. In 1992, there were only 330 newspapers in the country with a total circulation of 25 lakhs. According to the 38th report of the Registrar of Newspapers of India (1994) there were 3,954 daily newspapers with a circulation of 572 crore and the individual newspapers formed the biggest share (42%) in circulation (Table).

Although the number of newspapers has increased along with their out-reach and influence in the country, newspapers spend only 3% of their revenue for news gathering (Bhattacharjee, 1994).

Ownership pattern of daily newspapers as on 1993.

Table

Form of Ownership	*No. of Dailies*
Individual	2,746
Society/Association	288
Firm / Partnership	233
Trust	121
Joint stock company	486
Govt. central/state	31
Others	49
Total	3,954

Source: Report of the Registrar of Newspapers of India (1994).

News pertains only to urban areas is given importance as access to news events and filing of reports even later in the night is easier and can be accommodated in the news pages. In the process, reporting from rural areas gets neglected.

Importance of Newspaper

In view of the theoretical perspective about the role of the press in accelerating development in a country, scholars in the Third World have researched the role of the press in development. Researchers have examined the use of developmental news by print media in a variety of settings. These informative studies have provided descriptive information on the production of developmental news. These studies, however, suffer from conceptual and methodological problems.

One problem is the definition of developmental news itself. Experts in the field differ on the concept of developmental news, *e.g.*, Vilanilam (1975), Haque (1986) and Shah and Gayatri (1994). Vilanilam (1995) defines development news as news relating to administrative reforms, agricultural development and food production, economic activity, education, employment and labour welfare, family planning, health, hygiene and medicine, housing, industrial, scientific and technological development, mass communications, national integration, rural and urban development, social reforms, telecommunication, tourism and transport development. Haque (1986), in his study of Indian newspapers, defines development news as positive or negative reporting on health, education, literacy, communication, agriculture, industry, housing, population planning, national integration, energy and ecology.

Shah and Gayatri (1994), in their study of Indonesian newspapers define development news as those relating to development priorities outlined in the fifth five-year plan of Indonesia.

Shah (1988) mentions some studies that defined development news as all good news or news about economic and social problems as well as other studies that used lists of development topics based on a survey of people's needs, the opinion of experts, existing theoretical frameworks or pretests conducted by researchers. Most development news studies have assessed the quantity of development news appearing in different newspapers in a region or a country. They have used content analysis to find the percentage of development news. They have neither tried to analyze the direction of the news themes nor to compare the extent of coverage among different categories of news. The following pages present the studies in this context in different countries.

Available studies reveal that the coverage of developmental news differs from country to country. For example, Mustafa (1974) found that Malay language newspapers devoted half of their newshole to developmental news while the English language dailies devoted 32%. Emmanuel (1976) in his study of Ghana press observed that developmental news content was greater in the wire services than in newspaper reports. Sutapo (1983) examined six Indonesian national newspapers and concluded that Indonesian newspapers used, more developmental than non-development news and that each newspaper in the study had a different view about which development issue was most deserving of attention. Shah and Gayatri (1994) in their study of two Indonesian newspapers found that nearly 45% of the total newshole was devoted to developmental news. In contrast, Barghouti's study (1974) of Jordan media found that political news got more prominence than agricultural news. Maslog's study (1996) of the Philippines newspapers revealed that the newspapers gave more importance to politics and sports than developmental issues.

The performance of the Indian press, however, seems to be quite different. Although India is a developing country, its newspapers act quite differently from their expected role. Overall, the studies analysing newspaper content reveal that development news coverage is not significant compared to other Third World countries such as Malaysia, Ghana and Indonesia where development news occupies nearly half of the total newshole. However, Jordan, the Philippines and the Indian studies show that development news content is low and do not exceed one-tenth of the total newshole of a daily.

Quite interestingly, India's regional dailies, which are far ahead of the English dailies in circulation, are no exception.

Vilanilam's study (1975) of four Indian dailies revealed that the English dailies—*The Times of India* and *The Hindu* gave 9.2% and 18.8% of space respectively for developmental news, whereas the two native language papers *Aaj* (Hindi) and *Malayala Manorama* (Malayalam) gave 19.5% and 10.3%. However, this study concluded that all four newspapers devoted more space to government and political news than to developmental news.

The second Press Commission (1982) reported all the newspapers in the country consistently allocated more space to politics and conflict news than to developmental news. The commission observed that the English papers devoted nearly 50% of the space of front-page and inside pages to news on politics and conflict. Developmental news occupied only 12.2% and 17.2% on the front page in comparison to 52.4% and 42.8% for politics and conflict.

In comparative analysis, Mohapatra (1984) pointed out that the two news papers—*The Times of India* and *Samaj* (Oriya) devoted 25% of editorial space to developmental news. But, they were all about demands, complaints and opinions. Space devoted to serious issues of the country like family planning and literacy was insignificant.

Haque (1986) in his study of developmental news versus human interest stories in seven dailies in India, found that developmental news accounted for 10.5% of the news space across the dailies with a range of 4.9% to 18.3% and with a consensus ranking of *5* among the 10 subject categories of news. Among the seven dailies, only *The Hindu* devoted 18.3% of space to developmental news. However, political and government news occupied nearly one-fourth of the total space in all the seven dailies.

News items apart, editorials and letters to the editor also contain development-related issues. Researchers in India have analysed these issues because newspapers in their editorials focus on the policy decisions of the government as well as development-linked issues. For example, Ranade's study (1971) of editorials in six newspapers during 14 days revealed that out of 192 editorials, 35 (18%) (all papers put together) were on education, health/medicine, agriculture, science, social, cultural and sports while the rest were on political and economic issues. Another study of editorials of three national dailies— *The Hindu, The Times of India* and *The Hindustan Times* by Srinivasan (1985) showed that 27.3%, 27.8% and 46.3% respectively were devoted to cover politics. The study also analysed the treatment given to the issues in the editorials on a three-point scale-favourable, unfavourable, and neutral and noted that favourable editorials were more in all the three papers.

Similarly, readers express their opinions on development issues through letters to the editor column. Quite often, newspapers give attention to letters that contain references to political statements and conflict issues. Newspapers also publish columns meant for public awareness where readers can express their grievances and complaints through newspaper columns. In a study of letters to the editor, Devi Prasad *et. al* (1992) found that a majority of those letters that dealt with civic amenities such as power, communications, public transport, etc.

Rukmini (1979) in her study of letters to the editor published in three Andhra Pradesh dailies observed that the two English dailies—*Indian Express* and *The Hindu* gave more emphasis to national issues than local and state issues while the regional English daily *Deccan Chronicle* focussed on local and state issues compared to the national dailies.

Although women play a decisive role in the development of the nation, issues related to them do not seem to occupy prominent place in the Indian newspapers. For example, Dasgupta (1976), in her study of women's issues in four English dailies published in New Delhi in 1975, observed that women's issues received no attention in the six subject categories social, economic, political, art and culture, biographical and other issues. However, the study did not elaborate the methodology adopted for the study.

Even with the improvements in newspapers in terms of technology and growth, the coverage of women's issues have not received much attention. Bhatnagar's study (1996) of women's issues in six English newspapers published in New Delhi in 1987 indicated that only 280 (1%) items in the sample reported about the problems and welfare activities about women. Important terms like women's education, rights and wage rates of women workers did not receive adequate coverage in any newspaper under study.

The growth of regional newspapers in post-independence India has been phenomenal. Though the regional papers outnumber the English dailies, the coverage of development-related issues has not received much attention in these papers. This apart, the regional papers also dedicate much space to local issues unlike the English dailies as evident in the following studies.

A study by Ahmed (1986) showed that the regional press devoted more than half of the space to regional news. This study based on the four Malayalam newspapers in Kerala revealed that regional press devoted a large proportion of the space to political news rather than news on development of the State.

Vilanilam's analysis (1993) of ten dailies (eight Malayalam and two English). during the period between June 1987 and May 1988 found that science and technology news including development news occupied less than 5 per cent of the newshole. Preetha and

Karippai's (1996) study of farm news in two Malayalam dailies in Kerala found that hardly 1.33 per cent of the newshole dealt with farm news.

Srivastava's study (1996) of coverage of environmental news in four dailies (two English—*The Times of India* and *The Hindustan Times)* and two Hindi dailies—*(Dainik Jagran* and *Nav Bharat Times)* in 1995 found that only 0.7 per cent of the total print area occupied environmental issues. No editorial appeared on the subject in the entirety of March 1995.

Bhatnagar (1996) who analysed the development news content of four Telugu dailies in 1991 revealed that among the four dailies, *Andhra Prabha* devoted more space to development news than the other dailies. However, regional news occupied more space than national and international news in all the sample dailies.

The present study presumes that the press as a social institution should play a crucial and decisive role in the development of a nation. To play such a role, the ' press should disseminate development-related information to the people. Studies hitherto conducted in different settings to analyse newspaper content on development have shown that such content in Indian print media is very low compared to some other Third World countries. However, the problem with these studies is that they have chosen developmental themes for analysis randomly without defining the concept of developmental news systematically.

In comparison to earlier studies, the present study offers a definition of developmental news consistent with specific issues drawn from India's planned priorities. Thus, the present study seeks to analyse the extent of newspaper coverage on the developmental issues envisaged in the eighth five-year plan. It examines the extent of development reporting by newspapers in Andhra Pradesh.

No previous research has attempted to systematically examine the newspaper content in Andhra Pradesh, particularly those published in Vishakhapatnam, the north coastal region. The focus of the present study is only on newspapers. It excludes electronic media because of the constraints of time and finance.

Aims and Objectives

A Manual For News Agency Reporters published by the Indian Institute of Mass Communication defines the purpose of development reporting as follows:

The purpose of development reporting is to create a sense of involvement, to spread the realisation that the future comes out of present efforts, that development can be nobody's gift, least of all of the aid given by affluent countries, but is the result of one's own labour. Destiny does not descend from above, it grows out of one's hands.

Development reporting must concern itself with the people. It must show them how to improve their bargaining power with society. It must make them realise that their future is in their hands. It must describe the process of backbone building.

Development reporting must describe the people actually at work in new projects and processes. It must describe the processes of change and modernisation, the new discoveries and the products. It must describe terms and concepts of development.

An important aspect of development reporting is success stories of people who have adopted new technologies, tried new methods, and benefited themselves and helped society.

Development reporting, by its very nature, is devoid of the kind of sensational interest that an eruption or a calamity or a political confrontation produces. Secondly, it does not carry the stamp of immediacy that 'events' do.

Development reporting, to be effective, requires considerable investigative and research skill on the part of the journalist, apart from firm grasp of trends in economic thought, planning, and development.

What is development? The removal of poverty, the lessening of disparity between regions and classes, the building up of the technological infrastructure, modernisation of society through shedding feudalism, tribalism, and superstitions, the gradual achievement of economic self-reliance.

Development is measured in the improvement of the lives of the people and the strengthening of the family's or the individual's capacity to deal with the rest of the society and of the nation's capacity to deal with the world.

Here we have not only a reasonably good definition of what development is and what is expected of development reporting, which is development journalism, but also of the very purpose of development reporting which is to improve the quality of life both of the individual and of society.

Success Story

Development journalism has been a part of the western journalistic scene for a long time. It gathered prominence in recent years in India because it was generally believed that Indian news papers were too preoccupied with political events to give much thought to what was happening in the economic field and that Indian political reporting took a substantial percentage of space in the daily columns. Newspapers were accused of not caring enough for development reporting especially at a time when India was making rapid progress in industry and commerce.

The problem with development reporting—at least till India became free—has been that there was little development to report. It was only after India went through a succession of Five-Year Plans that thought was at last given for assessing the results of planning. To what extent did planning benefit the common man? Did he get adequate compensation for the fruits of his labour? The Planning Commission itself had a house magazine: *Yojana*. *Yojana* was primarily devoted to development reporting. And while other magazines and dailies did report on economic development, sporadically as it turned out, it was only in recent times that development reporting has reached respectable proportions. It is not unusual these days to read development reports in the Indian press.

Development reporting is primarily socio-economic reporting giving the Why, When, Where, Which, What, and How of deep structural changes in our society. The publication of economic dailies like *The Economic Times* or *Business Standard* undoubtedly has given a fillip to development reporting but equally credit must be given to India's planning approach that first gave development reporting its due significance. In that sense planning, development and development reporting go hand in hand.

Development reporting has always been a feature of western reporting, especially in the specialised journals of the west, as can only be expected. It is now becoming quite fashionable in India, primarily because India is rapidly becoming a developed country itself. Inevitably, the Indian press has to take note of the processes of development and report on it for the edification of a new class of readers: the industrial entrepreneur.

Development journalism is not sensational by its very nature though the story of the building of the Rajasthan Canal has its sensational aspects. There was a time when India did not build ships; she had to buy them from elsewhere. Today India not only can build freighters or passenger ships, she can also build warships of different kinds. This would have been considered sensational news a quarter century ago but today is accepted as part of our industrial scene. People have become very *blase*.

Development reporting need not be confined strictly to socio-economic issues. Any reporting pertaining to development in fields as diverse as medicine, science, industry and technology would come under that heading. The stress, rightly, is placed on the term "development". Has Company X discovered a new process of instant photography? Has Company Y discovered a fresh use for lasers? What is the latest in heart transplants? Answers to all these must necessarily be part of development reporting. To think of it in narrow terms as pertaining or relevant only to developing countries is not only erroneous, but is self-defeating.

We will discuss a few examples:

The Instances

Now Delhi, May 23: The Union Labour Ministry, with a view to boosting workers' participation in industrial safety is in the process of building up a cadre of worker inspector. The measure is likely to form part of the amendments to the Mines Act.

Under the scheme, experienced underground workers of the level of mining sardars with aptitude for safety work would be selected and given special training. They would be able to function as workmen inspectors while continuing to perform their normal duties at other times.

The recent improvements in the concept related to associating workers in safety measures have been appreciated the world over. In U.K., workers take active role in safety of mines. Qualified and experienced mining engineers have been hired by trade unions to function as worker inspectors.

These inspectors are required to make regular inspection of specific areas and file their reports with the management. The management is statutorily responsible to scrutinise the report and take corrective action wherever necessary.

The Ministry in the recent past had discussions with the trade unions for associating workers with safety in the mining industry. It is felt that the trade unions have not appreciated the approach and consequently could not reach any unanimous approach to the problem of worker inspectors.

This report meets some of the criteria for development reporting. It should—and does—involve workers conceptually, in the idea that in improving industrial safety, their own personal commitment is not only important but also necessary and that the Government of India is aware of it. What this report which appeared in *The Economic Times* (May 24, 1980) does not specify are the names of the trade unions that apparently were sceptical. The report would have been more credible if the reporter had interviewed dissenting trade unionists and recorded their views.

Take another report:

Fuel Saving at RSP

New Delhi, May 23: A saving of 12 per cent in fuel consumption has been effected by Rourkela Steel Plant (RSP) in trials for reducing heating time for cold ingots.

The successful trials were undertaken with oxygen enrichment of combustion air in a test soaking pit of RSP which resulted in heating time for cold ingots being reduced by about two and a half hours. The trials involved use of full air throughout heating and soaking period.

The total heating time for cold ingots will from now on be 10 hours instead of 12 hours as at present. Similar reduction in heating time and saving in fuel consumption has been observed during trials at the Durgapur Steel Plant.

The trials have also been undertaken in pursuance of the target of 2 per cent reduction in fuel energy consumption per tonne of salable steel set for the public sector steel plants for the current financial year.

A number of steps have been initiated in this direction. Fuel engineers of the steel plants have been asked to ensure systematic follow-up of thermo-technical regions of fuel consumption units and to carry out periodic review of critical heat consumption rates in the plants to ensure optimum economy in the use of energy.

To economise on petroleum-based fuel, a techno-economic study is being undertaken to explore the feasibility of developing appropriate type of coal gas plant based on non-coking coal to use producer, gas where at present petroleum and tar-based fuels are being used.

Public sector steel plants at present use nearly 224,000 tonnes of petroleum-based fuels and nearly 215,000 tonnes of coal for fuel in addition to gas, coke and coke breeze.

Energy conservation awards are being instituted at the inter plant levels to make steel workers energy conscious.

This story should come under development reporting, but it has many questions that call for explanation. One suspects that the story is a "handout" provided by the Ministry of Steel to reporters in Delhi.

The story, in the first place, should have originated in Rourkela and not New Delhi. Secondly, the following points should have been elucidated:

(a) Who instigated the move to effect fuel consumption? Did the order come from the Steel Ministry or was the idea entirely that of the Rourkela management?

(b) Why was the target of 2 per cent reduction in fuel energy consumption set only for the public sector steel plants? Why isn't the target applicable to private sector steel plants as well?

(c) Who conducted the trials and what does he think of the results?

(d) What do workers, engineers and trade union leaders think of the energy conservation awards that are being instituted at the inter plant levels? Where does the inspiration for giving the awards come from? What is the nature of the awards?

Had the reporter who wrote the story been to Rourkela and interviewed the Plant Manager, the concerned engineers and the workers, he would have had a more complete and meaningful story bringing out the human interest inherent in it. As it is it looks like a hand-out that the reporter passed on to his news desk without taking the slightest trouble to inject in his story the human element.

On the other hand, here is a different kind of report *(The Times of India,* May 12, 1980).

Generation at Singrauli to Start by 1981-end

Shaktinagar: (UP): India's first super thermal power station, taking shape here, will have its first unit ready by the end of the next year.

More than 15,000 men and women are racing against time to ensure that the Singrauli project is commissioned on schedule.

If Singrauli starts generation on schedule, it will be a sort of record in the public sector, as power plants usually take seven to eight years to be commissioned. However, the record could be achieved in this case as the construction is being done by the National Thermal Power Corporation (NTPC). One day's delay in the commissioning of a 2,000 MW power plant can cost the country Rs. 20 crores in terms of production loss, and the NTPC seems to be very well aware of it....

Mr. R. Gupta, the youthful General Manager who earlier ran the Kandla Fertiliser Plant at 140 per cent of its capacity, is confident that the Singrauli project will be commissioned before time.

However, problems keep cropping up. A railway wagon, loaded with equipment for the plant got lost on the way and was found after several weeks in Asansol. The railways are finding it hard to move it to Mirzapur district.

The reporter, L.K. Sharma had actually visited the place where India's first super thermal power station was being set up. To start with, this is an improvement over the usual habit of re-writing hand-outs. But in an otherwise fact-filled report, the reporter refers to the General Manager only once and quotes him indirectly. No answer is provided as to how come a railway wagon got lost on its way and was only found "several weeks later" at another place.

Here's another example of development reporting:

Bombay Graduates: Rural Progress

New Delhi, May 14: The first batch of 400 students will graduate in "rural development" from Bombay University this year.

Drawn from 11 colleges, the students have undergone a five-paper course spread over three years as part of their degree work for B.A., B.Sc, and B.Com.

Dr. Ram Joshi, vice-chancellor of Bombay University, said here today that the rural development course, the first of its kind in the country, had attracted the attention of several other universities. The universities of Allahabad, Surat and Pune were among those who had written to him and asked for a syllabus to enable them to launch similar courses.

Highlighting the advantages of the course, Dr. Joshi told newsmen that the job-oriented programme included actual field work in villages to enable the graduates to get first-hand knowledge of conducting socio-economic surveys of villages, land ownership patterns, crop rotation, farm management and the organisation of cooperatives.

According to Dr. Joshi, such training programme would weaken the tendency to flock from rural to urban areas and also enable the students, many of whom hailed from farming families, to carry on the traditional work in a scientific way.

A large number of institutions in villages were looking for young graduates trained in this specific manner. These included rural banking institutions and those dealing with providing not only farm inputs but also technical know-how in a predominantly agricultural community.

Of the 18 papers that the students study, five are related

directly to rural development. This would also promote modern agricultural practices and improve food production. Of the 11 colleges from which the students were drawn, three are from Bombay city, eight from moffusil areas. Many more colleges were seeking affiliation to the university in view of this specialised course.

The report *(The Times of India,* May 15, 1980) is reproduced in its entirety. The reporter probably learnt that Dr. Ram Joshi was in town or was informed that Dr. Joshi was holding a news conference. Some points that could have been elucidated:

(a) Which are the three Bombay and eight moffusil colleges offering the course in rural development?

(b) What do the first batch of students graduating in the course have to say about their studies? Do they feel benefited or cheated by the course?

(c) How many of the 400 students in the first batch are from purely farming families? Do their parents have any opinion to offer? We are vouchsafed no answers.

Development reports should also provide readers with success stories, to indicate what is possible. Consider this report from *The Times of India* (May 28, 1980):

Vaijapur-dry Belt Model of Drought Control

Vaijapur, situated in a dry belt about 80 km from Aurangabad, seems to have achieved notable success in the management of drought.

In only two years, this taluka town is said to have progressed from scarcity to bumper crops of jowar during this year. How has this been done?

The answer, according to Mr. Uttamrao Patwari, affectionately known as the People's MLA may be found in the percolation tanks and nullah and contour bunding in the taluka. Mr. Patwari was returned from here on the Janata ticket in 1977.

An advocate of percolation tanks, Mr. Patwari was responsible for increasing them from 22 in 1978 to 77 today. These were followed by complete nullah and contour bunding. "So much so, we have exhausted all the sites for bunding" Mr. Patwari told us when we met him during a recent tour of the town in connection with the poll.

These works, undertaken as part of the employment guarantee scheme, have helped the thirsty taluka to make do with its meagre rainfall of only 30 cm. "Today, there is enough water for drinking and for irrigation" Mr. Patwari said.

Mr. Patwari pointed out that, while in the past two years the Vaijapur sugar factory had to get sugarcane from outside the taluka, this year the area under sugarcane had increased.

Similarly, he stated, there was a bumper harvest of jowar during the rabi season. Besides, this year no money was spent on drinking water, while earlier annually Rs. 10 crores used to be spent on this account.

Mr. Patwari's chief contribution to helping the drought-hit in Vaijapur is the provision of guaranteed employment.

Two years ago, he recalled, what with water resources exhausted and fields yielding little, people were clamouring desperately for work. He gave no peace to the government until scarcity works could be provided for the people in his taluka.

Thanks to his efforts, about 17,000 people were daily found work under the Employment Guarantee Scheme (EGS) and upto Rs. 75 lakhs was spent in two years on wages.

As part of the EGS, he successfully obtained sanction for the digging of the 55 km long canal between Vaijapur and Gangapur, to bring water from the Igatpuri Hills under the Nandur-Madmeshwar project.

The canal is ready, but the work on the dam is yet to get under way, although the Rs. 51 crore project has been sanctioned. Meanwhile, he has teamed up with Dr. B.D. Kaldate, another Janata MLA in persuading the Maharashtra government to obtain World Bank aid for the project.

"It is our desire that this project should be completed during the sixth Five Year Plan" Mr. Patwari told us.

Work on another project, too, had now started, he said. This is the Rs. 9 crore Shivna-Takle medium irrigation project in Kannad taluka. When completed, Mr. Patwari said, it would irrigate 18,000 acres in Vaijapur, 7,000 in Gangapur and 3,000 in Kannad talukas.

All this service to the people of Vaijapur has cost Mr. Patwari his entire savings. A low bank balance and bereavements in the family have led Mr. Patwari to withdraw from the election battle this time.

"My practice has suffered (he is an advocate) and my liabilities have increased I have withdrawn for personal reasons" Mr. Patwari clarified.

The story of Vaijapur is a success story. What was once a drought-ridden area has been transformed into an area of bumper crops of jowar. Mr. Kamalakar describes how this transformation was achieved within the short span of two years. What he failed to do is to assess how long it will take to repay the money spent under the Employment Generation Scheme through the new earnings of the peasants. Mr. Kamalakar quotes Mr. Patwari. Surely he could also have quoted some of the farmers who have benefited?

Now take this report *(Indian Express,* May 10, 1980):

Ahmedabad, May 8: India has by now acquired a strong grip over the core technology for offshore oil exploration, field development and production and it is no more possible for any of the highly advanced countries in the field or the foreign countries claiming sophisticated technology, to take this country for a ride.

This is the impression the ENS (Express News Service) correspondent gathered during a visit to some of the structures of the Bombay High gas as member of the team of journalists which was flown by helicopter to F Platform and the Sagar Samrat, the ONGC's self-propelled jack-up rig.

Purchased from Japan, the rig with insured value of Rs. 1 crore has earned many times more than it has cost. This is not only the fact about Sagar Samrat. It is true of the platforms that are set up right into sea. A platform costing about a few crores earns many times over all that was spent in a matter of about ten days, when it becomes functional. Apart from the value of crude and gas found in terms of money, the strivings are priceless in terms of strategic and other international implications in this critical area of oil production.

ONGC which started with a budget of barely Rs. 10 crores in 1974 has taken spectacular strides. It has a budget of about Rs. 300 crores.

It has had a run of good luck and the Bombay High has been one of the best pick. Naturally the structures here are given a "blue-eyed boy treatment" as the sulphur content is minimal in the crude.

Dr. A.K.Malhotra, Member, Offshore, who has taken over recently was confident that by mid-1982, production plateau of 12 million tonnes of crude (240,000 BPD) would be accomplished.

There is no doubt that the country is yet a long way off from utilisation of latest and sophisticated technology. Stupendous efforts would be needed to keep up the production at 12 million tonnes per annum by developing the support facilities for the purpose.

While the ONGC officialdom do not say it, other informed sources in the field feel that it may be possible for the country to reach production plateau of even 20 million tonnes per year if the supporting facilities and other infrastructure and designing and fabrication facilities grow to the dimensions they are required.... And now, one more story on development *(Indian Express,* May 28, 1980):

White Revolution in Rajasthan

Jaipur, May 27: White revolution has gained momentum in Rajasthan, bringing about a substantial increase in the incomes of milk producers.

A recent official survey in Jaipur district revealed that before the launching of the Dairy Development Programme, the average annual income of a milk producer was Rs. 595 which increased to Rs. 3,324 a year, after the implementation of the programme. The production of milk and fodder has also increased, benefiting about a lakh cattle breeders in the State. Cattle breeding and dairying are the primary vocations of many farmers in the arid-zone in Rajasthan and the secondary occupation of farmers in the remaining part of the State.

White revolution in Rajasthan was ushered in following a policy decision to organise dairy development activities entirely in the cooperative sector. Cooperative societies were organised at the village level. These were federated into cooperative milk unions at the district level, while at the State level the Rajasthan Cooperative Dairy Federation was set up.

A comprehensive World Bank assisted project was thereafter undertaken in six selected districts—Alwar, Jaipur, Sawai Madhopur, Ajmer, Bhilwara and Tonk—with an outlay of more than Rs. 41 crores. Earlier, the 'Operation Flood One' was implemented in Bikaner and Bharatpur Districts.

The Intensive Dairy Development Programme was organised as part of the Drought Prone Areas Programme, and the Desert Development Programme. The remaining eight districts have been covered under the 'Operation Flood Two' project.

Thus, nearly 10,000 villages comprising about 30 per cent of the villages of the State have been covered under Intensive Development Programmes. About two thirds of the farmers covered under the programme are small to marginal cultivators belonging to the Scheduled Castes and Scheduled Tribes.

Composite dairy development schemes are functioning at Bikaner, Jodhpur, Alwar and Ajmer. The total capacity of these plants is 3.3 lakh litres of milk per day which is likely to be increased to 4 lakh litres per day. This is in addition to the dairy already functioning at Jaipur with a capacity of 25,000 litres of milk per day. A new modern composite dairy at Jodhpur is expected to be commissioned shortly.

The daily milk collection in Rajasthan was about 4 lakh litres per day during the last winter. The State supplies over 2 lakh litres of milk daily to the Delhi Milk Scheme and the mother dairy at Delhi.

A modern cattle breeding farm has been set up at Bassi where Jersey cows imported from Australia and Denmark and Holstein and Friesian cows from Holland are maintained. A frozen semen bank has also been established at Bassi to serve as the focal point for artificial insemination programme. Veterinary and animal health centres have been provided through cooperative milk union for animal health cover and technical inputs to milk producers in Rajasthan.

The State Government proposes to increase the daily milk collection from 4 lakh litres at present to 10 lakh litres during the Sixth Plan period. Of this, about 4 lakh litres of milk is proposed to be supplied to Delhi. After meeting local requirements, the surplus milk will be converted into butter, ghee, whole milk powder, skimmed milk, cheese and baby food.

The Rajasthan Cooperative Dairy Federation has already finalised plans to undertake the marketing of dairy products throughout the country from the current financial year.

Positive Approach

A question that can be asked about development reporting is whether it always has to be positive. Human nature being what it is, corruption is a way of life in many developing countries where millions of rupees (dollars, francs, etc.) have often been known to have been wasted. Should it not be the duty of the conscientious reporter to write about corruption, inefficiency and embezzlement wherever it is discovered? One feels that a reporter is indeed duty-bound to report an administration's shortcomings so that they are expeditiously overcome. Development reporting is not "puff" reporting with no effort being made to find what is wrong where. What has not been achieved is as much news as what has been achieved. Here is an example:

Dehra Dun, May 9: The Rs. 168 crore fertiliser project of Indian Farmers Fertiliser Cooperative Ltd., set up at Phulpur (Allahabad) eight months ago, has not been commissioned so far for want of naphtha.

A spokesman of IFFCO told newsman here on Wednesday that production of the project depended on the situation in Assam and the functioning of the refinery there. The unit requires a regular supply of 1,000 tons of naphtha daily.

The annual product capacity of the plant is five lakh tonnes. Work on the plants began in 1976 with a World Bank loan of Rs. 100 crore for the import of machinery.

The Executive Director of IFFCO, Dr. K.S. Gill, refused to comment on the availability of naphtha from Assam.

Dr. Gill told newsmen that IFFCO had another fertiliser project in hand at Hazira in Gujarat, costing Rs. 700 crores.

The construction of the Hazira project had been undertaken by Krishak Bhartiya Cooperative Ltd., an independent organisation, also in the cooperative sector, formed at the initiative of IFFCO. It would be the biggest fertiliser factory in the sixth plan and its annual production would be 15 lakh tonnes of urea, using ammonia as raw material.

And here is another example:

Poor Response in Public Sector Units

Bombay, May 23: The experience of Board level representation in banks and some public sector undertakings is not exactly encouraging, whatever be the reasons, so far as the implementation of workers' participation in management is concerned.

An employer's representative feels that the concept of three-tier system of participative management is unnecessary and unrealistic at least at the present stage.

In support of this contention it is stated that the issue which directly affects workers at the plant level are not generally discussed or decided at the Boards.

It is pointed out that the Union Labour Minister has evinced interest in introducing a scheme of worker participation in management which is one of the items of the 20 point programme.

One needs to recall that a scheme was evolved in 1975 for association of workers and their representatives through joint councils at the shop and plant levels. It was welcomed by a wide section of management and trade unions ....

Employers opine that no scheme of labour-management cooperation, no scheme of safety or welfare promotion and no scheme of productivity will succeed or even get off the ground unless the primary issue of determination and recognition of a representative union is first settled. All our past attempts in joint consultation have been frustrated by inter-union rivalry and for lack of a strong, responsible and representative union, the employers say ....

This story is taken from *The Economic Times* (May 24, 1980) but it suffers from many shortcomings. Except toward the end, where the mention of Mr. Naval H. Tata identifies one employer, the rest of the time the reporter expects the reader to accept his contention that the implementation of workers' participation in management has not been up to expectations.

The story is written in Bombay and there are any number of public sector undertakings in and around the city who, surely, would be willing to talk to the report for the record. The report does not give the impression that the reporter has talked to employers' representative, company executives or trade union leaders, let alone individual workers. And while the report may be entirely true, it would have added credibility if names were named and if General Managers, Chairman of Boards, Trade Union leaders and workers themselves were quoted.

Most development reports seem more "idea" centered rather than "individual" centered. When a reporter takes recourse to such phrases as "it is believed", "it is stated", "the general impression is that", "the point has been raised" it must be clear that he has not done his interviewing of people involved but is merely passing on his own personal understanding of a situation.

The reporter and his report will gain more credibility—apart from readability—if he specifies *who* made *what* point and *who* stated *what.* Who raised the point? On what basis has the reporter come to the conclusion that "the general basis" is something or other? Did he undertake a poll? Development reporting lives or dies by its association with live individuals and live situations The reporter who "believes", "understands" and hears it being "contended" is more often merely trying to fill column space than telling a straight story.

Cardinal Norms

Certain rules may be laid down for writing a development story:

(a) If you are writing a development story, see that the story is meaningful to the community that your paper is serving. A development story that is readable but has no relevance to your readers fails of its purpose, which is to enthuse and inspire parallel action.

(b) Research the background of the story from the pre-development stage to its current status and find out whether schedules have been met, expenditure properly audited and if schedules have not been met, the reasons why.

(c) Give a patient and objective hearing to all those involved in the development project including government servants, plant managers, workers' representatives and the people for whose benefit the project had been undertaken in the first place.

(d) Mention names. Take down the complaints or excuses made by different parties and where possible check whether they bear scrutiny.

(e) Beware of public relations men who will provide you ore-digested material that is laudatory but could be misleading.

(f) Look for parallels. Has a similar project been launched elsewhere and how does it compare with the project on which you are planning to write?

(g) If two contrary opinions are advanced by two different sets of people, state them impartially. Do not take sides.

(h) Wherever possible, quote profusely. Let the reader know that you have actually been talking to individuals and not just generalising on what you may have heard.

(i) Be meticulous about providing facts and figures.

(j) Avoid the temptation to re-write hand-outs; treat these as basic raw material on which to build the superstructure of your own well researched story.

(k) Keep your personal hang-ups, likes and dislikes, prejudices and preferences strictly to yourself. Let them not intrude in your reporting which is for the purpose of informing your reading public of what is happening around.

(l) Be constructive where criticism is merited; be generous where praise is warranted. Remember, no matter how hard you have tried to get all the facts, the whole truth may still elude you.

You are a reporter, not God.

A book that dealt with development will help to remind us what it really means in terms of human lives. Kusum Nair wrote *Blossoms in the Dust* in 1961 but an extract from it serves to provide an example of how to relate development—or lack of it—to ordinary people.

Take a village in the district of Ballia, in eastern Uttar Pradesh.

It has had six years of "Community Development", and the Rasra Block in which it is situated has been retired into the "post-intensive" stage.

"How much gold have you hoarded by now—tell me truthfully," I ask of Rikhi Dev, a cheerful young man with one and a half acres of land.

"Gold you say?" he laughs. "Here I do not get even two meals a day and you ask how much gold I have."

"What do you mean, you do not get two meals a day?" "Honestly. I do not eat more than once a day," he replies. "How often?"

"Why, always. In winter, we take only a glass of sugar cane juice during the day and in summer we drink *shira*. It is made from molasses, which we get very cheap from the sugar mill. But *shira* causes diarrhoea and so throughout summer we drink *shira* and keep running to the field. The only meal we eat is at night."

"What do you mean by 'we'?"

"We—all of us." He gestures to indicate every one present. "And the children?"

"They also fast during the day. If some *sag* is occasionally left over from supper it is kept overnight, and they eat it the next day but without any *roti* or rice."

Even for dinner the bread is closely rationed. Milk is scarcely available because, they say, no grazing grounds are left since the abolition of *zamindari*.

"You will find it difficult to believe us" says Hardwar Ram, an elderly dignified man with a small gray moustache. "Why not see for yourself. This village has 85 houses and now it is noon. It is the normal meal time. You are welcome to go into every house and see if you can find a single fire burning or any cooked food."

And so I did. I went inside every single cottage in the village.

They are small mud huts with tiled roofs. The entrance is very low and many have no doors. Inside is a small wall-in yard, lined on one side with a little verandah and one or at the most two rooms. In each room lives a whole family. Inside the room there is usually an earthern silo for storing grain, but no other furniture.

The *chula* is in the verandah; straw lies scattered in the yard; in some,. a little grain is drying on the floor. But in none of the 85 homes is a *chula* alight or even with ash in it. In the corner near the *chula* are piled neatly, face downward, the cooking utensils, earthern pots and a rare piece of brass. In one cottage there is a little cooked *sag* in a pan, black in colour.

The children—mostly naked, with hair matted and faces caked with dirt—stand around chewing on sticks of sugar cane and spitting out the remnants.

The women are thin—their tattered sarees barely covering the body. Being of a lower caste than Rajputs, they do not observe strict *purdah* and they talk freely.

Holding me by the wrist, they take me into their homes saying: "Come and see the tasteful dishes we have prepared for our mid day meal," and lifting up their utensils, they shake them upside down.

When I have been in all the 85 houses Hardwar Ram once again asks: "Do you believe us now? This is how it has been ever since I can remember."

Local Periodicals

Most Indian states have their own information journals which provide facts and figures and the economic progress made during any period. It would be wrong to dismiss these journals as just propaganda. Lakhs, on occasions, crores of rupees are spent in developmental efforts and even given large-scale corruption which is endemic in the country, there ought to be something for the government of the day to show. The mistake one should NOT make is to equate development journalism with economic development giving only the positive side of the picture.

Again, should the term development necessarily have to do with the economic betterment of the people? Shouldn't the fact that people living in India's villages are not getting justice and are living frequently under the tyranny of the rich and the powerful, also be a part of development reporting? In a scathing article in *Mainstream* (March 1, 1980), Mr. D.R. Mankekar raised the issue of justice in rural India and the role of the media:

The lifting of the rock by the shocking Narainpur and Gaya incidents revealed under them writhing swarms of deadly germs, which indicated that there are many rocks all over, particularly in benighted Bihar and UP, shielding organised criminality, flourishing in the countryside with impunity, all along, in the last three decades.

As we all know, that which is not reported does not exist. And crime unreported is crime licensed and encouraged. And we also know too well that when lawlessness and crime go unreported, the law and order authorities and government feel that they could get away with it and therefore they could afford to do nothing about it.

Why is such a scandalous state of affairs possible? Because the Indian Press has failed in its duty—its duty not only to lift the rocks and expose worms but to cleanse the ground under the rocks by focussing light on them.

Even if the metaphors are somewhat mixed here, the main thrust of Mankekar's argument is clear: rural reporting is poor, halting and often non-existent.

The poor, the argument probably goes, do not make news for the urban elite. In a sense it is very hard to define "development reporting" unless one is willing to settle for the narrowest of meanings. Development brings in its wake a multitude of problems. Shouldn't they be part of development reporting? The problem of pollution, for instance, or the problem of displacement of a large number of people from their natural habitat as and when it is proposed to build a dam. The issue was raised by Bharat Dogra in an article on Hydel Projects, Environment and People (April 5, 1980).

Today the importance of generating more hydel power is increasingly recognised—but at the same time there has been a spate of protests over the construction of several hydel and other multi-purpose river valley projects because of the threat they pose to the environment and the hazards implicit in their construction. It is important that the engineers pleading for larger exploitation of the hydel potential and those highlighting the potential hazards of some of the projects should appreciate each other's point of view, so that the progress of hydel projects is not impeded and we do not also suffer at a later stage due to neglect of potential hazards and any threat to the environment.

As V.D. Saklani, who heads the Tehri Dam Opposition Committee put it to me, "We fully agree to the tapping of the vast hydel potential of the Himalayas. Our objection is only to the construction of large dams here, specially at this most unsuitable site (the Tehri dam site). . . .

Creation of the reservoirs can also lead to immense destruction to aquatic life in the rivers, proliferation of weeds, spread of new diseases in the surrounding region and the erosion of downstream land. Construction of the dam may involve submergence of forests, including ecologically invaluable stretches of forests as in the case of the Silent Valley Project. Or construction of a dam may involve submergence of densely populated areas and rehabilitation of thousands of people. In some cases entire cultures may be destroyed and invaluable historical legacy ruined due to submergence of vast stretches of land.

Dogra was not giving theoretical objections. What the Aswan Dam has done to Egypt is a case in point. And we have yet to hear the last word on the Silent Valley Project.

Diverse Steps

The point to bear in mind is that development has many facets, positive and negative, social, cultural, economic and even political, and that its effects are far-reaching. Developmental efforts can contribute to corruption. Isn't reporting on corruption, then, a part of development reporting? The nation ought to know how money spent has been transformed into the betterment of a given society: how many jobs have been created? By how much has the per capita income of a given village, taluka, district or state gone up? Are children better fed, people better clothed, granaries fuller stocked? Positive answers to such questions make for traditional concepts of development reporting. But consider the other side of the picture as well. *The Centre for Monitoring Indian Economy* in its April 1977 report on the standard of living of the Indian people has this to say about *Food: The First Need:* Perhaps, of all the indicators, next only to the per capita real income, the most significant single indicator of the standard of living would be the per capita availability of foodgrains; for, this item accounts for 66 per cent of the total consumptio.ı expenditure of an average Indian.

* According to detailed calculations by S.M. Kansal *(Changes in the Per Capita Availability of Essential Commodities in India Since 1951, New Delhi, 1974)* the per capita availability of foodgrains fell from 515 gasper per day in 1931 to 395 gms in 1951.
* So, the increase which we find in the post-1951 years marks, in effect, only a partial recovery from the decline of the preceding two decades.
* For vast poor masses, particularly those who take a little or no non-vegetarian food, pulses constitute the principal source of protein. The decline in the per capita availability of pulses should, therefore, be viewed with great concern.
* It is noteworthy that whatever improvement that was achieved in respect of the availability of foodgrains, was achieved by about 1965. Throughout the subsequent years, the per capita consumption has shown either stagnation or some decline.

Shockingly enough, according to CMIE calculations, while the per capita availability of cereals and pulses in 1953 was 350 and 63 grams per day, in 1977 it was 347 and 56 grams, a distinct fall. It is poor development, but good development reporting.

What it finally amounts to is that development reporting includes science reporting, investigative reporting and even legal reporting. While it may be argued that this is throwing the net too wide and that the reporter should limit his development reporting to clearly demarcated fields of progress and prosperity, it may be counter-argued that this would leave vast areas of development subjects untouched.

Politics. Furthermore, development is closely associated with politics. There can be no getting away from it. Can development reporting then, be divorced from politics? Take this report, for instance, on the *New International Economic Order and India's Development Experience* by R.C. Dutt *(Mainstream,* May 3, 1980):

With the passing of Jawaharlal Nehru in May 1964, the forces that had till then exploited the weaknesses of the Plans ventured into the open to attack the Plans and their objectives. With the Third Five Year Plan ending in March 1966, within less than two years of Nehru's death, a Plan holiday was demanded and obtained for the next three years. By the time the Fourth Plan came in 1969, the zeal for planning had lost its elan and the 'socialistic pattern' its shine. The nationalisation of fourteen commercial banks in 1969, the popular slogan 'Garibi Hatao' in the 1971 elections and the nationalisation of the coal industry in 1973 proved temporary and unreal and were followed by a misguided movement for 'Total Revolution' into which all the reactionary elements threw themselves to set the clock back.

What followed is recent history, but in economic terms the period from the latter half of the sixties saw spiralling inflation, emergence of a parallel economy based on black money (of which a rough but awesome estimate was given by the Wanchoo Committee in 1971) and a lowering in real terms of planned investment. What was more serious was that the concept of planning suffered a set back. The Fifth Plan was not allowed to run its course. It was lost in a haze of political controversy —including opportunistic re-assertions of pseudo-Gandhian values—and was replaced by the concept of a 'rolling plan' which negated completely the idea of a target-oriented, time-bound blue-print for implementation which is an essential feature of socialist planning.

The cumulative results of the slide-back in the post-Nehru period were increasing concentration of wealth and economic power and the growing poverty of about half the population. As the draft Five Year Plan (1978-83) has stated, about 48 per cent of the rural population and 41 per cent of the urban population, making a total of 290 million, live below the poverty line defined on the basis of calorie consumption....

Distortion of this order pose a threat not only to the stability of the social order which sponsors it but to growth itself, for sustained growth cannot be ensured by the affluence of a small section while the rest of the population has little or no purchasing power. . . .

Dutt here is not only reporting on development but is commenting on its results or lack of them. And this is very important. Healthy and reasoned criticism about not only the development process but the ideology behind the planning of development as well as the mechanics and ultimate results of planning are necessary ingredients of development reporting. To think otherwise is not to fulfil one's role as a reporter.

Corruption : One could take a step further and add that development reporting also consists of reporting on corruption. The tragedy is that in almost all developing countries—and, for the moment, we may confine ourselves only to this part of the world—development expenditure and corruption go hand in hand. The more money is made available for development the more corruption there seems to be, human nature being what it is. It is therefore important that the reporter makes himself familiar with both the nature of corruption, its extent and governmental efforts to prevent it. The Prevention of Corruption Act, comprising eight sections only, has, for its object "to make more effective provision for the prevention of bribery and corruption". Better said than done.

The Act extends to all of India and applies to all citizens, including Indian citizens living outside India. Section 4 of the Act lays down that when a charge of bribery or corruption, in the manner of gratification is levelled at an accused, a presumption of guilt is raised against him. He is then called upon to disprove the charge or accept its consequences.

Five kinds of acts which constitute criminal misconduct are specified under Section 5:

(i) Habitual acceptance of gratification,

(ii) the obtaining of any valuable thing without consideration,

(iii) misappropriation,

(iv) the abuse of position to obtain pecuniary gains; and

(v) the possession of pecuniary resources or property disproportionate to one's known sources of income.

As H.L. Mansukhani has ably argued in his book *Corruption and Public Servants*, "... it is difficult to describe the 32-year-old Prevention of Corruption Act as an effective piece of legislation." Mr. Mansukhani asserts that Central Investigative Agency reports —apart from the superficial impact made by their growing statistical data and the court-case stories thrown up—establish that the object of the enactment of the Act "has not been achieved in any measurable manner". In fact, he says, one may well state that in the general and wide-spread climate of corruption in the seventies, the high purposes of such a presumptuous piece of enactment could do pretty little to prevent corruption.

Corruption has largely acquired political colours and contours. To quote Mansukhani:

The hot and humid 'climate' for corruption has, of course, many causes and few solutions. In the first place, the halting words that K. Santhanam used in the early sixties in his *Report on Prevention of Corruption* with respect to ministers and politicians, *now* make cynical reading—mocking in every respect. Corruption of the most sophisticated kind is now the creation of the biggest politicians—both the haves in government and the have-nots outside government—who are so very jealous of the bounties of the insiders in power. They always snipe from their own little vantage positions, itching to seek and share in the spoils that are spread out over a vast area of controls, contracts, collaborations and other deals.

Those in power are not averse to 'sell' policy-making formulae and offer other rich favours for a purpose and for a price, as in the fields of quotas and licenses. A bait can be thrown here and there—for instance, that nationalisation being the avowed policy, such-and-such sector of trading, which thrives on manufactured goods cornered by a few tycoons or monopolists (and for which they depend heavily on imported raw materials) is the next hop. That may mean blocking the account number two avenues of those well-entrenched monopolists industrialists and businessmen in that line. Therefore, if they could buy or hire a lobby, even to stall that, the plus and minus of it works itself out even in the time context to earn more by spending a chunk of it and out of it.

This sort of thing does not hurt either the givers or the receivers.

This is the new dimensional exchange of money, and fast-moving circulation of a lot of it, that alone helps to keep political parties and politicians above 'need-based' and 'subsistence' levels. Call them donations and subscriptions or cuts and commissions; the free flow of this money alone makes for fertility in the political field, for cash crops and other multiple crops without any fallow areas or seasons suffering from the effects of dry spells.

What is significant about corruption reporting is that it is not recognised as development reporting—after all, isn't this just a case of a man taking a bribe and being hauled in by the long arm of the law?—and when it is reported, the space given is so scant that the reader hardly ever notices it when there are more exciting reports elsewhere. Nevertheless the point must be made that development reporting encompasses a vast field of economic and other activities and it is sheer blindness not to see the immediate connection between development and corruption. It is necessary to know how in village X or a Dairy Development Centre Y, there has been a remarkable upsurge in milk production. It is also important to know how many officials have simultaneously benefited in the process.

So far the presumption has been that development reporting is one-dimensional: the reporting of development in the country to the press. But that is taking a somewhat limited view of development reporting. The argument can be persuasively made that all development reporting, to be meaningful, has to involve transfer of information to those involved in the process of development itself. How is this information to be transferred for the betterment of the rural population? In his paper submitted to a seminar organised by the Indian Institute of Mass Communication and the International Institute of Communications, Dr. A.W. Khan pointed out that the function of communication in the context of agricultural development is to inform, educate and motivate farmers to accept new ideas and agricultural practices in order to increase production per unit of land. But acceptance of an innovation was determined, as Rogers and Shoemaker observed, to a large extent by its own attributes, which were:

Relative advance—or the degree to which an innovation was perceived as better than the existing technology or practice.

Compatibility—or the degree to which an innovation was perceived as consistent with the existing values, past experience and the needs of the receiver.

Complexibility—or the degree to which an innovation was perceived as relatively difficult to understand and use.

Triability—or the degree to which the results of the innovations were visible or could be felt by others.

Desirability—or the degree to which an innovation could be tried on a limited basis.

Innovation—The key word in the definition of the various attributes of innovations is "perceived". Any reporting to the farmers—or members of a developing community—in the circumstances had to be so modelled that it would help them accept innovation more easily, or else the information or "message" would largely remain irrelevant. It was Mr. P.R. Dubhashi who pointed out at the same seminar that "a critical review of communication planning and development in India suggests that despite the radical public pronouncements and policy statements, the rural masses, particularly the rural poor, have not yet been reached". One reason, he said, and a most telling one, was that "the rural and other backward people, for whom many of the development schemes were especially made did not have the necessary information processing capacity and skills to take advantage of the opportunities thrown up by development programme". As such, in a sense, new opportunities never existed for them as they had no information about these.

This, obviously, can be directly attributed to the failure of reporting to the people concerned. What needs to be understood in this connection is that communication by itself is not development.

What communication does is merely to facilitate the development process. The process, of course, can be hastened by a sound knowledge of communication in the special context of the rural masses and their level of perception, and literacy. The more literate the peasant is, the more easily can he understand what has been written for him. Development reporting for the peasant, then, must not only be in his *own* language but in language that is within his capacity to grasp. Even more importantly, it must not talk down to him. The message must be clear, simply-written, acceptable and graphic. It must come within at least the penumbra of the peasant's past experience and related to his needs.

The message need not always be in terms of the written word. Indeed, development reporting must make extensive use of illustrations for, even while it is true that one picture is worth a thousand words, in the case of the semi-literate peasant, one picture should convey the whole idea.

Finally, communication should be need-based. The communicator should know his audience, the special market for his ideas and stream-line his message to suit the needs of his particular client. As S.G. Raghu of the Small Industries Extension Training Institute, Hyderabad has pointed out: "One thing that emerges clearly from the study of information requirements for aiding industrial development in different regions is that, in a way, though the answers to questions may be different in each place because of differences in local resources, the economic geography of the region, the availability of infrastructures, etc., the questions on what categories the information should be collected, remain the same." For the communicator the important things always to remember are information to such basic questions as: (a) What are the resources of the place? (b) What are the skills available in the place? (c) What infrastructures, including physical communication facilities, are available in the region? and (d) What are the major demands of the consumers of the region for which local manufacture would be acceptable? Get answers to these questions and communication reporting would then immediately become relevant and meaningful.

4

PROCESS AND DEVICES

The following are the important telecommunication tools :

Telegram : A written message supplied to the department of telecommunication which in turn sends the message by telegram.

Telegraph: *A* system of sending message by telegraph using either wires and electricity or radio.

Telegraphist: Also called Telegrapher. He is a person who operates a telegraph and acts as intermediary between communicator and recipient.

Telegraphy : With reference to telecommunication telegraphy is the process of sending a message by telegraph. Telegraph wire by which telegraph messages are sent.

Telepathy : *A* quite different style of communication of ideas and thoughts directly from one person's mind without the use of audio or visual help. Telepathist is a person who studies or practises telepathy.

Telephone Booth : Other names used are telephone box, call box. It is a small room or compartment established at a prominent public place containing a telephone for public use.

Telephone Directory : The directory is a specially prepared type of volume containing names and addresses of a particular group. The telephone directory is a special book containing a list of names, addresses and telephone numbers of a group of all the people in a particular area who have telephones. The list is arranged in alphabetical order.

Telephone Exchange : A centrally controlled system through which telephone calls are directed. The telephonist in a telephone exchange on being given a number connects. The use of the telephone exchange is necessary in case of non-STD and in the absence of direct dialling operations.

Teleprinter: *A* machine in a communication system. Teleprinter is a machine, a specialised type of type-writer. A telegraphic system or instrument by which messages are sent out at one place and received at another place in a printed form. The typing is connected to a telephone line and the message typed at one place transmits electrical signal over wire and the same message is simultaneously reproduced, printed at a distant place by the machine. It is used as a private circuit or through the post office telex service system. The post offices give teleprinters on rent to form a part of private telecommunication.

Tele type : An electronic system of transmitting information in typewritten form. Used in operation of the various public relations, newswires, as well as by the Associated Press and United Press International.

Telex: Sending messages by teleprinters. Detailed discussion is given under the teleprinter paragraph.

The most popularly used speedy forms of external communication and mechanical devices are telegrams, cablegrams and telex messages. It is pertinent to remember that these tools are commonly and widely practised techniques of communication in every organisation irrespective of the form and nature of the business organisation. These communication instruments are used when the message must reach the receiver on the subject matter which is more important and urgent. Indeed it is to be noted that with the increase in the area of operation and the urgency of the matters on which decisions have to be taken telegrams, cablegrams and telex techniques are widely practised. The advantages of these techniques are that they help to get rid of the problem of distance, save time and the receiver draws immediate attention to the central theme of the matter. But while using these techniques care should be taken to frame the message correctly. The essentials of a good telegram, cablegram and telex are that they should be concise, clear, simple and selective with appropriate words conveying the correct theme of the matter to avoid ambiguity. The words are selected in such a way so as to economise the cost of sending messages. Undoubtedly, therefore, the transmitter of the message is to be well versed in precise writing, to follow certain principles to make the communication really effective. The message to be effective, the central idea should be identified, sentences should be short and economically worded.

General Devices

External communication is a part of the communication network of the organisation. Most external correspondence is through written communication. It is by post. The postal department is the important department of the Government of India which has established a wide network of communication services throughout the country. The communication services provided by the postal department is of immense value not only to the business community but also all sections of society. External communication is between the organisation and outsiders. In this mail service the department is very essential for smooth functioning and work. If the mail is delayed the office work is also delayed. If communication services are inadequate it leads not only to late delivery of correspondence but also disrupts office work.

Mail service keeps work effective and workers with work. Therefore, it can be said that efficient communication sciences must be provided by the postal department. A business house may receive several letters and may correspond with them. The object of the mail service is to carry written communication. The message so transmitted should be interpreted and the decision is taken to act on that. In order to meet the needs of different businesses the postal department has been rendering different types of communication services. These services are most useful, particularly for external written communication. The important communication services are listed as under:

Prepaid Postage : Prepaid means payment in advance to the postal department. It avoids the work of affixing stamps on each letter. It is an arrangement with the post office department to facilitate this work. Under this scheme the person or the institution availing this facility has to pay postage in cash. In case there are a large number of standard letters to be despatched the postal department provides this facility.

Value Payable Post (V.P.P.) : The post office value payable postal service is more useful particularly to mail order business houses or book publishers and sellers. In this service the post office acts as an agent in collecting money or value from the customers. For instance, a book publisher may despatch a book under V.P.P. service. This means the price of the book is collected by the post office for and on behalf of the publisher or seller.

Certificate of Posting : This is a mail service, under which the post office gives a certificate of posting. This certificate is evidence that a particular letter has been actually posted. For this service the post office collects a requisite fee. In all ordinary mail posted no certificate is issued. It is an additional service of giving a certificate which serves as proof in case of dispute regarding communication. Company meeting notices, interview cards etc., are generally posted under certificate of posting.

Post Box Number : The postal department gives a separate post box number. It is also known as post box, letter box or mail box. This service helps to take delivery of the post direct from the post office from the post box without waiting for the postman. A business organisation, institution or individual with an arrangement with the post office gets the number allotted. Their mail is directly put into the box provided the post box number is written in the address.

Business Reply Cards : Business houses engaged in the mail order business usually use business reply cards. The reply cards help the receiver place the orders in accordance with the requirements of the business. With arrangement with the post office under licence, this facility can be availed of. But a certain sum of money as fee is payable for this service. The postal department may prescribe certain standards and business reply cards or envelopes should conform to the standards.

Concessional Postage : Concessional rates of postage are another important mail service rendered by the postal department. A company engaged in a large number of letters, bulky, more weight and printed matters can avail of the facility of concessional rates of postage. The department extends concessional rates of postage in respect of books, samples, patterns, printed magazines and journals, registered newspapers etc. Thus concessional rate is very helpful to certain business houses.

Registered Post : This service helps provide security for delivering communication provided the correct address is given. Remitting money by money-orders, remittance through bank-drafts, cheques etc., can be despatched either through registered or insured letters.

Acknowledgement Receipts : When a particular letter is sent by registered post, with acknowledgement due, the post office gives the acknowledgement receipt of the addressee. This serves as evidence in case of dispute of communication.

Telegraphic Address : An abbreviated telegraphic address can be used in transmitting a message by the communicator to the receiver. The telegraphic address is to be registered with the post office. A word containing 10 letters or less is to be registered; it serves as a telegraphic address. In cases where a telegraphic address is used, the full address is not required to be written on the telegrams. This facility saves a lot of time and cost.

Cipher Telegrams : This is a fast communication service through telegrams. This message is transmitted in code language and the recipient has necessarily to decode the message. The receiver finds it difficult to decode the message, for which he should be acquainted with the code language.

Phonogram : A phonogram is used for sending and receiving the message through a telegram. The subject matter of the message is dictated over the telephone at either side. The cost of the phonogram will be included in the routine telephone bill.

How to Communicate ? : Written documents containing messages or subject matters are to be transmitted. The question often arises how to transmit written messages. In use there are two methods of transmitting messages.

By Messengers : This is a manual method of transmitting written message by the communicator to the receiver. A messenger is an employee meant for delivery of a message from one person to another person or from one department to another. The communicators call the messengers by using signals or a buzzer and instruct them to deliver the message to the directed person or department. Though a primitive method of communication it is still being used in all organisations.

Every organisation has an internal mail service under which a messenger or messengers are required to meet regularly at a particular place like a department or desk or both, to deliver written communications brought from other departments or desks, and to take the message relating to other departments or desks.

The Advantages

1. The time of the executive is saved.
2. Executives are assisted by messengers who bring messages from other desks or departments.
3. Under this system timely decision is possible.
4. There will be many messenger services of not less than 4 to 5 deliveries in an hour.
5. Messengers service method can be used for many purposes. For instance, messenger services from executives to individual subordinate. Similarly messenger services from one department to another.

Mechanical devices are also introduced for transmission of written messages. Mechanical instruments carry messages from one place to another. Therefore, mechanical devices are broadly categorised into four types for transmission of written communication within the office. They are:

A conveyor is a mechanical device that conveys communication. A moving conveyor with moving belt of rubber, metal used for carrying papers and documents from one place to another. The messages are put on the conveyor which travels on fixed routes where papers and documents are picked. Conveyors are most useful when forwarding a large volume of papers and documents. They operate by a motor driven belt under them, moves along its routes and stops at fixed stations. Overhead write conveyors, horizontal conveyors, roller conveyors and vertical conveyors are the various types of conveyors in use in offices.

A chute is a sloping channel for sending objects. A structure of wide diameter pipes or channels running downward from top to bottom or from upper level to lower level. A chute is made of metal or wood. This device can also be used for transmission of papers and documents in larger quantities from one place located at an upper level to another place at a lower level.

Devices operated electrically or hydraulically used to raise or bring messages. A small enclosed platform that moves up and down, as operated, carrying articles. The written papers or documents or files can be transmitted between floors continuously. Lifts for transmission of messages are most useful in case of an organisation located in a multi-storied building.

When pneumatic devices are desired to be installed, a cylindrical pipe is connected to various offices. The cylinders containing papers and documents are transmitted by suction from one department to another within the office. Plastic conveyors are also now in popular use. Pneumatic tubes may be of a radial type, or of a continuous loop type.

Others : (a) teleprinter, (b) Telewriter, (c) Telefax, (d) Television.

Recording Process

One of the important merits of written communication is that written message can he preserved as records and reference source. It has the capacity of being stored as a record. At times the records can be used as evidence. Reports, circulars, notices, manuals, memos and other printed written or typed documents can be filed and preserved for future reference and can be produced as legal evidence.

So filing of written communication is obviously important because there is a very large number of papers and other media of written communications which have to be handled and preserved. Generally, however, serious attention is not given to filing of messages because some people think that it is not a useful activity, but this is not a correct understanding of the importance of filing written messages. There are a number of advantages which a business house can derive from a proper system of filing.

Filing is a process of collection of papers of particular subject. Filing with reference to written communication is the systematic arrangement of keeping every business correspondence and records so that these may be found and delivered quickly when needed for reference in future. Thus filing written messages performs a library function and information service. Filing includes classification of messages, preservation of letters, circulars, forms, memos, records and other documents.

Filing also performs an administrative function by maintaining, supplying and protecting records, forms, circulars and other documents necessary for formulating broad business policies and objectives and preserving them for future reference and use. The efficiency of office administration depends upon the efficient and scientific way of preserving messages and quickly making them available when required. Messages of any media must not only be maintained systematically but also preserved with great care so as to prevent them from damage, loss, theft, or mutilation. Human memory is poor and limited. Sometimes one should not rely on one's memory for past messages which have no official support or which cannot be legal evidence in case of a dispute of a particular message. The important functions of filing messages are to (1) preserve messages, (2) perform library and information functions, (3) know precedences, (4) help in framing business policies etc.

There are various methods in use which can be used for filing written messages effected by any media of written communication. All filing methods may not be useful to all organisations. Some methods may have only limited utility and some are only useful for small organisations. Some methods of filing communication are useful only for large concerns where the volume of written communication is comparatively large. So a method can be used in some concerns most efficiently in comparison with others. Old methods of filing may be replaced by modern methods. Filing methods can broadly be classified in two categories, namely, old methods of filing and modern methods of filing.

Old methods of filing in practice are more popular and are still used in small offices where the volume of communication is comparatively small.

The following are the old methods of filing :

Metal folders and guard book are used as a method of filing. Under this method papers, letters, documents, circulars, memos, instructions etc., are held together by metal folders or are pasted in bound books in chronological order. They serve no special function and the work of filing is inconvenient and difficult. The same function is served by a letter register. So these filing methods of messages have been discarded by most of the big concerns.

Under this method packets are used to file messages. Expanding alphabetical cases are numbered packets in which written documents like letters and other media can be placed alphabetically. The alphabetical cases or packets can be used for sorting out correspondence or keeping documents collectively only for a temporary period. However, this is a good method but not suitable for large volume of papers as it does not serve as a permanent record. Before despatch documents can be kept in these cases or packets for the time being.

Also called a wire file or pillar and post file. Under this method a spike or wire is fixed to a wooden stand or a wall. They may be placed on the table or hung on the wall near the table. The documents are punched and fixed into a metal spike. Another method of this type is each paper is punched with two holes to fit on the spikes and clamped down in its appropriate file. The file opens like a book and can be opened when necessary.

Boxes are used for filing documents. Cardboard boxes about three to four inches deep are used for filing papers. A box file is used but only for a temporary purpose. The boxes are fitted with spring clips to hold the papers down and the papers are placed under the clip. Sometimes papers may be placed in manila folders which may be kept in a box file. Though under this system documents remain fully secured, box files are not suitable for permanent storage of papers.

Pigeon Holding: Also called docketing. It operates with the help of a cupboard. Under this system a cabinet containing some compartments is required. It resembles pigeon holes so it is named as a pigeon holder. Each compartment is allotted a letter of the alphabet. All papers before placing into holes are sorted, folded and tied into bundles easily identifiable. A brief description of the folder is written on the outer top. The writing of particulars on the outer top is called docketing. Docketing means writing on the outer top the subject of correspondence, residence, date and name of the correspondence. Though the system is popular, particularly in small organisations it is unsuitable for modern offices. Hence many companies have discarded this method. The Post office even today uses this method for sorting letters.

All communications which are transmitted out are copied in a book marked for this purpose. A press copy book may be divided either on an alphabetical or on a geographical basis. Since particulars are entered in a book the press copy book serves as good evidence in case of dispute of communication. However, this is a very old method and is not in popular use in modern organisations.

Old methods of filing were popularly used where the volume of communication was comparatively small. The importance of these methods of filing has declined by the passing of time. Some of the methods have been fast replaced by modern methods. Modern methods are found suitable and perform more efficiently in comparison with old methods. With a view to meeting the requirements of large organisations, new and improved methods of filing have been devised and introduced. Consequently, old methods of filing became outdated. All large sized business organisations have now come to use modern filing methods.

Modern methods of filing can broadly be classified into two broad categories. They are flat or horizontal filing and, secondly, vertical filing.

Horizontal Filing : It is called horizontal filing because the documents are kept in a horizontal position or in a flat position. It means one on top of the other. First papers are inserted in files or folders and these folders or files are kept in a horizontal position in drawers or shelves. The horizontal method of filing takes the following two forms :

Under the flat file method the papers are kept in a flat position under a file liver. The files are made of cardboard or thick paper. Each cover is allotted to each customer or allotted to a particular subject. All papers relating to a particular customer or relating to a particular subject are put in the cover in the order in which they are received. In cases where a particular message relates to more than one file, more copies of the messages are made out so that each file may have a copy. A punching machine is used to punch the papers to be filed. The files are placed in the cupboards or drawers one on top of the other. Easy location of files is possible by preparing an index. Thus under the flat file method papers are arranged horizontally and in chronological order. But proper numbering of files and indexing is necessary.

Also called the pilot or liver arch files. These files are either made of very thick cardboard or have filing cabinets. It is called a liver file because it is operated by a liver. It opens and closes when the liver is operated. Cardboard files are opened by a liver. "Era" file and "shannon" file are examples of this type. When a letter is to be filed the liver is moved upwards and after inserting the paper the liver is pressed down. The special feature of liver file is that a paper can be inserted at any place between two earlier papers without disturbing the order of other papers.

The Merits : The following are the merits of horizontal filing method :

1. Filing of messages is simple.
2. There is easy access to the document.
3. There is no risk of losing the documents filed.
4. Misplacement problem does not arise once the paper is inserted in the file.
5. Quick and easy reference is possible without disturbing the order and without removing from the file.
6. The operation of the arch helps to avoid mixing of papers.
7. Papers are fixed on the arch and there is no chance of changing the order.
8. Files are kept in chronological order so it is easy to find out a particular letter with the help of the index, or if the date is known.

The Demerits

1. There is no scope for expansion.
2. It is not possible to trace a filed paper at short notice because of its horizontal nature.
3. Flat files involve trouble removing the papers on the top in order to take out a particular paper.
4. Keeping a complete drawer or tray for each classification causes difficulty.
5. It takes more space compared with the vertical system.
6. The system is not very efficient for a larger business concern.
7. It is difficult to maintain data for each letter or paper to trace a particular paper.

Vertical Filing : Also called the upright system of filing. Vertical filing is the most modern system of filing. As such it removes the drawbacks associated with the horizontal filing system. It has gained importance essentially out of the limitations and defects of the horizontal method because under the horizontal method papers are arranged in such a way that it is very cumbersome to refer to them at short notice. Owing to its defects vertical filing has come to be adopted by most modern organisations. It ensures efficiency in record keeping. The papers and the files containing them are placed vertically in position or in a standing upright position hence the name vertical file.

There are two parts in vertical filing. The equipment needs two parts. They are :

Folders: The basis for vertical filing is a folder. A folder is a folded sheet of manila or some other strong but flexible substance. The back of a folder or a tab attached to it is slightly higher than the front sheet. The extended edge of the back sheet is used for writing the description of the contents kept in the file. The description takes the form of the name of the subject, number etc. A separate folder may be kept for each subject. All the papers relating to a particular subject or correspondence are kept standing in chronological or other suitable order in the folder. Any particular paper can be removed or inserted without disturbing other papers.

Usually clips or folders are used to keep the papers fast and together.

A wooden or steel cabinet is the second important part required for vertical filing. Folders are kept in the wooden or steel cabinet with a suitable number of drawers depending upon the volume of papers to be preserved. Hence the folders are to be placed in a standing upright position. The drawers must be deep enough to accommodate the folders. The folders are placed vertically on their left hand edge one on top of the other. It has a mechanism called expander which slides backwards or forwards and holds up the folders. A memorandum card is put in the place of a particular folder which is removed from a drawer for any reference purpose.

The Merits : The following are the advantages of vertical filing:

1. Messages filed in a vertical system have the merit of quick reference.

   The facility of ready reference is not possible in horizontal filling
2. Any particular document can be removed easily as compared to a horizontal filing system.
3. Easy to find the records, contents of each folder are visible from the extended edge of the back sheet
4. It accommodates handling of large volume of correspondence more conveniently and easily than the flat filing system
5. Vertical filing system has the advantage of saving time because there is no need to punch the papers.
6. The advantage of cost saving or economy cannot be overlooked. A large number of papers can be arranged in drawers meant for the purpose. When files are arranged vertically they accommodate more papers. Thus it ensures economy of space and expense.
7. The system has inherent merit which offers scope for expansion. There is a provision for expansion in the drawers. It has a mechanism of expander which facilitates accommodating increase in correspondence.
8. Vertical filing system has the advantage that there is no

fear of mixing up correspondence of one person with that of the other. Because they are kept separately for each individual.

9. The vertical filing system is more adaptable to any variety of classifications. The folders can be arranged subject-wise, area-wise, alphabetically or in any other suitable basis.
10. Safety of papers can be achieved under this system. Papers are kept safe from dust and insects in the manila folders and steel or wooden drawers.
11. It has the merit of side applicability. Vertical filing systems can be used for preservation of all media of written communication such as letters, folders, orders, memos, and other documents.

One-shelf Filing : To find a paper in a cabinet, one has to lean over in a cabinet to open it. It also takes more floor space. In view of these difficulties, there is a recent trend towards open shelf filing. It is in popular use in the U.S.A. This is particularly so where materials have been accumulated in packets or large envelopes. The drawbacks of folder and cabinet method can be solved by making the shelves nine to ten feet high and providing ladders to the operator.

The Essentials : A good filing system is one that facilitates easy reference, preservation and maintenance. The following are the essentials of a good filing system :

Simplicity : The purpose of the filing should be clear and simple. It must be simple to understand, so that all clerical workers may operate it without any difficulty. The system must ensure quick reference, without any training and knowledge of filing.

Suitability : A particular type of filing should be followed which will meet the requirements of the organisation and which is in conformity with the nature and objectives of the organisation. No particular type is suitable for all types of organisations and as such, it is the problem of the management to devise a suitable system according to the needs of the business.

Accessibility : The written messages so filed should facilitate ready accessibility to documents, so that the communication required may be available quickly as and when required. The messages may be picked up without loss of time.

Economy : Budgeting of filing of communications is the important factor in selecting a particular filing system. The cost of labour, equipment, and overheads should be reasonable. As such filing should be economical. The cost should not be more than the benefits derived from it. Space is a problem; the filing system should not take too much. Economising space, and preserving documents but not beyond their proper life are the two important principles.

Compactness : A good system must ensure that the area must be compact so that only the required space is occupied. In big cities the cost of office space is very high.

Flexibility : The system of filing should consider future requirements. So it should be capable of expansion to accommodate the expanding needs. When the activities of the concern expand, an inflexible system is useless. The system must be suitable even after a certain limit is crossed, and adaptable to meet changing circumstances.

Identification : The system should be in a position to permit ready and quick location and identification of messages otherwise the system is not only a waste but also costly.

Cross Reference : Cross reference of filing is yet another essential of a good filing system. Sometimes communications may be filed under two different heads. The messages should be classified under various headings with cross references. The cross reference helps the clerks to find out the message in another file where it is kept.

Classification : A communication filing system should follow a suitable classification. There are many methods of classification of messages such as alphabetical, numerical, geographical, subject-wise, alphabetical, numerical and chronological. A proper and suitable classification should be adopted.

Safety : One of the merits of written communication is preservation of messages, which serve as future reference and evidence. *So* a good filing system is one which must try to achieve this objective. The system must provide safety to documents and prevent unauthorised persons from tampering with them. It should protect them from the dangers of insects, rain, rats, and white ants.

Indexing : A ready guide to locate a particular file is necessary. A good filing system should facilitate introduction of a good index system. The system of classification of files and the type of filing method adapted will decide the method of indexing to be followed.

Movement: Communication movement from one place to another is a common feature in the organisation. An indicator or guide is to be used when a particular message is removed from a file. The indicator should be inserted in its place with particulars of the part of the message removed, date, to which section it is sent etc.

Serviceability : It is obviously important that a good filing system should be capable of filing papers speedily and traced speedily. This is what is known as convenience of filing or serviceability of filing.

Up to Date : The messages should also be filed to date. This is possible to achieve with an efficient office forms control.

Mechanical Trick

Modern mechanical equipment and machines play an important role in efficient and speedy communication. Mechanisation of communication work is fast taking place. Messages are required to be transmitted to the inside tall network and flat network as well as to outsiders. It is no exaggeration that there are rapid changes in communication management because of growing scientific and technological innovations. The age of communication has brought about many changes in different fields, to keep pace with mass communication. Also to transmit messages to distant places with considerable speed, accuracy and quantity of messages to enable quick and correct decision making. All this has necessitated the installation of a number of time and labour saving electrical and electronic mechanical devices in written communication. These machines right from the typewriter to the sophisticated computers and teleprinters are required for transmitting information.

Network for Communication : Mechanisation of the communication network is for the accurate and speedy communication of messages. Even office work inside the organisation is mostly indoor desk and manual work. The process of communication is routine, continuous and monotonous in nature. The routine manual work may adversely affect efficient performance. This also necessitates the adoption of certain equipment and machines suitable for efficient written communication. Therefore, the most appropriate communication work can be done with machines at a comparatively minimum cost. More accuracy and speed not only improve general efficiency, but also increase the goodwill of the organisation among its visitors and other outsiders.

Today a wide variety of writing and communicating machines are available in the market. A management has to procure and install suitable machinery depending upon organisational requirements and working staff. There are a number of advantages associated in mechanisation of communication, like saving in cost ensures accuracy and speed in transmission. This reduces monotony, achieves uniformity, better appearance and easy record and reference.

The various types of machines which are available for the purpose of written communication are listed below along with a brief description.

Type-writer : The type-writer is a machine with keys for printing letters on a piece of paper. The type-writer is the most popular and commonly used machine in all types of communication work. Type-writers are now available not only in English but also in regional languages. In every organisation the type-writer is seen as a basic requirement now a days. The typed copy is the writing produced by the type-writer. It is called a typescript. Different companies make type-writers with different type faces. Type faces are a set of letters for printing, cut in a particular style. A typist is a person whose job is to type. Type-writing, *i.e.*, writing produced by a type-writer is a form of written communication.

There are various types of type-writers which are used in type-writing.

Standard Type-writer: It is the most commonly used type-writer in all organisations. It is most suitable for routine business correspondence and general typing work. Typing work can be done with considerable speed. It is more compact and more matter can be typed on a page comparing other types. The typescript is easier to read, clear and, if necessary, a clear carbon copy can be produced.

Portable Type-writer : A machine of comparatively small size, a portable typewriter can be carried or moved easily from place to place. A handy, lightweight machine. It can be used mostly for personal work of limited quantity. It contains all fundamental elements of the standard typewriter. Economically also it is cheaper.

Noiseless Type-writer : This typewriter produces no noise or less noise compared to the standard typewriter. Type faces are pressed rather than stamping and produces less noise. So it is called a noiseless typewriter. Generally used in meeting rooms or executive chambers where there is always some disturbance with telephone calls. A greater number of carbon copies cannot be produced.

Electric Type-writer : This typewriter is operated electrically by the typist. This kind of typewriter is basically in the structure of the standard type-writer but connected with electricity, fitted with an electric motor. It saves the energy of the typist and reduces monotony. The semi-electric machine is another variant form.

There are different types of type faces with various sizes, shapes and styles. Now a days a machine has been developed by which typing of letters with types of various sizes, shapes and styles is possible. The name itself indicates that it performs variable functions. The machine has differential space justification.

Automatic Type-writer : This type of typewriter functions with the help of punched paper type or paper roles or cards known as master cards. An automatic type-writer types individually typed matter from a punched tape or paper tape or roles as the case may be. The tape or roles are placed on the machine and the matter punched on the tape is automatically typed on the paper.

Type-writer with Other Devices : The machine facilitates continuous typing of standard and routine work. It is a common standard type-writer with a special fitted device. Continuous stationery can also be typed provided such stationery is inserted in the machine.

Teleprinter : Yet another type of typewriter is the teleprinter. The teleprinter not only types but transmits electrical signals over wires. At receiving point at the same time a machine prints the matter. It is used for transmitting messages to distant places. A machine in a communication system. A teleprinter is a machine, a specialised type of typewriter. A telegraphic system or instrument by which messages are sent out at one place and received at another place in a printed form. The typing is connected to a telephone line, and the message typed at one place transmits electrical signals over a wire and the same message is simultaneously reproduced and printed at a distant place by the machine. It is used as a private circuit or through the post office telex service system. The post office gives teleprinters on rent to form a part of private telecommunication.

Stenographic Type-writer : This is not in a strict sense a standard typewriter. Though is appears to be like a typewriter, not only is it portable but also makes less noise. It is used by a stenographer to take down short-hand dictation. It reduces monotony and work can be done at a considerable speed.

Continuous Stationery : This is stationery of long run routine forms, a long strip of paper folded in a zig-zag manner. A separate part called an attachment is fitted to the typewriter carriage. When there is a large quantity of work, continuous stationery is used to cope up with the volume of work. It ensures speedy typing and the greatest cleanliness.

Duplicating machines are used in offices and facilitate reproduction of a number of copies of letters, reports, circulars, memos, notices etc., for circulation. Duplicating machines ensure reproduction promptly and efficiently with secrecy. They are a substitute for printing. Usually these machines are used to produce more copies which an ordinary standard typewriter cannot produce. With the help of a master impression, a number of copies can be obtained. There are various types of duplicating machines. The important duplicating processor and machines used in offices are us under:

Hectograph

(a) Flat Bed Type

(b) Rotary Type

(c) Mimeograph

(d) Multigraph (Photographic Film. Electronic Stencil)

(e) Offset-Litho Duplication

(f) Copying (Photostatic Process. Diazo microfilming)

Imprinting Machines : Imprinting machines and their process contribute an addition to the existing copy. The difference between imprinting process and duplicating process is that the duplicating process merely reproduces a number of facsimile copies. They include :

Impression Stamps : Rubber stamps. For instance, stamp bearing impression as "paid", "date", "numbering" etc.

Addressing machines are useful when a number of letters are to be posted. When hundreds of bills, circulars, notices or wrappers are to be addressed, addressing machines are used. Addressograph machines are used for the respective printing of the same address. They are of two types : (*i*) Fibre stencils and (*ii*) plates. Metal plates are prepared on special embossing machines called graphotype. These plates when prepared can be preserved for future use and repeatedly used.

Signature Machines : These machines can be used for imprinting signatures on cheques, circulars or notices.

In order to affix stamps over covers or letters franking machines are used. The machines are used for imprinting postage marks in large numbers. The posts and telegraph department supplies these machines on hire for use in business premises. A cover is inserted in the machine and with the help of a handle it is possible to mark the letter with the required denomination of the postage. It saves time handling large quantities of stamps. There is no scope of risk of theft and mutilation in stamping.

The date and time recorder is used so that all incoming mail is stamped with the date and time of its arrival in the office. The mail is inserted in the recorder which automatically prints the time and date. It is used both for incoming and outgoing mail.

These include computing, accounting, tabulating machines, mailing scale, folding machine, inserting machines, sorting devices, adding and listing machines, billing machines, book keeping machines, punch-card machines, and other statistical or tabulating machines.

Telefax : This machine is used for transmitting sketches or drawings. The chart or diagram is originally drawn on a paper. The paper is wrapped round a cylinder in the machine. The machine upon switching on transmits the facsimile to the machine at the other end where it is reproduced simultaneously.

Telewriter : Also called a Telautograph or Tele-autorgraph. It also operates on the principle of a teleprinter. A message is written on a metal plate attached to a machine which is reproduced electrically on the machine at the other end.

Indexing : Communication is a continuous process involving the original message, followed by clarifications, explanations, corrected messages etc. We have presented a detailed picture of methods of filing communication, classification of documents and the essentials of a good filing system. Unless a particular filing system itself has an index, every filing system must be supplemented by a well designed index plan. The method of index to be adopted will depend upon the nature of organisation, media of communication in use and system of classification of files. So indexing is the most important and one of the essentials of a good filing system.

Indexing with reference to communication files refers to something which indicates or points to a particular piece of fact, figure, idea, opinion etc. In other words, it shows the indices. It is an alphabetical list of correspondence at the end of the file or beginning or on separate cards. The index is a guide which helps to locate the required file or records. In a business concern with the help of the index it is possible to ascertain names, subject and other particulars under which documents are to be filed. The index helps to find out documents easily and without delay. It indicates as to where communication in detail will be available. So from the above discussion on classification, it is clear that indexing and classification are different. Indexing indicates and points out the location. But classification is only a method of filing. For instance, when files are arranged alphabetically that itself serves as an index. In all cases where files have self-indexing there is no need to have separate index. But still it is good to have a good indexing system even if the files are arranged on a self-indexing system. The only purpose of an index is to facilitate the location of the papers. A condensed record of the customers, credit rating etc. Indexes are used with ledgers and accounts. It is common to have indexes in libraries, banks, insurance companies etc.

Types of Index : Different types of indexing are in use. The following are the various kinds of index systems in use.

This is also called an ordinary page index or bound book index. As the name indicates it is in the nature of a bound book or register. The book is divided into alphabetical divisions in which names of customers or correspondents are entered into. Each page or more pages is/are allotted to one letter or more letters of the alphabet. Each page or section has pages cut away at the right hand side, so that letters are visible at a glance. All entries relating to a particular letter will be arranged on the same page maintained for it. The arrangement is in the strict alphabetical order. The index may be maintained by different methods such as: (a) an index in the front of the book, (b) an index at the back of a book, (c) an index in a separate book or (d) a series of loose sheets inserted in front of each section of a file.

Advantages

(i) Under this system of indexing it is very easy and simple to operate.

(ii) It is not an expensive system.

(iii) It is possible to maintain the records for a long period.

(iv) A bound index is not generally misplaced.

(v) No scope for torn pages, lost or disarranged.

Disadvantages

(i) The system is not flexible or elastic and cannot meet the changes and expansion. Increase in correspondence cannot be accommodated in this system. More entries cannot be entered.

(ii) There is no scope for any other information to be inserted in bound book index.

(iii) Deletion of ceased and outdated entries of certain correspondence makes the system ineffective.

(iv) It also needs some knowledge to operate.

(v) Under utilisation of book is a serious problem in many cases.

This is an improved method of the bound book index method. Each page indexed for a particular letter is divided into six sub-divisions and each sub-division is earmarked for a vowel captioned A,E,I,O,U and Y.

Each sub-section has a separate page of letter 'A' and then a separate part of the page is allotted. The name of each correspondent is entered on one page reserved for its initial letters. The sub-division is meant for the first vowel in the name after the first letter. For example, the name Ranjit will be recorded in the section reserved for 'R' and in the vowel of section 'A'. Though the method theoretically appears good it suffers from certain drawbacks. For instance, entering of names on each page must be in sequence in which they have first occurred. Similarly the system is not flexible and elastic and does not permit addition of new entries.

This is similar to loose leaf ledger. It is a variant form of a book index. Under this system individual sheets can be inserted into metal, hinges, or scrows. It permits the pages to be taken out or to insert additional pages. The book index may simply be unscrewed and anew leaf can be inserted. A loose leaf book index has certain advantages such as:

1. The system is elastic and flexible, meets changing needs.
2. It is easily adaptable to meet different circumstances.
3. The system operates with locking so that no leaves are taken out without proper authority.
4. The loose index sheets may be inserted at the beginning of each alphabetical section of a book.

The card index system was invented by A. J. Rozier. The book index and vowel index have certain difficulties it their operation. In order to overcome the limitations the loose card index system has been introduced. Under this system a separate card is allotted to each *message. Here a card index is an index in which each item occupies a separate card.* All cards are in uniform size. The cards are arranged in some classification like alphabetical, numerical or geographical. The card index method is followed in libraries, banks etc. The cards so prepared are put in steel or wooden drawers. Generally a rod is put through them to hold the cards in their places.

Forms can be put either in a vertical or horizontal position. On each card is written the name, address, number and other particulars. The cards are arranged in such a way that the top portion of all cards bearing the main subject heading will be visible simultaneously. The cards are generally of uniform size, say post-card size or four inches into two and half inches. A card index is used particularly for the following purposes:

1. The addresses of the customers are maintained.
2. Index cards of books according to title or according to the name of the author in libraries.
3. Banks maintain a card index to keep specimen signatures of customers.
4. Index to the ledgers in which accounts of various customers are maintained.
5. Index is used to record employees particulars.
6. To record financial position.
7. Card index of store items.
8. To maintain particulars of title deeds, contracts and other documents.
9. Indexing of price list, catalogues.
10. To keep the accounts of stores items.
11. To maintain record of investment particulars.
12. For maintaining the record of transactions relating to hire purchase and instalment sales.
13. To maintain a record of the period of credit to be granted.

Advantages

1. New cards can be inserted easily and quickly.
2. The system is more flexible and elastic, so accommodates increasing work.
3. Adding and insertion do not disturb the order.

4. Old cards or cards of ceased customers can be removed from the drawers.
5. The system is easy and simple to operate and understand.
6. Any card can be taken out for reference. It is also helpful to find out a particular card. The sub division under the vowel index further facilitates reference.
7. As the cards are arranged in alphabetical order it saves time to locate any name or subject.
8. Card indexing is cheaper compared to the bound index method which takes more renewal cost.
9. Cards can be grouped and regrouped in any manner and in any order.
10. Cards can be ruled according to convenience or to the particulars desired to be recorded.
11. Different coloured cards can be used to classify various purposes.
12. It is possible to maintain the system neat and tidy.
13. Indicators or guide cards may be used to group cards to draw attention.
14. Blank pages will appear in case of a bound index. There is no need to insert blank cards in the cabinets.
15. A number of persons can use the index simultaneously.

Disadvantages

1. A serious draw back of the system is when cards are lost, misplaced etc. It is very difficult to find them.
2. The system is also known for delay as many cards have to be seen before the desired card can be traced.
3. It cannot be afforded by small concerns since the installation cost is very high.
4. When cards are kept for keeping the ledger there is a danger of fraudulent substitution, concealment etc.
5. At a time only one card can be seen, as all the cards cannot be seen at a glance.
6. When cards are freely taken out, checking is very difficult

7. The facility given by guide cards and dictionary arrangement is thus reduced

Visible Card Index : To overcome the difficulties of the card index method, the visible card index system has been introduced. If the visible card index method is adopted, the operational difficulties associated with the card index can be removed. Under it a large number of cards cannot be seen at a glance, as pointed out earlier. Under this method, the cards are laid flat in a shallow or in metal trays. In other words, cards are put in transparent covers and then arranged in trays. Each card is arranged in such a way and fitted into a metal hinge so that it overlaps the one before it. Overlaps its neighbour in such a way that a narrow strip at the bottom containing the name or title remains visible. The trays may be fitted horizontally or attached vertically to metal stands. The cards can be classified either by usual systems like alphabetical, numerical or a combination of them. There are two variant forms of visible card indexing such as "card wheel" and "Strip index".

Advantages

1. This system saves considerable time.
2. A large number of cards can be kept at a time.
3. It permits speedy reference of cards, because the names or subjects are visible.
4. Easy location and speedy posting in cards is possible.
5. The system operates in a very compact way and occupies less space.
6. It is possible to write on each card either in front or on the reverse without removing the card from its place.
7. Speedy and ready reference and information enables the management to control effectively the sales, purchases, credit etc.
8. Listing of correspondents or subjects can be done smoothly.

The Division

There are different forms of classification of papers or other written messages. In order to make communication messages available promptly, it is indispensable that pieces of communication messages be properly classified or divided and grouped according to some prescribed basis and by giving proper titles. The purpose of written communication can be achieved only when the documents are properly classified. On the other hand, the success or failure of a filing system largely depends upon the selection of the most suitable method of classification of documents. The following are the main methods of classification of papers and documents placed in files.

Various Modes

Alphabetical classification of files is popular, and the method is most widely used in every organisation. With this method, each file containing papers bears the name of the correspondent. The arrangement is in strict alphabetical order of the surname. It starts with the first letter with which the surname of the correspondent begins. Each file bears a letter like A or B or C etc. All the letters of customers whose surname begins with 'a' Are put in the file bearing letter A. And all those beginning with letter 'b' are placed in the B file. This method is very easy for the clerks to operate.

Advantages

1. Alphabetical method is simple and easy to understand.
2. There is no need to have separate indexing. The system itself is the index.
3. The system is flexible and more elastic. It accommodates changes and expansion.
4. It can easily be operated.
5. Any method of filing like vertical or horizontal can be adopted.

Disadvantages

1. The system takes a longer time for filing.
2. It may not be suitable to a larger organisation.
3. Confusion arises when spellings are not correctly given.
4. Congestion under common names is a serious problem.
5. Wrong filing of documents is possible under different headings.

6. Forecasting of documents under each letter is not possible.
7. If there are a large number of names of a particular letter more files are to be kept.

***Numerical*:** As the name indicates this classification facilitates operation with numbers. Under this method each customer or correspondent is allotted a number. In other words, a number is allotted to such a file. All documents relating to a particular customer or subject are put in one separate file which has a distinct number. For instance, 'A' is allotted number 25. All papers connected with him are placed in the number 25. The files are then placed in cupboards according to their serial numbers. But this system calls for comprehensive indexing. Index cards are maintained, which are also arranged in alphabetical order. A variant form of this system is that the filing cabinet is arranged in pigeon holes according to the alphabetical order.

Advantages

1. This is the simplest method to operate and understand.
2. There is greater accuracy in filing.
3. It facilitates and accommodates all kinds of communication media.
4. Under this system, it is possible to know the total number of customers or correspondents.
5. It is sufficiently adaptable to meet changing circumstances. It is more elastic and flexible.
6. Files can be arranged in an orderly way and can be easily located.
7. Any paper of a particular customer can be traced easily without disturbing the sequence.
8. The index is a full list and can be used for as an index address.
9. This system helps to expand or increase the number of files with the increase in the number of customers.
10. The files of ceased, old and irrelevant customers without any dealings can be removed

Disadvantages

1. It takes more time of find out when a particular number is given to a particular customer.
2. A separate index has to be prepared.
3. Documents of a miscellaneous nature, or residual category are difficult to arrange.
4. It takes more space.
5. Errors occur in filing in cases of transposition of figures.

Classification of messages under this method is a combination of the alphabetical and numerical method as discussed above. While filing, documents are classified in alphabetical divisions and numbers are then allotted to different classified documents. Giving numbers to alphabetical classification serves the purpose of their sub- classification. This combined system can be used suitably because it has many advantages. Guide cards or index cards can also be used to subdivide the holders into divisions or groups which help their speedy location. For instance Z_1 may refer to Mr. Kulkarni, Z_2 may refer to Mr. Saxena. This method is more popular and is commonly used in libraries for classification of books, and in banks for filing specimen signatures of the customers. This method combines all the advantages of the alphabetical and numerical systems of classification. This classification avoids serious problems of similar names arising in the case of the alphabetical system.

Under this classification documents are filed according to their geographical area or location. This classification is adopted when an organisation wants to keep the records according to the area. So this system facilitates that correspondence relating to a particular territory which is collected or pooled together and then classified according to alphabetical or numerical order. The documents are classified according to villages, towns, cities, states, countries etc. Under this system correspondence is maintained according to customers, records of the various areas and filing correspondence according to a geographical area. The sales department of an organisation can suitably classify sales particulars according to areas. This is the suitable method for all organisations which extend their area of operation to a wider area. Transport companies, export houses, mail order business houses, banks, insurance companies etc., can adopt geographical classification of documents properly. A company which has its business all over the world may classify documents according to the area or country. In home trade files can be classified and arranged according to state, district or taluk. These can again be classified and arranged in alphabetical order.

Advantages : The advantages of this method are :

1. The sales of each area can be known for planning.
2. Under this method documents can be easily located.
3. This method is very simple and easy to understand and operate.
4. It can be applied to all types of documents where area classification is necessary.

Disadvantages : The disadvantages of this method are :

1. It is very difficult to know all the addresses. Unless one knows the addresses it is not possible to locate the file.
2. It requires a thorough knowledge of geography.
3. Geographical locations are very difficult to know.
4. Sometimes a separate alphabetical index may be needed.
5. It is costly as clerks have to be trained to understand geography.

The subject matter of a message is important in the classification of documents. This method is adopted where the subject matter of the correspondence is important. The names of the correspondence and geographical area are of secondary importance. Under this method documents are classified and arranged in accordance with the subject matter like sales, purchases, royalty, taxes, commission, rent etc. Therefore, all correspondence relating to a particular subject may be collected together and put in one file. Similarly, documents of contracts, legal proceedings, income-tax etc.

Advantages

1. This method is most useful to lawyers, architects, educational institutions etc.

2. It automatically reveals useful information about the subject.
3. This is the simplest method and can be easily understood by all.
4. Ease of reference and location.
5. It can be adapted to changes. This system is more elastic and flexible.

Disadvantages

1. Difficulties may arise if the subjects are not fully known.
2. Under this method it is not possible to arrange miscellaneous papers
3. When a particular subject is allotted to a classification has to be found out, some time has to be spent.
4. A separate index is required to be prepared.
5. Sometimes cross reference may be needed.

This method operates with dates. Under this method documents are collected together and put into a container according to the date. Papers are kept in files date-wise. Date-wise classification takes place in case of newspapers, magazines, shipping lists, share price, market report invoices, and this method may also be used in filing vouchers. So chronological classification is useful for files of letters which have answers outstanding. The system is useful if dates are known.

Goals and Objectives

The systematic filing of written communication is one of the important aspects of communication work. Filing along with indexing is necessary because of the limitation of the human mind and memory. The object of preserving written messages is to provide necessary information readily and without any delay and when needed. However, the following are the main objectives of keeping messages :

Future Reference : The limitation of the human mind and poor memory cannot be overlooked. Changes of seats on account of transfer of employees also causes problems. Written messages can be preserved as records and reference source. Various media of communication can be filed for future reference. Thus keeping records is essential for continuous operation of the business.

Record of Evidence: Word of mouth is not believable and in a number of cases oral messages have no legal sanction. Written messages have the capacity of being stored as records. At times the records can be used as evidence. Papers can be produced as proof in case of dispute of communication.

Measurement of Progress: Properly filed messages are useful to know the progress of the concern. The records provide relevant and basic information; from this it is possible to know the progress of the organisation. It also facilitates comparison with previous years and also comparison with other firms. In other words, filing messages serves as a barometer of progress which supplies information for the purpose of preparation of annual reports and other periodical reviews.

Precedents : Maintenance of communication provides necessary information on earlier activities and decisions. Past messages are helpful for future decision making. They may act as a guide or rule in the future. In making decisions the decision maker has to follow a precedent set in the organisation earlier.

Avoiding Mistakes : In transmitting messages earlier records help in reducing mistakes and errors. So there is no need for correction, issue of amended messages, instructions, clarifications and explanations. Effective internal control is possible. So keeping and maintaining written messages minimises the chances for errors and prevents the occurrence of fraud.

Effective Decision Making : Old documents help effective decision making in a great way. The decision making process becomes easier if old records are available. Because the messages provide necessary information for the decision making purpose. Decisions may go wrong if the old communications are not followed. Past records may serve as a guide in the decision making process.

Organisational Efficiency : Organisational efficiency cannot be achieved with confusions and lack of guidance. Those records are most useful which guide the employees to take decisions to motivate effective internal control. Preparing classification of messages and suitable filing and indexing in this respect would be helpful in maintaining organisational efficiency.

Legal Requirements : There are certain documents which are required to be preserved compulsorily under the provisions of different legislations. To meet legal requirements the documents should be preserved and maintained. For instance, the maintenance of certain records and books is compulsory under the Indian Companies Act, 1956 and the Banking Regulation Act, 1949 etc.

Necessary Factors

Lajuana Williams Lee, Sallye Starks Benoit, William Colins and Celests Standfield Power, predict the importance of written communication in the future in the following way :

(1) The direct approach will be used more and more to save time and energy for the busy executive.

(2) The use of visual aids will increase and the text decrease in written reports and oral presentations.

(3) Research will be faster and more economical through technology's expanding data-based systems.

(4) Use of office memorandums for dissemination of information will increase.

(5) Increased data provided by advanced technology will demand skill and competence in handling and storage on microforms will eliminate heavy file cabinets.

(6) Information will be disseminated through computers Equipment will display information on screens, which will enable persons to correct errors before messages are sent. Teletypewriters transmitting electric impulses over telephone systems will reproduce written messages simultaneously on machines in neighbouring or distant offices.

(7) Computers will maintain the majority of business records. Primary storage will be in computers and in microfilm equipment.

(8) Business will begin to move closer to a paperless society. There will be electronic delivery rather than postal service deliver. Business letters and reports will be read from machines, not just paper.

Black and white is the most important vehicle used in

communication in all organisations. Information through paper can be transmitted in a written form. Written communication as a means of gathering and disseminating information is generally used more extensively particularly in formal communication. A considerable part of the executive's time is saved. Thus written communication enjoys certain advantages over verbal communication; some of the useful merits of written communication may be outlined below :

There is no scope in written communication to be influenced by self-interest and attitude. The employees have to care only for their work. The subordinates have to pay great attention to the written matter and the messages are formal or official, directly relating to their work.

Written communication is more reliable, and one can trust it. It has official recognition. Oral communication is not believable but written information is correct and reliable. This principle is equally important otherwise at times it tends to reduce the effectiveness of the message; Thus reliability of the communication in the mind of the receiver is a factor of great significance.

The dangers of oral communication are that they may lead to distorted information without any official sanction. Written communication does not suffer from the dangers of being distorted. In every tall network there is organisational distance, written communication is the best media. But in the same structure oral communication may lead to possibility of distortion which goes up with every increase in the organisation structure.

Written communication is a formal method of transmitting messages and they are best suited for long distance communication. This is the only way out if both the communicator and recipient are located geographically in far off places beyond oral communication media, or even beyond mechanical oral device range.

Written messages can be preserved as records and reference source. They have the capacity of being stored as records. At times the records can be used as evidence. Reports, circulars, manuals and other printed, written or typed documents can be filed for future reference and can be produced as legal evidence.

A bulky message cannot be transmitted fully and clearly by oral media. But a lengthy message can be effectively circulated in black and white. The problems of missing points, forgetfulness, lack of memory and use of improper words in speaking are the problems which can be avoided in written communication.

A number of business transactions takes place through writing, where oral communication has no place and is not believed. Written communication covers all kinds of subject matter like notices, deeds, minutes, resolutions, contracts, complaints, financial statements, legal documents, proposals, pleadings, charts, communication intelligence, memoranda and articles of association, and many other transactions concerned only with paper work.

Written communication usually carries no rumours and inaccurate and partial information. It has official sanction and may not even turn into gossip and rumour. It is routine, formal and will continue to exist for all time to come.

The written media are also useful for dissemination of certain information which cannot be transmitted through oral channel. There is every possibility that word of mouth is heard by others. Secrecy can be maintained in written communication.

As pointed out earlier, in real world situations oral communication does not always save time. Written media not only save time but also cost. The cost is greater in case of conferences, and meetings. In oral media the time of many people is wasted in conversation, but in written communication copies of written messages can be placed on the desk of the employees.

It has permanent value. It promotes upward communication for clarification, correction of error and other amendments. It is more orderly and binding on subordinates and superiors.

The Demerits

The purpose of communication is to understand the message. Written communication may sometimes lead to confusion and misunderstanding. The chances of communication being misunderstood are more. Everyone may not have the same understanding capacity.

Written communication is comparatively less effective because there is no instinct of personal contact. Everything is in black and white and better and immediate impressions cannot be created. It takes more time to see clarifications and explanations. There is no scope for exchange of feelings freely, and reactions cannot be understood immediately.

One-way communication implies giving information flowing from top to middle, and from middle to operating level. Most written communications are orders and instructions issued by superiors, imposed and enforced. The communication to be effective must be a two-way channel. One way directs in a definite manner the employees to understand what the management intends them to do. So it is rigid and lacks the quality of flexibility.

The importance of informal communication cannot be overlooked. Written communication is purely formal and generally expressed in writing in manuals, orders, reports etc. There are many messages which in the general interest of the organisation cannot be put in black and white. In such cases informal oral media are more useful. The executives should make effective use of the grapevine for the purpose.

Written communication moves 'comparatively' with little speed and often not faster than oral communication. Messages get disseminated improperly and impersonally. The element of personal touch is absent.

It does not offer the executive insight into what the subordinates think and feel about the message. The absence of personal interaction makes it difficult to get clues of the reactions of the receiver of message. The written communication represents no natural desire of people in the organisation to interact and communicate with each other. It does not grow up spontaneously and lacks flexibility.

Feedback is one of the important essentials of good communication. In written communication in respect of many matters, like objectives and policy matters, there is no scope for feedback. Feedback in the process of communication calls for making it a two-way process. Feedback is an inherent quality in oral communication. The communicator cannot ascertain whether the receiver accepted or rejected the message. The reaction of the receiver of the message can be assessed effectively in oral communication rather than through written communication. Getting feedback information is easier in verbal communication.

Written communication does not give subordinates a feeling of belonging and a sense of a personal importance. So it does not help in morale building and motivation. In times of insecurity and uncertainty there is not an outlet in written communication freely to express their fears, attitudes and thoughts.

The characteristic of bureaucratic administration is another drawback of written communication. It leads to delays and redtapism. Executives act in a bureaucratic way and do things officially, strictly according to the letter rather than the spirit.

Incompleteness of the message leads to a chain of clarifications. This delays action and the decision-making process. Organisational efficiency is dependent not only on effective writing but on clear interpretation by the receiver. Owing to the problem of the language, the receiver of the message does not interpret it in the same manner as the communicator. Differences in status, in formal education, vocabulary and the cosmopolitan nature of the organisation etc., make the written communication ineffective.

Speech Communication

.Among various forms of communication, oral communication is considered to be the earliest and common medium of communication. In oral communication, speech is a widely adopted tool of communication. The sender, the medium, the receiver and the message are the four basic factors associated with communication. Socrates and Demosthenes were great and renowned in giving speeches. The world is busy with speeches. Everyday, in educational institutions the students and the taught come into conversation. In offices the superiors talk to the subordinates, the subordinates to superiors, superiors among themselves. In productive and service organisations the customers come into conversation with the suppliers, lawyers, doctors, auditors, consultants etc., with their clients and so on and so forth.

Effective Means

Either in business communication or otherwise the oral communication should be clear and effective to achieve the objects of communication. Speech is an art for which there are no fixed rules which can be uniformly followed always and in all circumstances. There are a number of factors which influence effective oral communication. Factors like the conversation style of the speaker, language, medium, the temperaments of the receiver and speaker, size of audience, importance of message, fear of superiors, etc. are important. For instance, an important person appearing on TV or Radio or at a public meeting chooses his words selectively because if words are wrongly selected and used they may damage his image.

Human relations is the fundamental element of public relations. It is with speech to get along well with the public both internal to the organisation and external to the organisation. The public stands divided into three categories of people: (a) There are those who know you and like you. (b) There are those who know you and do not like you. (c) There are those who neither know you nor care for you.

The technique involved in the process of communication is through speech to do business with all types of people. The essential basis of all cross sections is the communication process. It is the transfer of information from one to another. The message is transmitted by spoken or written words or by image or a combination of these or other media such as music, colour, mimicry, design, odour, and sense of touch.

In a competitive and dynamic market economy there are information gaps which cannot be filled up by the interaction of supply and demand through prices and costs. This is where Communication activity steps in.

Some Basic Issues

The capacity to communicate effectively and clearly is an important skill. The speakers have to make the message clear and easily understandable both in work and outside. In any profession it is not possible to get through without communication. Communication is a valuable asset for most people in the modern-day busy world such as for lawyers, teachers, auditors, consultants, administrators, politicians, business executives, parents and children etc. Thus speech or talking is basic and indispensable in any group activities and civilized society. Speech is for others to understand. The confusion and misunderstanding in conversation are due to ineffective and bad speech.

There are no standard rules to be followed in oral communication once and for all time to come. However, effective oral communication calls for certain principles to be followed. Whatever the circumstances, however, the following are essential ingredients of good oral communication.

The essential of good oral communication is clarity. Clarity of message is of the first and foremost importance among principles. The three most important qualities of oral communication style are: first clarity, then clarity and then clarity. Before you start talking think and rethink ideas till they are clear to the speaker. Then put ideas in conversation in a clear-cut order. Clarity can be achieved with simple words, short sentences and common words. Daniel Defoe, the author of Robinson Crusoe, said that clarity is a matter of style in which a man speaking to five hundred people of all common and various capacities, idiots and lunatics excepted, should be understood by them all.

A message must be brief. Lengthy sentences confuse and may lead to misunderstanding. It should be a short one. One can achieve brevity by taking pains and framing sentences to serve people rather than indulging in lengthy and complex ones. We do come across people who give speech short in a sentence. Conversation in short sentences gives the listener time and opportunity to follow what the speaker endeavours to pur across. Using precise words, simple and familiar words and avoiding superfluous words are important factors in effective communication.

Precision is the most important principle in effective communication. Using precise words mean speaking in exact detail. Using right words at the right place in the context will alone convey the meaning intended by the speaker. In oral communication the precise words which are often the concrete words express the real and correct meaning. As far as possible using vague words should be avoided. But in practice it is difficult to replace one word for another. No two words give exactly the same meaning without changing or diluting the meaning. People may substitute a simple word for a difficult one. It is better to have full knowledge of synonyms and antonyms of words.

Cliche means a phrase which is used too often, and has some meaning. The cliches are now stale in oral communication. An effective good communicator avoids cliches. A speaker may use them unconsciously when he is involved in a serious mood of conversation. Examples of cliches are 'I mean', 'oh really', 'ok', 'quite fine', 'yes' etc.

Presentation of matter in a logical sequence is yet another important principle of effective communication. The speaker does not jump points or change the sequence. Consistency, continuity and logical development of the subject matter should be there. The manner in which a speaker said something is more important than the matter itself in communication.

In our conversation we must be conscious to avoid jargon. Jargon is a field applicable or relating to a particular section of a profession. It means language or terminology relating to law, commerce, sports, defence etc. It may be called legal jargon, military jargon, commercial jargon etc. Only people who are versed in a particular subject can understand. But in public and general conversation the words used must be clear to other people as well.

To convey meaning is more important than using superfluous words. Verbosity in oral communication is a great danger in conveying a message. Using more words does not assure greater clarity. Using more words will take more time and the time of an audience is wasted. The listener may tire and may misunderstand the meaning.

Seven C's of Communication : Francis J. Bergin advocates that there are seven C's to remember in spoken communication. They are : 1. Candid, 2. Clear, 3. Complete, 4. Concise, 5. Concrete, 6. Correct, 7. Courteous.

Use of unnecessary prepositions should be avoided. For instance, all employees must follow the safety regulation in regard to work. Here the word " about" can be used in place of " in regard to". Some other examples are : in connection with, with reference to, in relation to, with regard to.

Adjectives and adverbs should be used where necessary. They emphasis the meaning with the degree of importance. For instance, the problem is under *active* consideration; a *positive* decision will be taken; *definite* results; *comparatively* the results are poor.

Various Methods

Certain techniques should be followed to be a successful communicator. He must build into his speech an element of goodwill to which the listener will react favourably. A speech creates goodwill provided a message produces a favourable reaction from the listeners. A positive favourable reaction from the listeners can be achieved by promoting a friendly, kind attitude, cheerful consent towards listeners. Listeners are many and human, of all common and various capacities, idiots, lunatics. They should be treated as such, and the message capable of being understood by them all. A favourable effect of a message is important. One principle is being courteous, which is fundamental in all oral communication and good relations.

"Courtesy consists of putting yourself in the other person's place and showing every consideration, as well as showing good common sense in getting along with other people. It is an attitude of mind based on kindness, respect and understanding. It comes naturally to people who are considerate of another person's feelings, needs, and reactions, and impresses the other person favourably."

However, the following are the important techniques in oral communication to be successful :

Friendly Atmosphere : It is the responsibility of the speaker to create a friendly or kindly attitude, benevolent atmosphere at the place. A sincere speech should be in a conversational manner. The message should be capable of being put into writing. Cheerful consent, feeling of warmth of the listener are necessary.

The speaker must use a personal greeting while starting a speech, the salutation in oral communication to the listener.

It is always desirable to call the person by name say "Dear Mr. Saxena" but not "Dear Sir". Use the person's name once or twice during oral conversation.

Showing appreciation towards listeners is a technique for building goodwill. It involves being grateful to the audience. The speaker must wish to show his personal appreciation for what they have listened. It means giving thanks to an appreciative audience. Every listener likes to be appreciated. The success of speech depends entirely on the speaker's satisfaction with his listeners. The listener likes to be treated as an individual and to feel recognised as a person.

Showing awareness and interest in listeners as individuals is the desirable quality of successful communication. He can say: It gives me great pleasure to inform you. I am happy to learn that you are joining the organisation. He must make honest efforts to make the other person feel better or more important.

The communicator has to open his speech with a smile. It involves showing pleasure. It is an act of a smiling speech or the resulting facial expression. It gives clues to feelings and meanings. In the process a happy frame of mind when speaking means that pleasantness and friendliness will pass through what is spoken. This is particularly necessary when taking favourable action. It demands a happy attitude to be apparent from the very beginning.

Another technique for building goodwill among the audience is to make the listeners feel important. Due importance should be given to the listeners. The purpose of speech is to make them understand the message. This can be achieved by showing appreciation for listeners and by taking a personal interest in listening to them and clarifying their doubts. It is an art and tact of the speaker to make them feel important. Speaking from their point of view and mentioning various practical instances also makes them feel important.

Goodwill is a friendly and kindly attitude. A listener's goodwill is a major object of oral communication. Indicating acceptance of suggestions by the listeners will go a long way towards achieving a successful speech. Indicating attention and acknowledgement of what is being suggested will produce positive and favourable reactions from listeners. It will create a friendly confident feeling towards the communicator. Creating impression is a very difficult task. It is reciprocal and can be applied in all speeches. A speech can be given, but one must remember the listener's goodwill.

Empathy is important in a speech to a group or audience. Empathy means ability to understand and share the feelings, experiences, opinions etc., of listeners. A certain empathy must exist between the speaker and the listener. It is necessary to show every consideration for the listener that will create interest and persuade the listener. To show empathy with listeners is the projection of one's personality into the listeners in order to understand the listeners better.

Language is very essential in good communication. A person can adapt his own language but should speak at the listener's level. This will make message pleasing and interesting. An individual listener is interested in listening to anything which satisfies his purpose and desire. A pleasing message not only puts the speaker at ease but also relaxes his listeners.

Honesty : If the speaker is genuinely interested in the listeners' viewpoint, then the speaker should be honest in his response. Honesty in speech promotes confidence among the listeners.

The style in which a speaker dresses communicates something to listeners. Communicating with acceptable and gentle dress is one of the most direct and silent ways of communication.

John Molloy believes that the way a person dresses communicates something to others. He is a dress consultant with major corporations. In his interview with a series of questions of more than hundred top company executives revealed many interesting features on communicating with good personal appearance. Some of his findings in his book *Dress for Success* are as follows :

(1) He showed executives five pictures of men each wearing expensive, tailored, but high-fashion clothing. He asked the executives if this was proper dress for a junior business executive. Ninety-two said no, eight said yes.

(2) He showed them five additional pictures of the same people neatly dressed in conservative clothing and asked if they were dressed properly for a young executive. All said yes.

(3) He showed them five additional pictures of the same people obviously dressed in lower-middle class attire and asked

if these people were dressed properly for a young executive. Forty-six said yes, fifty-four said no.

(4) He then asked the executives if they thought that the people dressed in the middle-class suit would succeed better in corporate life than those dressed in the lower middle-class suit. Eighty-eight said yes, twelve said no.

How physical movements or keeping still stand in relation to the audience one is communicating with has a real impact on communication. A message or idea is often communicated through action. A person's gesture also communicates meaning. The movements give us clues to a person's self-confidence or interest in the topic. If a person is not interested in a subject he may more likely lean on chair.

The technique of being amusing is a very important characteristic that most good communicators possess. The ability to amuse people when speaking means that pleasantness and friendliness will permeate what is spoken. Especially, when taking any decision, or action, let a speaker's humorous attitude be apparent from the very beginning, opening with a smile. It is the most desirable feature of oral communication. Being amusing, conversation and speech naturally not only puts the speaker at ease, but also relaxes his listeners. Understanding the right situation and using the technique of humour whenever an opportunity arises will increase the speaker's speaking ability.

Making a speech humorous or witty is a technique to build goodwill, provided the wit is relevant to the context and effective. Jokes or anecdotes are recommended when used carefully otherwise the image of the speaker goes down. Corwin's Law: "Never make people laugh. If you could succeed in life you must be solemn, solemu as an ass. All the great monuments are built over solemn asses." "Never try to make people laugh at the wrong time or just for the sake of being entertaining make joke teach a point." Markel says "Humour is okay, wit can be dangerous, wisecracking is disastrous."

Sometimes, it may be necessary to use visual or audio-visual aids in support of speech. Their use is recommended for effective presentation of matter. It is practically possible to use electrical or electronic tools. The speech is nearly always combined with media like charts, graphs, tables, TV, visual projections from equipment etc. The speaker must see where they can be used rightly, and use only those aids which will carry the message.

Prepare a brief note of the subject matter of the speech and distribute it to the audience. Handouts serve the audience and act as permanent reminders of the speaker's message. Whatever is heard in the meeting may be forgotten soon after the speech is over.

Accent is another important factor to be achieved in good speech. It is a thing which may prevent meaning from being clear. If a person is speaking in an accent which is not familiar to the hearers, they may be worrying about the meaning of a word which he has used while he is saying the next phrase, and so they do not even listen to the second phrase. The word accent covers two separate meanings. It is used in some contexts to mean extra breath-force on a word or syllable (stress) : it is also used to indicate the differences of pronunciations heard in different parts of our own country.

Now we all hear our own voice and speech from inside ourselves while other people hear us only from the outside, so it is difficult to know, without a mechanical aid, how we actually do sound to others. Now that so many people own tape-recorders, it is a good idea to listen to ourselves through one of these useful instruments. Listening to a record does not, in itself, make speech better; it only makes us aware of good and bad points in our own voice and speech and in our use of speech, as mumbling, hesitation, dullness and repetition are noticeable on a record especially in an unprepared conversation. When we have become aware of our faults, hard and concentrated work is usually required in order to alter our habits.

A point about speech which is beyond the very practical points raised above, is the actual quality of the voice itself. Some people are more sensitive to this than others, or perhaps it would be truer to say that they are more consciously so. A beautiful voice in itself is interesting and pleasant to listen to, but here again another warning must be given: the owner of a lovely voice often takes great pleasure in listening to himself and anyone who does this is apt to go off the track. Another point is that he may be talking of something ugly or unpleasant, and then the unsuitability of a lovely tone makes him sound insincere.

In fact suitability of voice and speech to the subject is even more important than the acoustics of the room. In addition, the style should be suited to the audience and to the situation: a good speaker uses different styles when he is speaking, for instance, to small children, to adult students interested in his subject or to the guests at a wedding reception.

Dressing by people differ from place to place and from country to country like the dress of army men, naval personnel, airport personnel; dressing by religious heads, political leaders, lawyers, doctors, sports people etc. Likewise thoughts are so dressed by speakers as to gain the attention and interest of the audience. This is a fundamental principle of motivating the audience. Swami Vivekananda began his address at the Parliament of Religions in Chicago as "brothers and sisters"— Not "distinguished ladies and gentlemen", as others did before Swamiji's turn had come. Similarly it is more apprcpriate to quote the speech of the great Congress leader Chittaranjan Das to a vast audience, "I feel the weight of iron chains over my body, the handcuffs in my wrist; it is the agony of bondage; the whole of India is a vast prison...."

The Directions

Audience : The communicator should know his audience and accordingly put ideas across. If the audience or listeners are not able to understand, it is an ineffective communication.

Ideas : The transmitter should have clear information to be communicated. One must be clear about the ideas, opinions, facts to be communicated, otherwise one cannot make these clear.

Ambiguity : Using words in current use is important and to avoid words which convey vague meaning. A vague communication gives confusion in communication.

Conditions : Necessary physical conditions, facilities and environment are to be provided to both the speaker and listeners.

Not to Talk and Talk : Speak only that much sufficient to convey the central idea of the subject matter. A verbal communication should be short, clear and simple to pass message.

Gestures and Tone : The style in which the message is conveyed is as important as what is being said. There must be an integration between facial expression, voice, gestures and mood to the action of what is said.

Not to Talk to Impress : The purpose of communication is not to impress but to express, to inspire confidence and to make people understand. Expressing and conveying a better message makes an impression. It is not a good communication if the speaker tries to conceal, confess, intimidate and to impress.

Feedback : Feedback is probably the most important method of improving communication. Two-way process ensures feedback. The communicator has to obtain feedback from the receiver.

Emphasis on Purpose : The subject matter and its theme should be greatly emphasised to draw the attention of the listener.

Avoid Extremes : Some subject matters are too good or too bad. It is desirable to avoid extremes in speaking.

Cultivate Listening : Listening is different from hearing. Listening and understanding require a lot of reasoning and attitude. The reasons of non-listening are boredom, bias, fear, interruption etc.

Clarify Ideas : The communicator has first to clarify his ideas himself before : think on the message clearly and clarify ideas to ensure effective communication.

Purpose : The purpose of communication is to make others understand the subject matter. The communication is ineffective if the purpose is not achieved.

Physical and Human Setting : An atmosphere of confidence, mutual trust is to be created in the process of communication. It is mainly the responsibility of the superiors. The informal relations is the best weapon to promote physical and human setting in the organization.

What is the Basis ? : In oral communication, the important question arises is as to what are the different forms of tools of oral communication. Media of oral communication means tools or vehicles of communication. The instrument or instruments used or applied in conversation, speech, talk to convey a message is/are termed as medium/media of communication. The problem of misunderstanding in group activities or improper implementation of business objectives or broad policies laid down by the top management arises from poor communication. The aims of an organization can be achieved with effective communication. Transfer of message by any medium available is essential in any organisation like, private, public, productive, service, educational institutions, Government departments, undertaking, assembly, etc.

However, it needs to be emphasised at this point to account for the important and popular media of oral communication.

To make communication effective, appropriate medium or media may be selected to meet a particular situation which the speaker endeavours to put across. All media may not be useful in all circumstances. A particular medium or instrument may be more useful as a conveyor belt carrying a message to a particular group. Any medium may be considered good only when the listener receives, understands and responds to that or acts accordingly. Diverse educational background, mental aptitude, position occupied, responsibilities, importance of the message, urgency etc., call for different media of oral communication. As such a particular medium of communication cannot be applied to all cases. The chief executive's medium of communication is different to a medium applied by a foreman. Similarly, the medium of communication would certainly vary when the politician wants to convey his ideas. Similarly, the medium of communication would also vary when the Government wants the public to be informed about the welfare and development programmes and achievements during a particular period. Again, the medium of communication would definitely vary when a teacher wants to convey a message or to educate about a subject.

In this connection it is, therefore, very necessary to choose an appropriate medium, because the success of communication depends upon the selection of an appropriate instrument or instruments to make effective communication. Oral communication has mostly and primarily been adopted as a media for many purposes. The forms of oral communication are many and varied which may be briefly discussed below.

Issue Discussion

Face to face conversation is the most effective type of communication. It has certain advantages. Certain things can be done orally more effectively than written communication, Though modern scientific machines like telephones are used as a device for verbal communication it is not a face to face communication. There are many media in oral communication in which there is no personal contact. It is only in face to face communication that information can be satisfactorily conveyed. Explanations, notes etc., as used to written communication need not necessarily be used in this method because necessary clarifications, explanations and doubts can be exchanged orally without loss of time. A face to face communication gives an opportunity of observing facial expressions, reactions and gives effective feedback on the matter. When the communicator and the recipient are talking together sitting face to face there is a definite understanding. Opinions can be expressed freely, opposed, offers and counter offers and clarifications take place then and there only which are most essential for effective decision making. The verbal words are more direct and personal. Word of mouth exposes feelings and actions. The acceptance or rejection can be better understood and necessary clarifications can be given. But the communicator must choose words so that the receiver will be sure to understand them correctly. The following are some of the important principles of effective face to face communication :

1. To avoid waste of time and thought of both.
2. The message must reveal the necessary facts.
3. The vocabulary level of the receiver must be considered.
4. To convey the message in the way we feel towards the receiver.
5. The manner and style and temperaments are equally important.
6. Appropriate fitting words to be chosen to convey the central message.
7. Short sentences, clear words, currently in use should be used.

Benjamin Balinsky put it : "If there is any short-cut to executive effectiveness, it is the mastery of the art of face-to-face communication."

Telephonic Consultation

A telecommunication device. A communication device for speaking directly to someone at a distant place. The instrument may use either an electric current or radiowave.

The telephone is an instrument for speaking to someone from a distance. The message is transmitted using either an electric current which passes along a wire or radio waves. One speaks to another by means of a telephone. A telephonist is a person who operates a telephone switchboard at a telephone exchange. Telephone exchange is a central control through which telephone calls are directed. Under the direct dial system one can speak to someone from a distance directly without the assistance of the telephone exchange. Telephonic communication is very essential to create a good impression. It has a good potential for providing two-way interaction between the speaker and listener. This medium is particularly useful when people are scattered over a vast area in an organisation or otherwise. Telephone has thus in recent years come to be used for direct contact. Under this one can hear a natural voice and is more clear in telephonic communication. It is recognised that the telephone is one of the oral communication devices to save time and get things done quickly. But in telephonic communication one should be precise, clear in presenting the message. Similarly it is not desirable to allow the telephone to ring for long because it leads to annoyance. In recent years in many organisations the intercom system has been introduced. Intercom is a system of communication within an organisation usually by means of microphones and loud speakers. The telephone directory is a book containing the list of names, addresses and telephone numbers of all the people in a particular area who have telephone facilities. It provides quick reference of a particular number required. The directory may be compiled covering a limited local area, a taluk, district, state and may also be a national telephone directory.

Prior Meetings

Another medium of oral communication is a conference. A

conference means a meeting for discussion. A conference is the pooling of thoughts of two or more individuals to assist in solving problems. The conference of political leaders, conference of chief executives, conference of press reporters, conference of scientists etc., is convened to discuss and find a solution to the problems of their interest. In a conference mutual problems constitute the subject of discussion. Eminent and expert participants contribute their thoughts and experience in solving a problem. It is a joint effort of the people gathered. They interact, exchange with others, teach each other and learn together.

Thus a conference is an assembly of a group of persons gathered to exchange information for some particular purpose. The words conference and meeting are generally used interchangeably. The group may be small or large. Similarly there is no difference between speaking in a conference and a meeting. A conference is also called a convention when it is attended by a large number of people. In a conference the speaker speaks his own ideas and opinions on the subject on which the conference is conducted. All the speakers present their own solutions or opinions and the leader of the conference summarises the proceedings. In this type of oral communication the success is based on the thought process and how well the members are stimulated.

Press Conference : It is a gathering of journalists and press reporters. In a press conference journalists and reporters from various news agencies are invited to participate and to listen and cover in the press. A press conference may be with politicians, Government, corporate executives, local bodies, educational institutions, voluntary agencies etc. The purpose of a press conference is to appraise a situation, problems, achievements, progress, public matters etc. Press reporters are supplied with pamphlets covering information and statistical data so as to enable them to cover in the press. The conference enables the press to carry messages to the public. The press is entitled to raise questions and solicit replies or explanations. In a democratic set-up the press conference is the powerful media of mass communication.

Operative Acts : Action and message is a communication medium called a demonstration. This media is mostly adopted by corporate marketing strategy. Demonstration is also used to educate the voter as to how to exercise his franchise. The demonstration is the part of the sales presentation where a salesman proves that his company's product will do all. The purpose of the demonstration is to maintain the interest that was aroused on previous occasions and to build desire in the mind of the prospect. The salesman shows and states the benefits that the prospect will receive, supported by facts. He places the product in the hands of the prospect for his examination. The demonstration gives the prospect the opportunity to experience for himself the benefits to be obtained from using a particular product. Everyone would rather enjoy a pleasant experience than just be told about it by another person.

Radio's Role

The radio is a vehicle of a mass medium. It is a type of communication technology. Radio is extensively used for broadcasting many programmes mainly because of its wide accessibility and relatively low cost. It is a one way communication system. But some institutions in the advanced countries like New Zealand and Australia have evolved radio tutorials and radio conferences. It is the only audio medium. Nassif suggested that the audio-visual electronic programme used must be complementary to other media. The effective use of radio for correspondence courses began in Japan in 1976.

Recording is a process which involves recording a programme at a particular place. The process of making a record of something like a message, talk, interview especially on a record or on a tape. A record player is an electrical instrument which reproduces the sounds recorded on records. The information or statements recorded are intended to be repeated or made public. It is written down or recorded for future reference. Recordings make it possible to capture a speech or radio programme and replay it by radio before an audience or over a public address system anywhere. Some recordings are made on the spot at special occasions or events. In other cases special programmes are deliberately produced at a recording studio.

In-oral communication a mechanical dictating machine is called a dictaphone. It dictates correspondence read for another to write down through the dictating machine. Dictating machines by a combination of electronics and mechanical means record the voice. The transcriber reproduces the voice. The machines are most popular and used for dictation of correspondence, recording of proceedings, conferences, recording of interviews and are used for market research. The advantages of using dictating machnines are : (1) They save time. (2) Reduce the cost involved in corresponding work. (3) The mistakes in hearing by typists are avoided. (4) Speed and accuracy can be achieved. (5) Personal presence of the typist or stenographer is avoided. (6) Because of inter-room connections dictation is possible without the presence of a steno. (7) The advantage of centralisation can be achieved.

Thus there are many types and models of dictaphones. The main function is to record the dictation and transcribing to play back and transcribe the dictation by switching on the machine which is recorded on a magnetic tape or plastic disc. Making use of the dictaphone to be effective in communication demands and calls for following certain norms. They are : (1) Clear pronunciation, *(2)* clarity, (3) simplicity. (4) short sentences, (5) stop when interruption takes place. (6) avoid pipe, gum, cigar in mouth while dictating, and (7) dictation should be read back.

In a real world situation meeting are yet another media of oral communication. In a democratic set-up meetings are a common method. In a restless age of communication meetings are business. A message can easily and understandably be communicated through the media of meetings. Message is carried in family meetings, street gatherings, samiti meetings, panchayat meetings, parishad meetings, municipal meetings, municipal corporation meetings and political meetings. Assembly and Parliamentary meetings. Meetings may be convened regularly and in extraordinary circumstances. In corporate management we frequently come across company meetings. A company may conduct several types of meetings to convey the ideas of the company for the purpose of taking decisions. The usual company meetings are statutory meetings, annual general meetings, extraordinary general meetings, Board of Directors meetings, shareholders meetings, debenture holders meetings, creditors meetings, etc. Meetings are gatherings of groups of persons belonging to a particular interest to whom, as groups, some common matters or issues are entrusted. At meetings information is communicated orally, discussed, deliberated and debated to come to a solution or decision. Meetings are supposed to be of democratic origin.

Sometimes special invitees, *ex-office.* Government nominees and institutional representatives are invited to have their specialised and technical advice for consideration. Meetings ensure collective decisions. Collective decisions are taken with oral discussions sitting in meetings, hence fear of authority being concentrated in one person is avoided. A meeting may be informational, advisory, or problem solving. In an informational meeting the object is to present ideas, and data to the members. In advisory types of meetings the purpose is to gather and seek advice, information, suggestions relating to a problem. The object of a problem solving meeting is to seek a decision, solution out of the collective discussion and mutual understanding of a problem. Thu is in meetings communication flows both ways. Discussion is an important object of a meeting. In this verbal form of communication the group acts as a team with responsibility since it helps in arriving at a collective decision.

A rumour is an oral information circulating something. It sometimes passes unfounded news from person to person. In a rumour, communication is a piece of news or story passed from one person to another which may not be true. A verbal general talk or gossip. A loud untrue sound. It is a talk or report of a person or thing in someway noted or distinguished. The fact of being generally talked about fosters reputation and renown.

A rumour is a verbal statement or report circulating in a group, of the truth of which there is no clear evidence. A rumour once spread is not soon removed. A rumour spreads like anything and may create wonders and miracles as a channel of informal communication. The two persons involved in a rumour are: rumour spreader and rumour bearer. The originator of a rumour is also called as rumour monger. In the grapevine the leader of a group tells the message to each person in that group. A communication leader recognises rumours. The leader must be trustworthy and have credibility.

The management can use rumours for effective communication.

The information can be fed into the informal channel to dispel rumours and to provide quick and easy access to the information.

Model Rumours

1. A rumour circulating that the managing director is going abroad.
2. Rumour passing from one person to another person about the change in holiday arrangements.
3. News that the secretary got a new job.
4. A person rumoured that a colleague has left the country.
5. It is rumoured that they are getting transferred.

Demonstration and Dramatization Method : This is a method in which "doing" skills may be shown, explained and applied. Demonstration is made and dramatized as a means of giving emphasis to the subject under consideration.

Public Message

In oral communication, the public address system is another important dimension. It is a mechanical system. It is a system adopted at meetings, shows, carnivals, meals exhibitions, gathering of employees or mass audience. Through the public address system if is possible mechanically to project the human voice spread among a large gathering. Mounted on a minitruck or any other mobile auto the PA system can be transported from place to place, presenting speakers and programmes as it goes, and reaching a widely distributed audience. Sound tracks can also be rigged up at stationary locations, providing facilities for meetings and special programmes in lieu of a permanently installed PA system. Portable bull horns afford great mobility wherever amplified sound is needed.

Informal Manners

Informal communication is termed as grapevine. So the informal medium in oral communication, as the very name implies, is based on informal relationship of the people in the organisation. A successful management must recognise and give importance to the grapevine. It is also known as grapevine communication and means an informal communication network constituted to pass a message speedily. When an informal channel is used to communicate, it is termed as grapevine or informal communication. It is not a deliberately created and officially prescribed channel for flow of information, hence free from all sorts of formalities. The network is formed out of personal relationships, social and group relations, but not out of position of line and authority, superior, and subordinate, or based on organisational hierarchy. It is a quick vehicle for a message. Informal communication may be conveyed by a simple glance, gesture, smile or mere silence. It is composed of a series of small groups of people linked to one another covering everyone in the organisation.

One person in the group passes the message to each person in a particular group. The individuals of the group in turn pass the message to someone in another group. Because of inter group links and chains the message quickly passes to everyone. There are communication leaders in the grapevine and the management can make use of them to communicate. On the other hand, management may create its own grapevine.

L. Brown clearly describes the advantages of the grapevine to the management in the words— "advantages to management include expediency — it saves time, gets immediate response; provides useful feedback for decision-making; generates ideas and suggestions that may prove helpful; disseminates accurate, factual information that needs to be relayed. In using the grapevine, management must be able to pinpoint the leaders and work through them, must feed in factual information, listen to the feedback response, and be discerning in not overloading the system and using it inappropriately."

Discussion in a Mess

In the context of group discussion it is more appropriate to quote Robert Bales who defines : "A small group is defined as any number of persons engaged in interaction with one another in a single face-to-face meeting or series of such meetings in which each member receives some impression or perception of each other member distinctive enough so that he can, either at the time. or in later questioning give some reaction to each of the others as an individual person, even though it be only to recall that the other was present."

In a group discussion members of the group are in interaction with one another. A group may be a small group or large group. There are no fixed norms as to the right size for a group, it all depends upon circumstances of a particular case. A group is headed by a leader generally called the chairman, controller of group discussion. A group may be a casual group, permanent group, learning group, policy making group and action group. For certain reasons groups are formed to take a decision or to carry out some activities. Communication in the group takes place in the form of deliberations among the leaders and group members. Group reaches decisions after discussion.

Group decisions are collective opinions. Group decisions through discussions are superior and better to an individual decision which is one sided. Group discussion is a process of decision making where communication exchange on validity, reasonability, practicability, time and cost factors are interacted. Thus group discussion involves defining a problem, generating solutions, analysing alternative solutions, identifying a balanced solution, selecting the best solution, implementing the solution and evaluating the results.

Audio News

Oral report means presentation of written matter before a group. One must have oral communication skills for oral report presentation. This method is used in every business activity and at every level. The originator of an oral report presents an informational and analytical message. The essentials of good speaking will equally apply to oral reports. According to L. Brown,' "The function of an oral report is to furnish he facts necessary to expedite action or to persuade someone or any number of persons to take the action the group decided on or to implement the group's solution."

Like in an oral message an oral report to be effective must carefully be planned and developed. When a report is orally read before a gathering it is similar to oral presentation and should be written in such a manner. An oral report is generally drafted for a particular group of people. For instance, an oral report to a welfare committee, an oral report to a conference of salesmen and an oral report to the executives of all the departments. Like a speech oral reports have an introduction, body and ending. With a view to clarify certain things or to create interest audio-visual aids may be used.

A successful and effective oral report must follow certain essential principles. Some of the principles are :

(1) A report should be complete, clear and short.

(2) To practise report reading by imagining an audience.

(3) To set a gentle style and tone.

(4) To know the audience.

(5) To fix a time limit to read.

(6) To divide a report into paragraphs, each paragraph should give a separate central idea.

(7) Other principles of good oral communication and written communication are equally applicable.

The following are logical steps to acquire self-confidence to present an oral report, suggested by Leland Brown :

1. "Preparing your talk carefully. Fear of forgetting result in stage fright.
2. Practising aloud you will know your talk better after rehearsing. Practise alone, going over it again and again, imagining your audience before you, or viewing yourself in a mirror.
3. By not memorizing your talk; a tape recorder can be helpful for it allows you to hear yourself.
4. Checking your appearance. Dress appropriately for the occasion and your audience.
5. When you face your group, waiting a few minutes before you start to talk. Think of your audience as your friends. They want you to do well. Do not think about yourself.
6. Beginning slowly; do not give up once you have begun. Stage fright disappears after you start.

7. Speaking louder than ordinarily, at least at the outset.
8. Speaking as often as you can. The more practice you get, the easier it is to speak with confidence.

A medium of oral communication operates by using a television set. The television camera is connected to the receiving set. The camera scans the picture to be transmitted. The camera converts the picture into electrical signals, i.e., video, signals video amplifier applies the range of frequencies Amplitude modulated picture transmitter is a circuit which places visual information on a career wave. The microphones convert audio signals into electrical signals. The complete process gives us continuous viewing of pictures and his to listening.

5

MAGAZINE SETUP

Magazines disseminate more specialised information; they carry articles and commentary to diverse readers. A newspaper generally reports the happenings of the last 24 hours. The tempo of work is very fast since it has to appear every morning. In comparison, magazines-weeklies, fortnightlies, monthlies, have more time to plan and publish. They attract wide and divers audience. The contents are marked by high quality and pictorial stuff. In India, we intermingle the terms magazines, journals and periodicals, although they have different connotations. The term "magazine" indicates a stitched paperback of writing by different authors and traditionally a medium of light entertainment. It includes articles or stories or both and it is published at regular intervals. Most magazines include illustrations as well as advertisements. Writings of different types ranging from factual or practical reporting to more personal or emotional accounts regularly appear in these publications. The word magazine is derived from the Arabic word. Makhasin meaning warehouse or khazane, that is, a store-up.

The word "Journal" means a diary or daily record and covers all periodical publications providing such information. These also carry serious or scholarly articles with or without illustrations and advertisements. The word "periodical" simply means a publication other than a daily, which comes out with a fixed periodicity-every week, every fortnight, every month and so on.

However, distinctions among these terms are fading out. Whether it is Sunday. The Week, India Today, Sarita or Malayala Manorama Weekly, they are called by any of these names. The periodicity of these publications can be weekly, fortnightly, monthly, quarterly and half annually. Even annuals are included among the periodicals.

Whatever be the term employed, these periodical publications contain some built-in merits. They provide a wide variety of information, opinion and entertainment. They are designed to be kept by the readers for a much longer time than daily newspapers. The magazines are centrally stitched and the publishers use more colours and variegated typographical and layout designs. They even print their magazines on better quality paper. Compared to dailies, folders or pamphlets, magazines provide reading material of enduring interest and contain different shades of opinion. That way they can better inform on a theme or event and stimulate more critical, pointed and segmented deliberations on it. Besides tantalising covers, the topics covered by the magazines vary from science to fiction, from current affairs to fine arts, and from social sciences to religion and philosophy. At the same time, they carry amusement of all sorts-stories, pun, satire, humour, cartoons, comics and various other types of light reading material. No wonder that magazines are purchased by as many as 36 million readers in India while dailies are bought only by 27 million people.

For their visual appeals, titillating covers, pretty graphics and typographical variety, decorative boxes, drop letters, neatly cropped pictures, and other innovative devices are employed by the magazines to hold the attention of the readers. With catchy titles, cryptic captions, racy or feature style of writing, the focus is on current controversies. Besides, fun and frolic make magazines highly readable. They cater to the states of a wide variety of readers. For discerning eyes, they have much more to offer. For these reasons, some people call magazines the TV of the printed word. The increasing race among the publishers to lure the readers by making their magazines more attractive and better than others turn magazines into a feast for the eyes. The readership of magazines is by and large confined to somewhat influential, affluent and discriminating sections of the people. They cover important events, in-depth and investigative reports and sensational revelations. For these characteristics the magazines are called the 4th Estate in Japan and are proving to be that in India also.

Media, as a Force

Magazines fast are becoming the strongest of the mass media. While individual magazines may find their growth limited by greater competition for advertiser dollars, magazines as a group are more prosperous in readers and in revenues than at any time in their recent history. Not since the so-called golden age of magazines in the late 1800s has this mass medium been so strong.

Three factors contribute most to the collective strength of magazines: specialization, technology, and innovation. Specialization refers to a continuing trend away from general interest publications and toward ..magazines ever more tightly focused on narrowly defined subject matter. Technology has supported the trend toward specialization by reducing the cost of publishing, primarily through use of computer-based systems. Innovation involves progressively more creative concepts to produce audiences attractive to prospective advertisers and therefore rewarding to entrepreneurs.

These factors yet may produce another golden age in which magazines are the nation's prominent mass medium. Industry performance since 1962, as described by the Magazine Publishers of America (MPA), suggests that magazines Publishers of America (MPA), suggests that magazines at minimum are becoming the nation's primary source of contemporary information. While MPA is a partisan source, the association's data are persuasive. The persuasiveness is heightened when the data are examined in the context of information published by independent sources.

At least one negative factor also is introduced by an dependent source, however, in the form of data regarding the comprehension of print communication. Researchers working under the sponsorship of the Advertising Educational Foundation have found print communications-specifically, magazines-to be less effective communication vehicles than some believe to be the case.

Miscomprehension : The researchers, Jacob Jacoby and Wayne D. Hoyer, examined a series of questions critical to advertisers and others who depend on the efficiency of mass media:

1. What is the average level of comprehension among magazine readers?
2. Does comprehension level vary with type of content?
3. Do socio-demographic differences influence comprehension?

Research data were gathered by administering quizzes to readers after they were exposed to magazine communication. Results were not reassuring to those who depend on the effectiveness or efficiency of printed communication.

Comprehension Levels : Only 63 percent of the questions posed by the researchers were answered accurately. Twenty one percent of respondents misunderstood the messages to which they had been exposed, while the remainder indicated they did not know.

Among the 1,347 who participated in the study, only 10 percent answered all questions correctly. Seventy four percent misunderstood a part of what they had read. The remainder of responses were in the "don't know" category. In general, the researchers found, only 63 percent of messages in magazines are understood. A small but significant variation in comprehension was found between advertising and editorial content. Normative miscomprehension of advertisements ranged from 15 to 23 percent while miscomprehension of editorial content was in the 19 to 28 percent range.

Socio-demographics : Differences in comprehension recorded among respondent subgroups were small. Miscomprehension tended to increase slightly in those over the age of fifty four. Those with less than ninth grade education experienced more miscomprehension than others, and a small inverse relationship was found between income and miscomprehension. No significant gender difference were detected, but facts were found to be markedly less prone to misconception than inferences.

Perhaps most interesting in terms of Socio-demographics are differences between the finding of this study and data gathered by the researchers during a similar project dealing with the electronic media. Sociographic and demographic factors accounted for far greater variation in comprehension in the electronic media than among magazines.

The Impact

Although less than perfect as channels of communication, magazines exert a growing influence among mass media. The most persuasive data concerning the influence of magazines arises out of a trend toward specialization. The depth and breadth of the specialization trend is most apparent in the several magazine directories used by advertisers and others. Standard Rate and Data Service's consumer magazine directory, for example, is little more than a third the bulk and weight of the company's directory of trade magazines. Within the consumer directory, in addition, are found a relative handful of what might be termed general interest publications. Magazines today might be better categorized as general interest, special interest, and super-special interest, with the letter category consisting of publications catering to business, the professions and academia.

Publications is the critical word in the sentence above. The word encompasses newspapers and newsletters as well as magazines. Definitions that might permit accurately sorting out the components of those categories are another matter.

Journalists generally are strict constructionists in defining the word newspaper. They apply broader definitions to magazine and newsletter, and the results can be confusing to lay persons. Many publications that appear to be newspapers are classified by professionals as magazines and, as a result, numbered as magazines by those who publish media directories.

Definitional Characteristics : Much of the definition problem has to do with criteria used in sorting out or differentiating between and among newspapers, newsletters, and magazines. Ambiguity is the prevalent characteristic of contemporary definitions, regardless of source.

Webster defines a magazine as "a periodical that usually contains a miscellaneous collection of articles, stories, poems and pictures and is directed at the general reading public" and as "a periodical containing special interest material directed at a group having a particular hobby, interest or profession (as education, photography or medicine) or at a particular age group (as children, teenagers)." The two definitions more or less adequately cover general and special interest magazines.

A newspaper, in contrast, is defined as "a paper that is printed and distributed daily, weekly, or at some other regular and usually short interval and that contains news, articles of opinion (as editorials), features, advertising, or other matter regarded as of current interest. A newsletter is defined as "a printed sheet, pamphlet, or small newspaper containing news or information of current interest to or bearing upon the interests of a special group."

Variables that these definitions address include (a) frequency or regularity of publication, (b) nature of content, and (c) nature of audience. None of these characteristics, unfortunately, can be defined with sufficient precision to circumscribe any media group. All publications that appear daily are newspapers but the newspaper category also encompasses weekly and bi-weekly publications. Many magazines and newsletters also appear at weekly intervals.

Differences in content between articles, as specific to general interest magazines, and news, as specific to newspapers, are more difficult to define. Much of the content of the major weekly news magazines-Time, Newsweek, and U.S. News & World Report-would be as much at home in newspaper as in magazine format. In like mariner, much of the content of a Sunday edition of The New York Times or The Washington Post could be published by one of the news magazines without departing from any apparent content standard.

Newsletters usually are readily identified by their relative brevity and format. Much of their content, however, could make the transition to a magazine or newspaper with little difficulty. A number of magazines in special and general interest categories, for example, contain pages composed in a manner resembling the typewriter format of the kiplinger Washington Letter.

Presumed experts have taken divergent approaches to defining types of print media. Some have managed to write extensively about newspapers and magazines without venturing concise definitions. Others who made the effort fell short of establishing all-encompassing categories to make discussions more easily managed.

Author and media critic Ben Bagdikian, himself a former print (New York Times) journalist, defines a newspaper as a publication that carriers information on newsprint for a general audience that is issued daily, weekly, or on Sunday. (There have, in the history of U.S. journalism, been several newspapers that printed only on Sunday.) Bagdikian's definition would exclude some publications that virtually every authority considers to be newspapers and would include others that few would consider worthy inclusion. The Wall Street Journal, for example, would have to be excluded from a Bagdikian list in that it is not directed toward a general audience. Many shoppers and advertising circulars would have to be included.

Among those who manage to successfully avoid definitions while dealing effectively with extensive descriptions of the media are two teams of textbook authors. Warren Agee, Phillip Ault and Edwin Emery describe newspapers and magazines at length in Introduction to Mass Communications, as do Ray Hiebert, Donald Ungurait and Thomas Bohn in Mass Media. In neither of these books are individual media precisely defined, and probably for good reason. No debate over the nature of specific mass media is apt to be productive in an era of rapid change. Historically, the word magazine was derived from the French and referred to a warehouse or storehouse. Early magazines, in fact, were compendia of information previously printed elsewhere. Newspapers, in contrast, usually contained originally written material.

Distinctions such as these today have blurred to a point at which they are all but meaningless. The blurring, moreover, is proceeding at a rate that raises questions as to the meanings of basic media language. Consider, for example, some of the publications serving the media industry. Editor and Publisher, most would agree, is a magazine. Advertising Age, however, appears in tabloid format and use a makeup style more akin to traditional newspapers than to magazines.

Any two individuals who agree on the basic nature of Editor

and Publisher and Advertising Age may want to entertain themselves by attempting to characterize TV Sports. This advertiser supported magazine was launched by ESPN, the cable television station sports station, primarily to carry broadcast listings. Is the result a competitor to TV Guide, an item of direct mail advertising, or a printed version of television content akin to the soap opera magazines?

Your conclusion concerning an appropriate label of TV Sports, or any other magazine, is unlikely to detract from the evident trend toward specialization in the magazine sector as a whole. Of the almost 500 magazines launched in 1987, only 180 were of the consumer variety and only 10, or about 2 percent of the total, were categorized by the Magazine Publisher Association as general interest.

MPA data are straightforward but may be somewhat misleading, as indicated by the definitional questions addressed above. This is especially so in MPA's city and regional interest category. Broadly defined, city and regional interest can cover a host of publications that might as readily be assigned to special interest categories. What category, for example, is logically home to an entertainment magazine oriented to a relatively small geographic area? Both its and regional interest and entertainment categories would be defensible choices.

Different Aspects

While numerical estimates vary, history and logic suggest that only a small percentage of magazines launched each year will survive. New launches continue, however, because of magazines' ability to target and deliver specific audiences to waiting advertisers. Targetability or selectivity is the most attractive feature of magazines from the viewpoints of publishers and advertisers. Magazines also are attractive in that they are better "attended" than competing media. Magazines are sought out and selected by their readers. Rather than being casually watched or scanned as a matter of course, magazines tend to be closely read. More than three quarters of all magazines are purchased by subscription rather than in single copies. In addition, magazines tend to be closely read. More than three quarters of all magazines are purchased by subscription rather than in single copies. In addition, magazines equal or outperform newspapers in exposure to white collar readers.

Finally, magazines are best equipped to deliver complex information and provide high quality reproduction. Magazine audiences are interested in the in-depth treatment of subject matter in which their publications specialize. The nature of magazine production processes enables publishers to provide better reproduction than is possible in newspapers for advertisers and readers. These attributes collectively have triggered a growth pattern that continues to accelerate.

Magazines have increased consistently in number, in total circulation, and in advertiser patronage through the last half of the twentieth century. The growth pattern apparently persists because of the relative quality of magazine audiences from user as well as advertiser standpoints.

Both perspectives were illustrated by a 1986 study of magazine and television advertising conducted by Audits and Surveys. Men and women both rated magazines superior by significant margins.

Magazine circulation in the United States has grown more rapidly than the nation's population since mid-century. From 197 million in 1962, magazine circulation increased to 236 million in 1972 and 291 million in 1982. By 1987, the total had reached 336 million.

Advertising revenues grew at approximately the same rate as circulation during the 1960s and early 1970s but increased rapidly during the 1980s. From $850 million in 1962, revenues grew to $1.3 billion in 1972 then more than tripled to $3.42 billion in 1982. The 1987 total was $5.39 billion. Numbers of magazines increased by almost 28 percent during the same period, from 9,062 to 11,593, and the pattern promised to continue. A total of 477 new magazines was published in 1987. More impressive than numbers of magazines established, however, are data about magazine circulation in comparison with the national population. While the population increased by less than 70 percent between 1952 and 1987, magazine circulation more than doubled on a per-issue basis.

Magazine reading, as a result, is pervasive in the United States. Ninety four percent of the population eighteen years old and older read an average of 9.6 magazines each month. More than 96 percent of readers attended or graduated from college, and the same percentage enjoy household incomes of $40,000 or more. The extent and affluence of readers, in fact, doubtless is the primary factor that motivates publishers to launch more and more magazines. As long as advertisers are interested in publishers' affluent audiences, proliferation of magazines will continue.

The magnitude of the proliferation pattern was described by New York Times columnist Wayne Curtis in early 1989 with a summary of the previous year's statistics:

Magazine publishers seem undaunted by the fact that only two out of 10 new magazines survive beyond their fourth year. Indeed, in 1987, 477 new consumer magazines appeared on the newsstands, a 28 percent increase over new launches in 1986.

Growth continued apace in 1988, although figures have yet to be tabulated. And the activity shows no sign of abating. In recent days, the information hot line at the Successful Magazine Publishing Group, an association of magazine executives, fielded one phone call a day from prospective publishers requesting details on how to start a new magazine.

Most of them are bent on developing specialized publications to develop narrow reader groups for waiting advertisers. Only rarely will a publisher launch a magazine as broadly oriented as People. Among 1987 start-ups, sports, music, and automotive magazines were among the most popular, but entrepreneurial publishers are prone to move quickly from one area to another in keeping with perceived profit potential.

Levitt Communications is exemplary of the sort of entrepreneurial organization often could in magazine publishing and elsewhere in the communication industry. Founded by American Stock Exchange Chairman Arthur Levitt, Jr., and consultant James K. Glassman, Levitt Communications took a broad-spectrum approach to publishing. The firm publishes Roll Call, a newspaper for Congress, and owns University Press, an academic book publisher as well as half of Battery News, a weekly serving- Battery Park City in New York.

Entrepreneurism is no less prevalent, however, in other sectors or niches. Observers of the mass media during the late 1980s have found no shortage of material concerning new publishing ventures. The start-ups came so frequently, however, that editors were discouraging articles other than those that focused on some trend or otherwise newsworthy development.

Soap Opera

Battles for market position or circulation then became media reporters' favorite subjects. Magazines oriented to soap opera fans, teenagers homemakers, the over forty woman, the wealthy, the computer user, and the business community proliferated. Media writers and critics responded accordingly.Their efforts also included a number of lengthy features concerning the major media organizations' efforts to prosper in increasingly competitive environments.

Among the more aggressive of the media moguls is S. I. Newhouse, Jr., who inherited Conde Nast Publications in 1979 and proceeded to build on that base. Newhouse launched Self and Vanity Fair and acquired New Yorker, GQ, and several others. By 1989, Newhouse owned more than a dozen magazines and probably would own more. Unlike those building media empires for their own sake, he selected publications based on his own interests and took a long developmental view rather than aiming for short term profits.

Newhouse nevertheless was in the thick of the battle for magazine markets. His Vanity Fair and Conde nast's Traveler (the Diner's Club magazine renamed) fought for circulation with the likes of Elle, M, Connoisseur, and Millionaire. Similar turk wars raged over the over-forty woman, the soap opera fan, the business executive and others. Lear's, Memories, Modern Maturity, 50 Plus and others are competing aggressively for a growing "seniors" market. Soap Opera Update, Soap Opera Digest, and Day-time TV are among major competitors for the soap viewer. In New York, New York City Business, Manhattan, inc., and Crain's New York Business compete with Business Week, Nation's Business, Barron's, Dun's Review, and a host of other publications for the business market.' The same pattern prevails in the business sector across the country, with more than one hundred publications competing for executive attention.

While battling for new audiences, publishers also were competing for increased shares of existing markets. Competition for homemaker readers, for example, accelerated sharply during the late 1980s. The field had been dominated by the so-called seven sisters: Ladies Home Journal, Good Housekeeping, McCall's, Better Homes and Gardens, Family Circle, Redbook, and Woman's Day. Bauer Publishing, a division of Germany's Heinrich Bauer Verlag, then announced plans to introduce First for Women, aiming at a circulation of two million. At about the same time, Newhouse's Conde nast announced plans to buy woman, and news Corporation announced plans for Mirabella, an upscale fashion monthly.

Battle lines even extended into magazine design, once an area ruled by tradition. Successful designs then changed rarely and at a glacial pace, presumably to avoid offending existing readers. Fresh faces became the rule in the late 1980s, with magazines undergoing almost wholesale rest-lying. During 1988, for example, Ms, Esquire, H.G., Mademoiselle, Good Housekeeping, Glamour, Fortune, Self, and Mother Jones were only part of the horde of new faces that appeared on newsstands. The flurry of redesign projects was prompted by a perceived need to adhere to contemporary standards and by competitive factors. Advertisers' reactions are as important as those of readers, especially in the early months of a refurbished format. Redesign can help or hinder in advertising sales as well as on the news-stand.

Day-to-day competition among magazines within and across reader categories in the 1980s partly obscured the passing of the era of general interest magazines. Something of an epitaph appeared in The New York Times on September 10, 1985. In an article written by advertising columnist Philip H. Dougherty, The Times recorded Reader's Digest's decision to reduce its circulation rate base by 1.5 million to 16.25 million and, thereby, yield circulation leadership to TV Guide. The Digest's move, in a sense, marked the end of an era in magazine publishing. Not only did few mass audience magazines remain, but no longer did one of them lead in circulation.

Strategy for Competition

Redesign, is a basic competitive strategy in publishing.

Magazines and newspapers long have sought to capture reader attention with more attractive type dress or graphics. In recent years, innovation has moved beyond graphics and content formats to several non-traditional areas. In magazine publishing, most such efforts have taken one of two forms: other components of the communication industry have used magazines as extensions of their services, and magazine publishers have extended their operations into other communication sectors.

There remains one other area, however, in which magazine publishers have become increasingly active: innovation within traditional magazine formats. Innovation here refers to relatively radical departures from traditional mechanical processes to enhance the attractiveness of publications to advertisers and/or readers.

The origins of the first mechanical innovation-peel-apart advertisements containing perfume samples-are lost in time, although the technology continues in use and presumably remains productive for users. With scent strips now commonplace, advertisers are introducing a broad range of what some term high tech advertisements. Some consist of nothing more than pop-ups of the sort long used in pre-schoolers' story books. Others are more innovative.

Advertising pop-ups first appeared in the mid-1980s. Honeywell was among the first users with a model of a factory complex that appeared in Business Week. Pop-ups since then have been used by Disney World, Dodge trucks, Transamerica, Corporation, Chicago's Northern Trust Company, and Hennessy cognac.

Toyota Motor Sales went beyond traditional pop-ups in 1987 by inserting 3-D viewers in advertisements introducing a new model of the Toyota Corolla. Carillon Importers, and Brown-Forman Beverage Company used microchips to create musical advertisements playing Christmas carols. IBM used music and blinking lights in an advertisement introducing its PC microcomputer in France, and there seems no end in sight.

Publishers are using computers to insert subscribers' names into magazine advertisements. The process is tricky in that mailing labels must match advertising content, but the technique has been applied successfully by several publishers.

Where does it end? Business Week's Amy Dunkin reports that some expect microchips to someday permit magazines to mimic television and quotes advertising executive Jerry Delia Femina: "The limit is when a pair of hands reaches out of the ad, grabs you by the throat, and pulls you in."

Recent Wave

Publishers' openness to new technology in advertising is more than equaled by their internal applications of technology. Many have become involved in electronic information distribution and some firms in the electronic sector have expanded into magazine publishing. In other cases, magazine entrepreneurs first have developed innovative published products and have subsequently moved into the electronic sector.

Perhaps most innovative in the latter group has been Christopher Whittle, chairman of Whittle Communications of Knoxville, Tennessee. Whittle in 1988 launched Special Report, a quarterly magazine that comes in six parts and is circulated exclusively through physicians' offices. Special Report departed from tradition by selling category advertising directly to producers rather than by working through advertising agencies, and allowing only one company in any retail category to advertise in each of the six magazines; guaranteeing advertisers that magazines would be placed in the waiting rooms of at least fifteen thousand obstetricians, pediatricians, and family practice physicians, all of whom would be required to have no more than two other magazines in their waiting rooms; selling advertising in twenty four page units (one page per year in each of the six magazines) at $1.25 million per unit.

The magnitude of Whittle's enterprise was unprecedented, but he was not alone in applying the free circulation principle to magazines. Many others have done the same. Ford Motor Company's Ford Times was a pioneer in this area. Farmers Insurance Group distributes Friendly Exchange to some four million policyholders, and United Healthcare is publishing Healthscenes for distribution by member hospitals to their patients.

The same pattern is followed in somewhat different fashion by magazines such as Avenue and Seven Days in New York and

Dossier in Washington. These magazines cater to the affluent. Their publishers, who prosper by delivering large affluent and/or well-educated audiences to advertisers, have elected to use free or controlled circulation to boost their distribution figures and support high advertising rates. The technique thus is neither new nor innovative. While the jury was still out as to the long term success of Special Report, Whittle was in the process of launching "Channel One," a broadcast product intended for high school audiences. Whittle Communications proposed to provide receivers free of charge to participating schools. The schools would agree to have students watch educational programming and accompanying commercials that Whittle presumably would sell to sponsors.

"Channel One" brought a small deluge of protests from authors and others concerned over the future of literacy, literature and reading but Whittle appeared little concerned. Time, Incorporated had agreed to pay $185 million for a half interest in Whittle Communications and an option to purchase an additional 30 percent. Within months, in addition, both Turner Broadcasting of Atlanta and the Discovery Channel had announced plans for similar projects aimed at the high school market. The destiny of classroom-oriented broadcasting remains uncertain, however. "Channel One" has been banned by the New York Board of Regents from schools in that state, and California authorities have discouraged schools from using the programme.

Other Techniques : Whittle's was not the only move on the part of a publisher from print to electronic media. Several others attempted to follow the same path, in one direction or the other. While publishers were moving into the electronic sector, some in the electronic world were moving into publishing.

Some moves across traditional media boundaries were logical in light of other factors involved. Whittle Communications' "Channel One" effort, on the other hand, appeared motivated purely by economic factors. The logical category included moves from publishing into the electronic world and from the electronic area into publishing. PC Magazine organized "PC Magnet," an interactive magazine extension that readers can dial up on computers by accessing CompuServe Information Service. The Magazine's editorial involvement with every aspect of personal computers, including, communication, made the move quite logical. McGraw-Hill, doubtless for similar reasons, offers Bix (Byte Information Exchange), primarily for readers of Byte, the company's computer magazine.

PC MagNet and Bix both have been productive for their sponsors in nonmonetary terms. Byte has recruited writers from among Bix users, and PC Magazine has used MagNet to conduct user surveys subsequently incorporated into the magazine. Most magazines have not sought to develop cash flows from their electronic ventures, viewing them instead as contributors to magazine growth.

The same sort of motivators apparently prompted Online Today, a monthly printed version of CompuServe Information Service's Online Daily. Online Today is published to encourage subscribers to expand their use of CompuServe. Content consists primarily of feature articles about CompuServe services and advertising for computer-related products and services.

Online Today is not the only publication for users of on-line computer services. Most of the magazine's competitors are entrepreneurial publications seeking to capitalize on growing interest in computer utilities. Link-Up, for example, is a bi-monthly tabloid newspaper that calls itself "the news magazine for users of online services." Other computer publications also dedicate significant amounts of space to online services and technologies of concern to the magazine publishing industry.

Yet another innovation came from the nation's catalogue publishers, who were experimenting with publications that resembled magazines. Lands' End, Inc., was among pioneers in the area, adding employee profiles to clothing catalogues in 1981. Williams-Sonoma's cookware catalogs feature recipes, and Spillage, Inc., produces self-improvement video tapes designed to sell items in its catalogs. Alternatively called "Magalogs" or "Catazines," they are yet another experiment in a fast-changing media world.

Technology's Role

Some similar events have been spawned by changing technology. Most technology influencing the magazine industry relates to processes used in magazine production. In at least one case, however, technology has spawned a competitor. "Videozines," as they have been called, are nothing more than magazines delivered on videocassettes. They are designed to be watched and listened to rather than read. And while they "have some problems" at the moment, they someday may be part of the world of magazines-video or otherwise.

Most early videozines dealt with sports although one "publication" called Travel quest was aimed at travel agents. All face major developmental obstacles, primarily in high costs and equipment limitations Costs of twenty dollars a copy are not unusual, and magazine publishers wonder whether readers can be attracted to "publications" that limit "reading" to rooms equipped with videocassette recorders. A portable player might encourage greater acceptance, however, as has been the case in Japan.

Computer's Role

Any new technology that erodes traditional magazines' market shares will be insignificant when compared with technologies that help publishers. Magazine proliferation has been fueled in large part by the microcomputer and the tools that it made accessible to writers and editors.

Microcomputers put magazine publishing within the economic reach of a large percentage of the population. These conditions result from he fact that tasks now performed by microcomputers once could be accomplished only by skilled workers through extensive manual labour, or both. The work of designers, writers, editors, advertising sales persons, commercial artists, and printers has been reduced in volume, has increased in productivity, or has in part been replaced through the workings of the microcomputer.

Designers : Computers enable designers to easily create as many different looks for existing or proposed magazines as owners or publishers care to contemplate. Once loaded into a microcomputer, through a scanner or otherwise, every component of the magazine readily can be modified for management review. Each resulting version can be quickly reproduced in hard copy form through laser printers. Where editors or publishers experience difficulty in visualizing results, slides or photo positives can be made from computer screens, slides or photos can be reproduced in any size using state-of-the art copying equipment. Publishers or editors considering changes in the look of their publications thus can have almost any number of graphic variations in front of them in minutes.

Further modifications are just as easily accomplished. Microcomputers permit every proposed design to be saved in electronic form for subsequent use. Each can be further reviewed and modified through additions or deletions. Two or more features from separate versions can be combined to create still another variation. Finally, entire pages can be produced in nearly finished form for final reviews.

Preparing final review versions usually involves executing preliminary designs in virtually the same form in which they would be prepared for printing. Articles are set in type and placed in page form by computer. Alternative type faces may be used in the pages. Computers permit both processes to be completed in minutes at negligible cost.

Illustrations can be prepared separately or as a part of final review copies. Photos and artwork can be quickly and inexpensively edited and resided by computer. Graphic elements can be maintained as separate electronic files and integrated with others to create final products.

Computer-generated photographs have yet to achieve the clarity necessary to the final product. Some illustrations require alternative production techniques as well. Computer-managed illustrations are more than adequate for review purposes. However, and production technology is advancing at a rate that soon should overcome the last barriers to high fidelity computer graphics.

Photographers : Devices that ultimately will overcome the photo fidelity barrier already exist in a new imaging technology that replaces photographic images with computer files. The process requires a device externally resembling a 35 mm camera and equipped with a lens. The resemblance stops with the lens, however, in that the "camera" records images on miniature floppy disks rather than on film. Resulting files can be loaded into computers, shown on video display terminals or television screens, printed out on laser printers, and combined with words to create newspaper or magazine content. Images also can be transmitted in digital form via microwave or telephone lines.

The technological feasibility of the system was demonstrated during the national political conventions of 1988, when a University of Missouri team transmitted images to their campus for reproduction in student newspapers. Image quality arguably was inadequate for magazine reproduction, but advancing technology can be expected to soon overcome these deficiencies.

While imaging technology will continue to improve, the process will not soon eliminate the photograph. Results will remain inferior to professional photography for some time to come. The cost of computer imaging, in addition, will be beyond the reach of individuals for some time. Equipment necessary to reproduce images in a form similar to photography costs several thousand dollars. Images can be displayed on television or VDT screens at lower costs, but television images fall short of photographs in many respect.

Photographers and photography at a minimum will continue to prosper as artists and an art form. Photogrpahic training doubtless will be necessary to those using imaging equipment during a transitional period. Photography ultimately will probably disappear, however, as a mass media technique.

Mechanical Artists : Computer technology already is leading mechanical artists to the brink of extinction. Magazines and, to a lesser extent, newspapers long have employed mechanical artists to handle paste-up duties. Paste-up involves taking reproduction proofs to type set in metal or by photo typesetters and, literally, pasting them up in final page form.

Type for articles and advertisements today is more easily and more rapidly manipulated by computer than in proof form. Sizes and leading the space between lines of type, can be changed at the stroke of a computer key. Where necessary, type faces can be changed with equal ease. The finished product can be printed out on a laser printer in camera-ready form for use in lithographic printing or, through more sophisticated equipment, can be converted directly to negative or plate form.

Mechanical artists, as a result, have become or have been

supplanted by computer operators. Writers and editors who came first into the computer age more often than not have been replacing mechanical artists in their traditional roles. Specifications prepared by graphic designers are readily followed by writers or editors, eliminating the need for mechanical artwork.

Writer's Role

Adaptation to computers came easily to writers because of advantages they derived from the technology. Computers permit rapid and efficient reorganization of work in progress. Changes an be made easily in words, sentences, paragraphs, pages, chapters and books. Consider, for example, the doctoral candidate making last minute changes in a dissertation. Pages and footnotes in such documents must be consecutively numbered and precisely positioned. Minor changes, in the precomputer era, often required retyping dozens of pages of manuscript. Computers eliminate such problems. Footnotes are renumbered and repositioned, pages are renumbered, and indexes are modified in keeping with other changes, all in a matter of moments. A few key strokes then direct the computer to generate a revised manuscript.

The benefits are even greater for those who write books or engage in projects of similar magnitude. Paragraphs, pages, and entire chapters can be moved about at will. Changes that must be carried out repetitively throughout a manuscript, such as those in which specific words must be replaced, can be accomplished automatically.

Writers who prefer their own typographic specifications to those imposed by graphic designers or other also find the computer environment hospitable. At little cost beyond the time required to learn a graphics programme such as Page-Maker or Ventura Publisher, writers can specify type faces and sizes to their hearts' content.

Finally, writers enjoy the portability of computers and the capability to transmit files by telephone. Portable computers are smaller and lighter than typewriters. More important, they can be equipped with internal modems-modulator-demodulators-that permit them to be quickly plugged into telephone lines.

Editor 's Role

Ease of content management by far is the most attractive attribute of computers from the standpoint of magazine editors. Where writers find computers helpful in transmitting information, editors find them even more beneficial after information has been received. What earlier would have been a typewritten document that would have to be rekeyed by a typesetter now is an electronic file that needs no rekeying. Editors can examine and revise electronic files on their computers hold them in electronic form for further revision, or convert them almost instantaneously into page form for printing.

Those in advertising sales enjoy the same benefits that computers create for writers and editors, and others as well. All writing, editing, and file management attributes that assist editors and writers help advertising sales personnel and managers. Perhaps the most productive computer-based devices for those in advertising, however, are software packages that permit several individuals to work on the same electronic file at the same time from different locations. An advertising sales person and his or her client, for example, together can make changes in a proposed advertisement, each from his or her own office.

The sales person can transmit an electronic file containing an advertisement to an advertiser in the same way that the writer transmits an article. The two of them then link their computers by telephone using a two-party editing programme and employ a second telephone line for accompanying conversation. Each sees the advertisement on his or her computer screen while the other makes changes. When final changes have been made and approved, the finished file becomes camera-ready copy ready for insertion into the appropriate publication page.

Savings in time are considerable in the exchanges between advertising sales persons and their prospects alone. Savings increase when computers also are used in preparing copy and converting that copy into advertisements. Where start-up magazines are involved, computers and software enable the same personnel to handle editorial and advertising content with equal ease and economy.

While helping the advertising department, computers replaced printers. Printer is a term with multiple meanings. Traditionally, the printer is an individual who operates a printing press. In the magazine industry, however, the printing press operator is a pressman, or press person if you prefer, the printer, in contrast, was the individual who took metal type prepared by typesetting machines and placed it in forms from which press plates ultimately were made. The printer, in other words, did what the writer and advertising person now can do more rapidly and more cleanly by computer. The printer and the typesetting machine operator were displaced by the computer.

Since independence, the periodical press in our country has been expanding and exploding, diversifying and professionalising, and thus becoming enriched in contents, looks and impact. This sudden growth during 1970-80 is called the magazine boom. Even otherwise, during the last 45 years, magazines of all categories and periodicity, expanded nearly six times and touched the figure of 28,000 in 1992. They commanded a total circulation of over 36 million copies. Delhi and Uttar Pradesh were among the top producers of the periodicals in India. The number of actual readers was, of course, much more because each copy of a magazine passes through the hands of at least twenty persons.

You must have seen many beautifully produced magazines at a stall or in a library: India Today, Frontline, The Illustrated Weekly of India, The Week, Reader's Digest, Sunday, Gentleman, Business India, Marg, Dharam Yug, Saptahik Hindustan, Chitra Lekha, Sarita, Manohar Kahaniyan etc. During air travel, you may have even got copies of Swagat and Namaskar, the in-flight journals of Indian Airlines and Air India. Thanks to the new printing technologies and photocomposing, these magazines wear a bright look and create a riot of colour in window displays of book-sellers and new stands or even on the pavements where magazines are displayed for sale.

Unlike the above colourful package, India's two largest circulated magazines Malayala Manorama (over 11 lakh) and Mangalam, (over 8 lakh) both Malayalam weeklies, appear in black and white. Recently, Malayala Manorama has undergone a pleasant change by making its cover in colour. Malayala Manorama, which has won over a record number of readers in India and abroad, publishes articles on social and cultural subjects, light romantic pieces, two serial cartoon strips done by their staff cartoonists, poetry, literary columns and the most attractive feature is a serialized novel for which readers wait eagerly week after week. It also has a sports piece. Mangalam started comparatively later but is fast catching up; it also thrives on melodrama by serialising works of novelists. It carries love stories, features on film stars, poetry, murder and crime stories. They are largely following the Malayala Manorama model but have added somewhat spicy material to attract a larger audience. The two magazines have been resorting to aggressive promotional campaigns.

Promotional drives have been launched by almost all important groups of papers. Even India Today, a celebrated English fortnightly and a leading illustrated magazine, now carries a typically Indian promotional ad. Take a pick of the world for a partner through its classified matrimonial column.

So you can see how the publishers of periodicals in the country are adopting vigorous business and promotional techniques to find a progressive or stable place in the market. At the same time the magazine industry in India is subjected to marketing and advertising pressure for better looks, attractive layouts and appealing contents and even for gun powder.

Nevertheless, for reasons of low literacy, lack of purchasing power and the widely common shared readership, no magazine in our country touches the seven figure mark in respect of either circulation or advertising revenue; seven figure circulation is a common feature in periodical journalism in the West. No single magazine here approaches anywhere near the aggregate sale figure of the multi-edition Reader's Digest. The Indian magazines have to go a long way to reach the production standards of the Life and the National Geographic of USA and Sunday of U.K.

Quality Factor : A good or a bad periodical is basically a matter of opinion and individual taste. Broadly speaking, a good magazine must be the readers' forum. It should satisfy their needs as well as fancies. In a vast and multilingual country with ethnic variety, it should also fulfil the aspirations of each segment. For that, readers' surveys and preference polls are necessary so that the contents and design of the journals are close to the readers' hearts.

Apart from being imaginative and creative in the treatment of topics, a better quality periodical should reflect a sense of advancement and excitement about life in general and about events, issues, values and literature in particular. The other essential qualities of a good periodical, besides its slick production and titillating illustrations, are its liveliness, clarity, insight, probing investigative reports and individual character. It is heartening that some of the periodicals have attained standards comparable with the good western periodicals but the bulk of magazines and journals in the country still lag behind. Most of the magazines, as critics point out, seek to lure the readers by providing juicy and sexy stories, gossip columns, morbid sensationalism and exposures of the private life of VIPs or stars.

Let us consider the Hindi magazines and journals which are the largest in number and carry the highest circulation. These magazines cover a variety of subjects and are widely recognised as potent in reach, power and influence in certain areas. However, one eminent journalist observes in a professional journal that "news value that Hindi periodicals adopt are dubious". According to him, "the effort seems to be to ponder to the lowest common denominator with little attempt to enlighten and educate the readers". He adds that the most disquieting feature is the condition of the Hindi journalists themselves; in his view they have appalling working conditions. He further observed that "the proprietors spend less money on news-gathering and are generally content with making money as and when they can." These observations were reinforced by the editors of Saptahik Hindustan in the same journal who maintained that the growth of Hindi journalism has not really been proportionate to the growth of professionalism or growth of self-discipline within Hindi media circles."

Some small irresponsible newspapers and periodicals in various languages, including English, thrive on yellow journalism. This is supported by some of the complaints that have come before the Press Council.

Magazines fulfill the need for a medium of information,

instruction and entertainment. They also interpret issues and policies. They have many accomplishments to their credit: During India's freedom struggle, opinion magazines like Gandhiji's Harijan played a vital role in moulding public opinion and mobilising it against the foreign rule. Magazines have helped strengthen social, regions and national bonds. They provide excellent entertainment at an affordable price. Magazines act as an effective medium of education and instruction by interpreting issues, events and developments and putting them in proper focus. They help in bringing about social, cultural and political reforms on rational lines.

Cheap quality journalism exists in various regions and language belts and it co-exists with good journalism. One authority sums up well by saying that the Indian periodical journalism presents a many-splendoured congregation varying from the good and the professional ones to the dirty rags, all set in the same tapestry. There are no professional organizations and professional journals of stature, actively and systematically engaged in promoting professional standards in the sphere of periodical journalism.

Some authorities in the West classify periodicals into two main categories: trade or specialised magazine and consumer magazines of general interest. In India, however, the Registrar of newspaper's Report categorised periodicals into 21 groups. The second Press Commission report, on the other hand, preferred to classify them into ten categories: (1) News and current affairs journals (2) Opinion journals, (3) Farm journals, (7) Women journals, (8) Children journals, (9) Sports Journals, (10) Film journals.

In the Commission's calculation, news and current affairs journals constitute the largest group India Today, The Week, Frontline, Sunday, The Illustrated Weekly of India and Probe are the most-bearers of this group. Features of such periodicals, as witnessed in recent years, have been the emergence of investigative reporting, backgrounding, incisive comments and team-based and interview-based reports, with effective pictorial and graphic support. Such quality reporting, however, is confined to only Some top journals and is not a group virtue. Literary and cultural magazines constitute the second largest group. The bulk of these magazines, particularly those with a large circulation, follow a formula of mixed contents in order to appeal to diverse tastes and thereby attract more readers. Malayala Manorama. Malayalam weeklies, Kumudam, a Tamil Weekly, Aajkal in Hindi and Urdu are the examples of this group.

Opinion periodicals are distinct from news magazines as also from journals of entertainment for leisure time reading. They are generally concerned with one or more themes of current interest. Seminar and Mainstream are illustrations of this category. Farm journals, as the name implies, deal with agricultural and other allied activities. Shetkari and Gramsevak belong to this group.

The economic, financial and other trade journals are of recent origin but are coming up well. The Hindu Survey of Industry, Business India, Business World, Business Today, Vyapar udyog represent this class. The growth of science journals, to which below Vigyan Pragati as also the better selling Science Today, has not been quite satisfactory in terms of their number and quality. The number of women journals in India is not commensurate with the strength of the women population in the country. Vanitha, a Malayalam fortnightly from Kottayam, has the highest circulation in this category. Femina, an English periodical, is also gaining importance.

In the group of children's journals, Chandamama and Indrajal comics are the leading examples. Bal Bharati, a government journal, is also popular. Most magazines in this section provide entertainment, short stories and some articles on current events and sports publishers try to lean on cheap circulation gimmicks instead of resorting to originality and creativity.

The sports magazines had a low rate of expansion till recently. But now sports magazines have started improving with experts contributing columns and the journals giving quizzes, interviews and illustrations. Sports Star, an English weekly, is a leading examples of this category.

The number of film journals has increased since the sixties, but professionally and circulation-wise their record does not show much improvement. Mayapuri, a Hindi weekly, Stardust, Filmfare and Cine Blitz from Bombay touch a respectable circulation figure.

Official Magazines : Among the periodicals in India, 706 were brought out by the government in 1992. Language-wise, the largest number of periodicals in the government sector appeared in English, followed by those in Hindi. The largest circulated government publication was Shraya (50,000), a bilingual bi-monthly of Canara Bank, Bangalore. The second largest one was Shrivir Patrika, a Hindi Weekly of Bikaner. As far as the contents are concerned, 139 periodicals were concerned with news and current affairs; 65 journals dealt with social welfare and 55 with agriculture and animal husbandry. The government periodicals climbed a total circulation of 2.45 lakh copies, being less than 1 per cent of the total circulation of the Indian press.

The inadequacy of science and technology journals is obvious. They are necessary for a developing country like ours. The Press Commission felt that the number of science journals in inadequate, besides, they lacked the technique and style to inculcate scientific temper among the people by telling them in a simple language as to how they could advance in certain hi-tech areas.

Women in India constitute nearly half of the population. Press Commission study found that there journals address themselves to the urbanite or working women. Children constitute the future leaders of tomorrow. Stories abound in these journals but contributions on how our children should become enlightened, healthy and democratic citizens and forge ahead as world competitors in sports, technology and modern business are lacking. Cheap serials or comic stories borrowed from the West are allowed to fill in the columns of some of these magazines.

Film journals which are read widely are full of gossip stories and rumour mongering. They deal less with professional matters. There have been times which witnessed direct confrontation between the film world and film journals. A study of the Press Commission revealed another interesting facet-that many juicy articles are written by the PR men in the payroll of film producers.

Professional and research journals dealing with mass media are few and not of a high standard. These journals are essential for building up the academic and professional base of journalism in the country. One critic rightly remarked that journalists revel in criticising others but are allergic to any criticism of their own work.

In recent years, interesting and encouraging trends in the field of periodical journalism have been witnessed. Some of the more significant ones are: Popular and widely circulated magazines branched out into regional languages and made a mark for themselves. Magazines like India Today, Femina, Stardust, Filmfare and others made their appearance in Hindi, Gujarati and other Indian languages. For example, India Today had five regional language editions including Hindi, Gujarati, Malayalam and others. These are largely independent publications with separate staff for each language edition and have definite regional slant. India Today, Stardust and a few others have made a mark by bringing out successfully international editions. In these editions, the editorial content is largely similar to the national editions, but advertising is different. The practice is in line with world famous magazines' trend of bringing out editions devoted to different continents. Time and Newsweek bring out editions like Asia editions. Europe editions and so on. The motive is to earn more revenue from advertising. The emergence of city magazines is yet another interesting trend. Big cities like Bombay, Delhi, Calcutta and Pune have exclusive journals that focus attention on metro affairs, events developments and problems. Bombay has Island, Delhi has First City and City Scan. We can hope this rend will multiply.

Among the Indian periodicals, both giants and dwarfs co-exist. So do the pretty looking and the drabs. The giants are not only fatter in size but elegant to look at. By and large they are well managed and are in sound financial health. Their printing is by the latest technologies like multi-colour offset. They have well-known columnists to contribute besides their own staff. Occasionally, they bring out special numbers. Sometimes good local scoops also appear.

By comparison, the small and medium magazines have not been able to maintain professional standards. They lack trained journalists and an adequate number of reporters. This affects their news gathering and reporting standards. Most of them, therefore, lean heavily on fiction, gossip columns, detective stories, sensationalism, cheap humour, sexy pictures and western comic strips. Some political magazines find it more paying to write on factional fights and resort to who-on-whose-side kind of political analysis. Similarly, most of the tabloids, which thrive on explosive, critical, daring or expository reporting or titillating make-up, concentrate mostly on sex, scandals, inflated rhetorics and fabricated juicy material. Some film magazines bank on film politics and rumour mongering about the stars. They seek to thrive on pornography, both in pictures and script.

A few journals carry humorous or otherwise light hearted stuff but generally these constituents appear as an appendix rather than an integral part. Some periodicals of course carry regular doses of contributed humour. Among them are Sunday, Mukta, the Illustrated Weekly of India, Eve's Weekly, Dharam Yug and Femina.

Advertising revenue is crucial for the periodical press. So a mad struggle is on to get a larger and larger piece of the cake. The sudden increase in advertisement revenue, especially on consumer goods, motivated the leading periodicals to improve their production standards and editorial contents. As the colourful display of ads is possible in magazines, a large number of advertisers are attracted to such; magazines. In this game, the large general interest magazines, specially the English ones attached to newspaper chains and combines of big business-houses, get the better of the smaller ones. The government has pursued a liberal advertising policy of offering special rates to Indian language newspapers and small newspapers. It has also extended to them newsprint facilities, rebate from excise duties and so on but the big papers still have an upperhand. Lack of adequate newsprint continues to be one of the main problems for the small periodicals. The recently announced liberalisation policy regarding the import of e newsprint will give an added advantage to big papers-and rich units. The small magazines will have to trap the local or regional advertising and bank on contents which are dear to their segmented readers.

The bright image of a magazine is one important factor which goes to build up its circulation. Other factors are its appearance on time, its price and the distribution network to ensure its availability to: readers at home and on news stands. Income from advertising may keep a magazine going for some period but if circulation drops, for whatever reason, so would the advertiser's enthusiasm to buy space in it. As bulk of the periodicals have low circulation, their financial viability constantly remains in doubt. Most of the small and tiny periodicals brought out from the mofussil areas survive from one publication to the next by sheer passion.

The high price per copy, a large number of readers sharing the same copy, inadequate development, of road transport in the interior parts of the country and unsatisfactory distribution facilities limit the circulation of magazines, besides, illiteracy, poor purchasing power and low reading habits of the rural population are the broad-based reasons for low circulation. These are the chronic problems of the small periodicals.

Public relations and scientific promotion are new dimensions in the publishing trade though these are still in an infant stage in our country. The adoption of proper circulation drives can make the magazines more acceptable to potential readers and thus accomplish larger sales. The introduction of reader surveys can result in improved contents of the magazines and thus promote their commercial interest. The National readership Surveys by the Indian Market Research Bureau and the Operation Research Group already cover the press, radio, television and film media to gauge the reading/listening/viewing habits and their socio-economic backgrounds. Many of these ventures are primarily for advertisers. Only a few newspapers and magazines independently conduct readership surveys with the objective of improving the contents, writing style and design of their magazines.

There are some irritants which require PR application. The editorial staff does not explain to the writers while soliciting an article, the nature, length, style and scope of the write-up and the type of illustrations to be used. Other flaws are delayed payments and replies, heavy editing without taking the author into confidence and blunt refusals.

Most of the periodicals do not have even attractive readers' columns where the readers could come out with their comments, suggestions and contributions. This is important for establishing a two way communication-between the readers and producers of magazines.

Poor payment in the case of articles perhaps explains the reluctance on the part of well-known writers to accept magazine assignments. They accept these assignments only when they do not have other lucrative assignments and mostly as a short term arrangement.

With literacy increasing steadily and the country making economic progress, both in rural and urban areas, there is a tremendous readership potential in India. Publishers can adopt ingenious promotion techniques. They need not make loud claims, but resort to persuasive and credulous pleadings or appeals tied to the needs of the target readers. Here are some promotional devices which could be employed profitably: Promotion of sales on news-stalls, sales depots of other public places; Soliciting advance subscriptions by issuing appropriate direct mail literature; Simulation of the sale of advertising space; Building up of goodwill or corporate image; Promoting understanding of the contents of the publications; Making editorial contents more affective and problem solving; Seeking wider involvement of readers; Making advertisements more attractive and creative.

Comparative Study

Periodicals are exposed to competition from the electronic media, including video magazines. Satellite TV and cable TV pose quite a challenge. These media re captivating the mind and time of the people. To play its due role, the magazine publishers must make their magazines still more attractive, vibrant and satisfying. The soaring prices are no doubt a great hindrance but that makes it all the more necessary for the magazines to step up their efforts to improve their quality, enhance their popularity and ensure adequate circulation and advertising support.

It is a professional obligation on the part of magazines to cater to the needs of diverse readership, from the elite to the common man, from the urbanites to ruralites, from people with deep interest in specialised areas to people with superficial interest in many areas. They must also evoke brand loyalty. Different magazines in different areas and in different languages must evolve their own promotional strategies based on readers' polls. In fact, what is important is that the magazines should woo their readers by satisfying their curiosity and by giving them the type of detailed information and lively entertainment which they wish to have.

A periodical is a strategic informational and cultural institution. If developed on sound editorial and management principles, it will endear itself to the readers. It should certainly mirror the society but not succumb to conformity or mediocrity. It should be creative, educative and even controversial. It should speak its mind even at the risk of becoming unpopular.

On issues of great concern to the public it should not hesitate to take a stand which may offend the authority or a section of the readers. If a periodical makes readers and public interest its major concerns, advertisers will come in a procession. A combination of bright ideas and attractive design accomplished through new printing and layout techniques would result in more stimulating, attractive and saleable periodicals. The planners should study the market and the reader's mind to evolve the right formula, to determine the lines along which their magazines should give information and education to the readers and serve the interest of advertisers. A sound periodical cannot remain static, it should ensure continuous freshens, improvement and enrichment in contents and presentation.

Right Topic: We have already explained that a writer always remains alert to the environmental stimuli that are bombarded on his mind. Read newspapers and magazines on a daily basis. Meet celebrities and learn how they have become famous. Talk to other authors and editors. Look for opportunities in the field of magazine publishing. Watch TV regularly. Remain sensitive to events and happenings that are directly related to your field. These stimuli would churn your thoughts. These thoughts would boil in your mind due to this churning effect. Finally, you would arrive at a goal—the topic on which, you would be very keen to write and express your views. You could be willing to explain a problem. Alternatively, you could be motivated to present a solution to the set of problems that were given to your mind by the environmental stimuli. You should be confident about the topic selected by you. Write a few topics on a piece of paper and analyses them carefully. Then, arrive at a conclusion by visualising how efficiently you would be able to collect data and facts about each one of them. Naturally, those topics would be eliminated about which, there is no or minimal data. Finally, you would be left with one or two topics. Out of these, choose the simple one even if the data of the difficult one is much more accurate and abundantly available. The second topic (selected by you) may have poor data back-up. However, do not mind this lacuna. Try to pick a simple topic to begin with. When you become adept at writing fine articles, try the difficult topics.

Before you plunge into the ocean of words, talk to a magazine publisher. If you already have one who would publish it, talk to the sponsoring editor of that publisher. Two situations arise now—either the publisher gives you a topic or you define a topic. Let us discuss both these possibilities:—

The article has to be written to serve an objective of the publisher. In fact, he would discuss why he wants an article of a particular genre to be published in his magazine. His readers may have asked him to present data and facts on a specific topic. They could have written to the publisher, "Sir, please publish an article on Indo-US relations; we have to prepare for the IAS or UGC examination." The publisher and his staff must oblige their regular readers. That is why, they would invite you to write on a specific topic. If the publisher or his sponsoring editor has already given the topic (and you are confident about it), your job is done.

You can also inform the publisher that you can write an article on a particular topic. If the publisher is not aware of the topic, send a note to him or his sponsoring editor (along with the title of the article) and tell him in briefly what you would like to write. This note is a kind of rough draft for the publisher or his sponsoring editor. He may change the topic as well as the basic hints that were sent by you. He knows the markets, not you. Therefore, obey him and alter the title and contents after telephonic conversation or across-the-table negotiations. You may have to make some compromises; you may not be allowed to write on exactly the same topic that was selected by you. Be prepared and get going; the real work starts now!

Research: After the finalisation of the topic, you would be expected to collect data or undertake research activities. You would be required to visit libraries and read various books on the topic. You may have to buy some books and magazines too. The publisher may also give to some books, magazines, and photocopies. He can also give you the addresses of scholars, researchers, professors, media celebrities, movie stars, or other professionals who would give you vital data, clues, sets of information, or opinions on the topic. While you conduct the research activities and meet people, keep the title and rough draft of the article in your briefcase. Also, make a broad outline of the contents. This outline would emanate from the rough draft prepared by you in consultation with the publisher or his sponsoring editor. The data would have to be collected according to this outline. This outline can also be given to you by the publisher. If you are a novice in the field, it is better to ask for such an outline from the sponsoring editor; it would be a modified version of the rough draft submitted by you. When you mellow with experience, you would be able to write such outlines on you own.

The Structure: We presume that you have worked hard during the previous stage and that adequate data are available with you to write the article. Now, decide the structure of the article. Magazine publishers publish such articles as inform, motivate, or change perceptions of readers. Some articles are supposed to entertain, enthrall, or educate readers. Therefore, your article would have to be written according to a suitable structure, which would help the reader imbibe the thoughts with finesse. You have to take care of the needs of the readers by creating a suitable structure of the article. The readers should not be forced to accept your structure. The ideas and concepts should naturally flow into the minds of readers. Hence, the structure must be conducive for transmission of thoughts from the sender (author) to the receiver (reader).

Suppose, we have assumed that every paragraph has a word count of 125 words. The font is selected by the publisher. Magazines are usually printed in a type size of *10-12* points. Hence, your article would have an extent of *1,000* words. You may have to give tables, photographs, sketches etc., in your article to authenticate your facts. These would have to be embedded carefully at appropriate places. The simple rule in the context of these insertions is—as soon as you mention the table number or figure number, that table or figure must come up on that very page. It cannot or should not come after another figure or table. If this is not possible, mention the number of table or figure in the text and then, let that figure or table come on the very next page. The DTP operator of the magazine publisher is aware of these rules. All you have to do is to write the article, get it typed in double-space on foolscap paper, mark the places where the tables and sketches must be put, and submit this MSS to the publisher (along with sketches, tables and diagrams). If you cannot draw well, create rough sketches only and the DTP section would take care of the rest. However, tables should preferably be typed or legible (if you have created them with a pen). Alternatively, you can give the entire article in Word 2000, PM 6.5 or any other suitable software. You can give half-tone images and/or colour photographs along with this soft copy. The DTP staff would incorporate the same into the article (you have to define the figure numbers or photograph numbers carefully in the soft copy).

The Style: You have not started writing yet. Decide the style first and then, write the article. You must develop a unique style of writing. This style would give a typical shade to the:

(a) basic ideas and concepts;

(b) order and sequence;

(c) grammar, phrases, and sentences;

(d) paragraphs; and

(e) overall presentation of your article.

Your style should not be copied from those of others. Finally, you cannot develop a good writing style overnight. After years of practice, you would learn how to start the article, give headings, insert data and vital facts in the middle, and give conclusions in the end. When you write your twentieth article, we hope you would have developed a fine style of your own. Ask the reputed editors, authors and DTP specialists to help you in this context. You would become an expert that way.

The First Paragraph: The structure of the article is ready and so is its style. The structure is the basic outline of the article and there is no harm in using the rough draft to refine it. These rough hints were the same that were used by you during the data collection and research phase. In fact, the structure is based on these rough notes and the data collected during the research process. You should reflect whatever you have collected during the research phase. Now, start writing the article. Prepare yourself physically and mentally. Sit in a secluded room, which should have a writing desk (with a local lighting system). Do not sit on the bed to write. Bring all the books, journals, magazines, and data sheets on this writing desk. Remember you deity and pray to Him/Her. Now, write the title of the article. Write the first few lines of the first paragraph. Read them before you go further. If you do not find them to be up to the mark, change them. Alternatively, throw away the paper and write on a new one. This is the painful incubation stage of writing, but do not give up. Finally, you would be ready to start the first paragraph. We can give a good cue in this context—explain the data collected by you in a nice manner in the first paragraph. Also, give the idea of the problem in only one sentence in this paragraph. You would be able to make a fine background for the article that way. A positive punchy opening is the key that opens the door to a reader's heart. Attract the attention of the reader with the first two lines.

Example: *Dubyaman has opened a Pandora's Box by sending additional troops to Iraq. If Uncle Sam continues to rule the war-ravaged Mesopotamia, Saddam and his cohorts may seek the support of other terrorist groups to wreak havoc on the 'outsiders.'* Note that in this example, Dubyaman refers to George W Bush; the author purposely does not name the President because he wants the readers to guess who Dubyaman could be. Eventually, they realise that the term has been coined for President Bush. The opening must be lively, cosmopolitan, and declarative. It answers the first question of the reader, "What's this all about"? In technical terms, it is called Lead. In newspaper articles, the headline does the job of leading. However, in articles of magazines, you have to "make the lead" because a title would not help the reader tread the path of words you have created. You could use the quotation of a popular person in the first few lines.

Example: So said Oliver Goldsmith, "Where wealth accumulates, men decay." You can also narrate an anecdote in the first paragraph. You can even ask a question. You can give news that is thrilling and able to arouse the interest of readers.

The Second Paragraph: The second paragraph must maintain the pace and style of the first one. Long, rambling paragraphs are eschewed by readers and editors alike. Do not use difficult words, The reader is not keen to learn that you are the master of the language but is interested in knowing about the facts and data related to the topic. The second paragraph should really take him off ground and land him in a heaven of words.

The Third, Fourth and Fifth Paragraphs: Use short simple sentences. Give only one idea in one sentence. Do not use quote marks very often in the body of the article. Further, do not use too many adjectives as they crowd the verbs (Alan Jamieson). Be pertinent and dedicated to the topic. Key sentences should capture the important points. Do not use 'I.' Use 'we' or 'our.' Use the phrase "the author" instead of the word 'I,' if it is every much necessary to do so. Give facts and data in the third, fourth and fifth paragraphs. Further, note that the body of the article can be contained in more than *three* paragraphs. However, in that case, the article would be very long and could be ignored. The ideal length of any article should be *800-1200* words. You can complete the body of the article in four paragraphs as well.

All the Tables: Many articles require tables. Economic and technical data are presented through tables. Mention the number of the table and give the table below the line that mentions the table. In actual practice, the DTP man would make a table and let the text wrap around it in Corel Draw 10.0. If he uses PM 7.0 to process the article or book, he cannot avail the wrap-around tool.

The Figures and Graphs: You may have to insert figures and graphs to support the data. These would also be embedded in the text at suitable places. The DTP man would do the actual job. Figures and graphs enhance the readability of the article.

The Inset Boxes: Some vital data are given in the small decorated inset boxes. These may not be referred to in the text of the article. They look beautiful and engage the reader immediately. They contain facts, data, or numerical figures. The DTP man would create and decorate them.

The Photographs: Many articles contain half-tone, quarter tone or colour photographs. The DTP operator adds them at suitable places; the author must inform him where to insert such photographs. They normally have captions and numbers, just like all the tables, figures, and graphs. However, tables and figures in the article of a magazine do not have numbers, although they do have captions.

Sixth and Seventh Paragraphs: Give conclusions and recommendations in the second-last paragraph. Give solutions in the last one. The last paragraph is literally your own baby. Do not give vague suggestions. Do not promise heavens and stars while solving the problem. Simply write that the suggested solution can be implemented to get better results. Do not give ultimate solutions to burning issues like Kashmir, Palestine, the Basques, LTTE crisis, Afghanistan, Pakistan, the Taliban, north-south dialogue, deadlocks in the WTO conferences, deadlocks in the conferences related to environment etc. Give only rational or plausible suggestions. Align your views with those of the masses. Do not give funny conclusions. Do not state, "A solution eludes humanity." Instead, state, "Through collective efforts, XYZ would arrive at a solution in the near future." Do not give dates of solutions. Do not state, "The Palestine-Israel conflict shall be resolved by December, 2004." Instead, state," The Palestine-Israel conflict can be resolved due to the joint efforts of the Israelis, Palestinians and UNO. However, this issue may take more time to be resolved. Do not drag the farewell. A sharp finale can prove very effective. Create an environment in which, the reader should remain keen to read another article written by you on the same topic in the same magazine.

Bibliography or References: If need be, you can give bibliography, which is a list of books read casually by you to write the article or references, which are the clear indications/ addresses of the sources used by you to write it. You must mention the page numbers of those books, magazines, or journals from which, you had taken the data. This guideline should be followed for writing the bibliography as well as references. Further, reference numbers must be given on the phrases or lines within the text of the article. These numbers must correspond to the actual references at the end of the article. In general magazines, there is no need to give references or bibliographies. However, some authors thank the authors, researchers, corporate firms, government firms, or libraries in the end of the article. These gestures of gratefulness can be deemed references of bibliographies in magazines. In journals, you must give references or bibliography. Example: *Daniel Murphy states that the media are the most effective modes for altering human psyche.* Here, the number 1 is the reference number. It must come in the end of the article as the first item of the references, as follows: *Murphy Daniel, 1997, The Media: theory and practice, Holt Rhinehart and Winston, Chicago, PP 142-144,* In many magazines, especially in Indian vernacular magazines, references or bibliographies are not given. The authors of such articles may not have referred to any books or magazines to write the same. In any case, the writers of sets of knowledge should be given due credit in the bibliography and references section. Engineering magazines do not publish articles without references or bibliographies.

Rough Layout: In order to help the DTP staff, take the following steps (the decision of the art director or creative copy editor is deemed final and not that of the author):—

The First Page: This page has to be attractive enough to gain the attention of the reader. It gives a rough layout that should be used by the DTP operator to make the final CRC. It can also have figures, colour photographs, and tables.

The Second Page: This page is the actual body. It can have colour photographs, inset boxes, diagrams, sketches and other useful data.

The Third Page: This page can be filled with the conclusion and some parts of the body that would come before the conclusion

Fourth Page: This page would contain references or bibliography. It is the last page of the article. Another article can be started by the publisher from that page. However, type setting is done by the DTP staff of reputed publishers in such a way that all the articles start from new pages. In order to fill the gaps, other inset boxes, news photographs, quotations or advertisements are inserted by the publisher.

Processing the Article : Once you have completed the article, get it typed. If you are giving the soft copy, get it typeset. Give photographs, sketches, diagrams, and other inputs to the DTP staff. Label all of them clearly. The article or the soft copy must have the same figure or table numbers as well as inset box numbers that were handed over by you. The article of a magazine is processed by the DTP staff of the magazine. It is normally not returned to its author. Hence, give your best to the article and then, forget about its processing.

If you are able to put your hands on the first proof (with all the diagrams, photographs etc.) or galley (sans all the diagrams, photographs etc.) of the article, you would be able to edit it thoroughly. Take care of the grammatical errors and syntax. Grammar is important; so are placements of inset boxes and photographs. When the number of a figure is mentioned, that figure must appear after the text or on one side of the page (so that the reader may be able to refer to it while he reads the figure number in the text). Do not allow the DTP staff to put the figure on the next or any other page. Check and edit tables very carefully.

Further, in all probability, you would receive the second proof. The first proof may have been edited by the in-house editorial staff of the magazine publisher. Do not mind this practice, after all, they are publishing your article. Do not let the editors change the basic thoughts and spirit of the article. Also, do not allow them to fiddle with the data. For this purpose, you must be sure about the authenticity (and sources) of your data. After completing the editing session, return the proof to the publisher; you would not be getting another proof.

We hope that it would be a moment of pride for you! Read it yourself and find out the mistakes in its content, presentation and style. Get it read from experts and take guidance from them. Take a vow that you would write a better article the very next time! If your attitude is positive, you can be a winner all the way during the course of your writing career. Perseverance, toil, and dedication to facts would help you succeed!

What Merits should be in an Article ? : Alan Jamieson has given the following guidelines to judge an article:—

Purpose: What is it—to instruct, inform, persuade, amuse? Is the article successful in meeting its objectives?

Idea and Content: Is the idea original? Does the idea work in actual practice?

Order and Sequence: Is the paragraphing effective in the sense that one paragraph's theme leads into the next one?

Opening and Closing: Is the opening effective? Is the closure powerful and worthy of making an impact?

Style: What do you think of the style? Has the author used to be more forceful? Is there a razzmatazz of cliche's, tautology, and confused syntax in the article? Is the reader able to imbibe the basic concept for which, the article was written?

Did it Work?: Did the article arouse the interest of the reader in the subject? Was it able to impinge upon the mind'of the reader? Would he like to get more information on the same topic and, may be, from the same author? Did the article fade into the oblivion as a sluggish insipid comet of words, or would it remain etched in the memory of the reader as a star of vivid, pragmatic, and thought-provoking ideas?

6

ROLE OF PRESS

After it assumed power in 1989, the National Front government came out first with a Cabinet Paper and then introduced the Prasar Bharati Bill in December 1989. According to P. Upendra, the Minister for Information and Broadcasting, the Bill borrowed from the Prasar Bharati Bill of 1979 and took into account the changed circumstances and the present ethos. Many, however, felt that the bill was put before the nation in a hurry. A national debate was initiated, in many cases with the active encouragement of the government to arrive at a consensus on the framework and the modalities of media autonomy. The Bill, after incorporating some amendments, was unanimously passed in both Houses of Parliament. But following a change of government in October 1990, the lack of political good will to translate the concept into a working proposition was apparent. While there was no official pronouncement, the interim government headed by Chandrashekhar continued to maintain the status quo. The dissolution of the Lok Sabha in April 1991 signed the death warrant of the Prasar Bharati Bill, which then had needed only the Presidential assent for becoming Law. The death of Rajiv Gandhi and the advent of Congress rule in June 1991, under P.V. Narasimha Rao, put an end to any hopes about the issue. Meanwhile, the question of broadcasting autonomy has become irrelevant as other sources of information and entertainment viz.,

STAR TV, CNN and BBC have burst into view in the wake of the Gulf War. The invasion from the skies has begun.

Today, the rapid expansion of television in India in terms of availability (7 channels) and sheer expansion (545 TV stations) speaks of unqualified success by any standards. TV has often reached a high degree of professional excellence in its news coverage. The 32-hour continuous election telecast in May-June 1991 involving on-the-spot reporting from the counting booths even in the remote corners of the country and the swift shuttling between the national network and the local centres was a refreshingly dramatic experience for the viewers. But barring occasional and isolated instances, it has steadily developed an urban bias and an elitist approach, popularising, in the process, an alien life style and culture far removed from the realities of Indian life.

The Doordarshan has always suffered from the dichotomy between policy pronounce-ments (which emphasize the use of the mass media for social progress) and the continuous drift and departure from them in actual practice. In a developing and democratic country like India, access to television and the social benefit accruing from it, is a crucial test of the social relevance of such an expensive medium. The reason to the establishment of the Doordarshan in India, according to official statements, is to create a sense of participation in our efforts to usher in a new social order. As early as February 1973, a seminar on software objectives sponsored by the government recommended that, "Television must be used in the development process as an instrument of social change and national cohesion by unhesitatingly upholding progressive values and involving the community in a free dialogue. Indian TV has to shun an elitist approach and consumer value system and evolve a truly national model."

Officially the task assigned to the electronic media is three-fold. First, "the AIR and Doordarshan should inform people about happenings in India and the world, objectively, fairly and without any bias, as adequately and quickly as possible." Second, "the electronic media should get across to the people the policies and programmes that the government has framed for accelerating the process of socio-economic transformation." And finally, the broadcast media should pursue "an open policy and a policy that does not shirk issues and the responsibilities connected to these issues in order to develop an informed and participative citizenry; so that people know and think for themselves what is good for them and for the country." There can be no serious difference of opinion on these objectives. The reach of the electronic media together with the high percentage of the illiterate population make the broadcast media the most appropriate vehicles of national communication.

Mrs. Indira Gandhi, who played a leading role in the growth of TV in India, saw its role primarily as a promoter of development and education in a backward country. She repeatedly affirmed the national importance of utilising TV not just for the idle entertainment of the elite but for the uplift of the poor, especially in the inaccessible rural areas. But in effect and in actual practice, the purchase of a TV set is seen as wholesale investment in entertainment which obviates the bother and expense of going to an auditorium or a stadium. Even a cursory examination of its programmes during any week makes it clear that the order in which Doordarshan fulfils the three functions of the medium are entertainment first, information second and education third. This is true even after the introduction of the five Metro channels.

Even a casual viewer cannot but notice that the Doordarshan does not practice what it preaches and evidently such guidelines are honoured more in the breach then in the observance. The official media, despite occasional airs of openness, are generally identified as the propaganda wing of the party in power. These media do not present a balanced and non-partisan view of the events and happenings, which an average citizen so badly requires in order to arrive at an informed judgement. India may demand free and balanced flow of information at the international level. But at home, the distinction between the ruling party and the government, between the party interest and the national interest often gets blurred. In addition to the lack of objectivity and frankness, the news on Doordarshan also suffers from an overdose of elite and urban values.

From inception, broadcasting in India has been looked upon as a public service for the promotion of social objectives. The concept of advertisements for the promotion of consumer's goods was also considered incompatible with the prevailing philosophy of the "socialistic pattern of society." What causes alarm today is the proliferation in the mass media of these very advertisements for consumer goods.

In a developing country like India, radio and TV should be viewed as a national resource for the uplift of the masses. It is only through a strong media network that the right kind of information and education can be imparted to the people. But the media in our country, like elsewhere in the world, have buckled under the pressure of commercial interests. As a result, besides discrimination of information or the 'haves' from the 'have-nots', there is erosion of regional and cultural identities and ethics. Mindless entertainment with little or no educative value defeats the very purpose of building up a strong media network. For one, it is definitely not in the interest of the people to provide them with unproductive media fare. For another, it is nothing but unjustifiable use of invaluable resources.

The question that inevitably arises is whether we should use TV for promoting a humane social order or to create synthetic needs.

Under the existing system Doordarshan has become a tool for the promotion of crass consumerism. It is a strange paradox that this public investment, which facilitated the rapid expansion of the TV network in a poor country, is now being exploited by the big businesses for building their own corporate images. While it is conceded that ad revenue makes a network viable and independent, the same advertising also dictates the nature, form and content of the media software. Every noble intention to arouse social consciousness through the media gets traded for unhealthy programming. Here is an example.

Advertisers would always prefer to sponsor those programmes which create the proper mood in the viewers to buy their products. Their choice, invariably, falls on entertainment programmes. On rare occasions when serious programmes on topics like environment preservation, public hygiene or any significant social issues like land reforms or minimum wages are telecast, no sponsor is usually available. This is in stark contrast to the situation when advertisers lined up to spend a total of Rs. 35 crore on the serial 'Mahabharat' alone. To play the role of communicator-cum-educator in developing countries, broadcasting media have to provide software that would enrich the lives of the people. A communication policy would have to specify some guidelines to our communicators regarding balanced programming. Here, 'balanced' would mean the right mix of entertainment, information and education.

The press in a democratic country plays a vital role in creating, moulding, and reflecting public opinion. It is a fundamental institution of our society.

Though the press in India is free, it suffers from many ills. It has yet to identify its true post-independence role so as to ensure against haphazard growth and directionless expansion.

There are a few in-built handicaps such as vast geographical area, illiteracy, poverty, multiplicity of languages, and absence of adequate communication facilities. Some other bottlenecks exist, like the linking of ownership of newspapers with other industrial or commercial enterprises; limited newspaper ownership with closely held 'share interest'; urban-oriented expansion of newspapers leaving the vast country side population untouched, inadequate and expensive newsprint, and the lack of local advertisement support.

Eminent journalists have pointed out several drawbacks which stand in the way of making the press in India an independent and impartial instrument of communication of news and views. Some of these drawbacks are: the present system of accreditation of journalists; the government's allocation of newsprint; fixation of advertisement rates; favours to journalists in the form of perquisites such as subsidized housing, medical facilities, etc., heavy dependence of the press on official releases.

For a comprehensive and an in-depth examination of the state of the Indian press and the steps that need to be taken for its development on sound and healthy lines, the Government of India appointed the second Press Commission on 18 May, 1978, headed by Justice K. M. Mathew.

The appointment of the Second Press Commission had

become necessary as the Indian Press had undergone several changes, had taken new strides, and acquired an added significance with an ever-expanding readership.

One of the recommendations of the Second Press Commission was to include both positive and negative aspects of an event in development reports. This implied that these reports should investigate the reasons for success as well as failure at different places and under different conditions of various development programmes affecting the lives of the common people. But most of our newspapers merely carry official handouts giving statistics of man-days of employment provided, persons made literate or area brought under irrigation.

The reporting of non-official initiatives in rural development, education reform, struggle against superstitious beliefs. Evil practices like dowry and Sati or other areas of social campaign, is even less extensive than in-depth reporting of the implementation of official development programmes. The Commission says: "our newspapers usually become aware of such non-official activities only after they have been honoured by a Jamnalal Bajaj Foundation award or Magsaysay award."

Another long standing criticism of the press is that it carries too much bad news at the expense of the good. To gain maximum readership, the press emphasizes the exceptional rather than the representative; the sensational rather than the significant. Many activities of the utmost social consequence are not considered reportable incidents. But, as Indira Gandhi never tired of pointing out, "the meek may one day inherit the earth, but never the headlines." This brings us inevitably to the question of social responsibility. Certainly, the press has travelled a long way from the arrogant attitude of the newspaper owners who said, "A newspaper is a private enterprise owing nothing whatsoever to the public, which grants it no franchise. After all, responsible journalism is journalism with a conscience." Nikhil Chakravarthy, an eminent journalist, had said that, "Even if you don't like someone or disagree with him ideologically, you must be fair." A journalist is confronted with ethical decisions almost daily. Should a news source go unnamed? Should a "leak" possibly affecting national security be used? Does the public interest override individual privacy? Should a rape victim's identity be disclosed? Should communities be identified in a communal clash or gory details of violence reported? General professional codes call for truth, accuracy, impartiality and fair play. Unlike most countries where a free press exists, there is no universally accepted code of conduct in enforcement in India. Even the professional bodies have not been unanimous in developing any. Nor has any serious effort been made by the press to find out what the society thinks of it let alone identify the possible areas of disagreement.

The Indian press had always been known for its sanity over sensitive issues like communal disturbances. But on the threshold of the nineties, it appeared that a large section of the press lost its sense of balance and fairness while reporting such highly explosive issues and events. Barring a few glorious exceptions, most of the newspapers betrayed a distinct and dangerous slant in reporting the Ram Janmabhoomi-Babri Masjid controversy.

For all this, the absence of a code of professional conduct in our country is more or less made up for by the adherence of the press to the social responsibility theory. And the performance of the press can be evaluated on the basis of this single criterion. Such accountability to the public serves as a self-regulatory mechanism in place of an explicit policy.

New Approach

What is the role of the government in making the mass media truly effective vehicles of culture, creativity and expression? Whatever the nature of media ownership-whether government, public corporation, or private enterprise-it is the government which is ultimately responsible for ensuring the use of broadcasting frequencies in the public interest.

Programme content is based on the objectives of the medium, these objectives form the basis for media policies. In our country, the Ministry of Information and Broadcasting monitors the content of the print and electronic media to ensure that all the mass media serve their noble purpose; to be tolls in the process of development and change. The improvement and expansion of the media network is directly linked to this goal.

From time to time various Committees and Commissions have been set up for the purpose of evaluating the working of the communication network. Attempts have been made to formulate a mass media policy based on their recommendations, whether or not these suggestions will be incorporated to the working of the media system depends on the authorities. In response to some of the policy considerations the government may decide to make resources available through direct budgets, or grants or provided fiscal advantages to quality productions, or offer preferential customs duties when importing hardware or software, etc. Alternatively, the media policy itself may be the outcome of such decisions and regulations.

Public participation in the formulation of national mass media policies may be achieved by setting up Mass Media Policy Council, with representatives from among media professionals and others concerned with the role of communication in society.

To implement policy initiatives, institutions may be started or existing ones improved for training and research in the media of film, radio and television broadcasting, printing and book production, etc.

It is of utmost importance to chalk out a detailed communication policy to guide the growth of the communication networks. Piecemeal initiatives only harm the functioning of the media system. A comprehensive policy would help bring about more effective and purposeful communication.

For effective mass communication it is essential that mass communications have as much information as possible about the audiences or receivers. Although mass audience for each medium is seen as a large group of unknown people, there are also specific audience for particular contents.

Information technology has advanced so much in the years that it is now possible for people, while sitting in their drawing rooms, to witness the events taking place in any part of the world or even in space. We can watch the live coverage of sports events or music concerts taking place thousands of miles away. Indira Gandhi was able to talk to Rakesh Sharma in the space shuttle and the whole of the world could watch them in conversation. The war in Iraq was shown live by CNN. Teleconferencing makes it possible not only to watch events far away but also to participate in the action.

Technology has expanded the audiences manifold. Today we think in terms of audiences spread over the whole world, a phenomenon which Marshall McLuhan called global village. National boundaries hold no barriers for mass communication.

Still communication cannot be without targets. Mass communication is effective if it is produced for specific groups people. Thus, on the one hand, audiences of mass communication are spread across the national boundaries; on the other hand media content has to be target oriented.

We have seen that each of these media has certain advantages over the others. We have also seen that different people exhibit different preferences for media use.

The term mass in used to denote different things. In physics, the word mass refers to the quality of matter or material contained in an object. It may also mean a quantity of matter of indefinite shape and size—a lump.

Sometimes the word mass is used to refer to common people, specially the lower classes. Mass also has both negative and positive meanings. In the negative sense, it refers to the ignorant and unruly mass. Mass implies a lack of culture, intelligence and even of rationality. In socialist tradition, mass has a positive meaning. It connotes the strength and solidarity of ordinary working people when organised together for political ends.

In general usage, the word mass refers to people in a large number. If we say masses are ignorant, we mean that a very large proportion of the population ignorant. Similarly, when we say mass destruction means destruction on a very large scale. Mass awareness programme refers to a programme that aims to create awareness amongst a very large number of people. In fact, the important feature of mass is its very large size in terms of the number of individuals. It will be appropriate if we say that mass refers to an infinite number of individuals. The size of mass is very large and unknown.

Secondly, masses are geographically distributed. Very large number of large of people may be attending a public meeting. They are physically present anywhere and everywhere. When we say masses in developing countries are poor we refer to the people living in Africa, Asian, Latin America and perhaps some other and perhaps some other parts of the world as well.

Since the masses are very large in size and in physical terms the people are distributed all over, they are anonymous to each other. They are not even conscious of the presence of one another. There may be a vague feeling of others like us but it is not well defined. Since the people are anonymous to one another, the masses are unorganised. Unlike the people in a public meeting, there is not organisation and therefore no leadership or hierarchy in mass. Further, the masses are not capable of behaving as one unit.

We can conclude that for our purpose that mass to an infinitely large number of people who are physically located at different places and are not organised at all as a group. In fact scholars like Roymard Williams have summarised that masses actually do not exist, it is only a way of conceiving large groups of people as masses.

Society is a large and complex system. With modernisation the complexity of the society further increase. The traditional society has a well defined social system in which individuals are closely tied to each other, mainly through kinship ties. But industrialisation and urbanisation lead to the formation of society where interdependence of numbers in economic terms increase manifold but kinship ties gradually fade away. The individuals become more self-centred. The socially, economically and politically isolated. The modernising societies experience an increase in individuality. The individuals develop a strong alienation with the community as a whole. There is an increased growth of segmental and contractual relationships. Such a society which is very large in size but where members are isolated and relationships are contractual is called a mass society.

However, the concept of mass society is not to be equated with of massive society. It is more than the massive society. There are many traditional society that are very large in a numbers but are not necessarily mass societies. The individuals in a traditional and Selznick have explained the concept of mass society as follows.

Modern society is made up of masses in the sense that there has emerged a vast mass of segregated, isolated individuals interdependent in all sorts of specialised ways. Yet lacking in any central unifying value or purpose. The weakening of traditional bonds, the growth of rationality and the division of labour, have created societies made up of individuals who are only loosely bound together. In this sense, the mass society is something closer to an aggregate than to a tightly knit group.

In fact, as stated earlier, mass society has no continuous existence, except in the minds of those who want to reach as many people as possible. It will be useful to further understand the concept of mass society using a set of contrasts with other kinds of units in social life, like group, crowd and public.

In a small all members know each other. They are aware of their common membership, share the same value, have a certain structure of relationship which are relatively stable. The members of a group interact other for a purpose.

The crowd is a spontaneous collection of individuals. It is temporary and never reappears with the same composition. Members of a crowd may strongly identify with each other. More important, they share the same mood. But there exists no order or structure in the crowd. In many cases the actions of the crowd are emotional, sometimes irrational also. Crowd is physically present within observable boundaries, that is, at a particular place.

Unlike crowd, public is widely dispersed. Its size may be small or large. Generally public is identified with some cause, purpose or activity. Public may be quite heterogeneous and members may not be aware of each other. Usually public is identified by the people who want to perceive a large of people as targets.

Let us illustrate each of the above discussed concept with example from our day to day life. Each one of us belongs to many groups simultaneously. Family is the primary unit and basis for all social life. We are all members of our families. Along with this we are also members of class, team, peer group, club etc. On a railway platform we are a part of the crowd. A crowd is also formed when we together to protest against the non-availability of goods.

Political parties treat us as public when they tell us about their policies and plans. We are public for public for police when it informs us about the imposition of curfew. We move in small group of friends or families in a mela. In the mela, we become a part of the crowd but for those displaying their items we are a public.

The Patrons : The commonly used meaning of the term media audience is the aggregate of persons forming readers, listeners, viewers of different media, that is, the content of different media. In other words, audience is a group if individuals with a common pattern of media consumption. Such individuals share common access or exposure to the same mass communication products.

There are four different ways of looking at media audiences. These are media reach, media access, media exposure and media exposure and media effects. We shall discuss these approaches one by one.

Media's Range : The owners and producers of the mass media conceive the total population whom their communications can reach. The signals of All India Radio are available to about 95 percent of the population living in about 85 percent of country's area. So the total population of India may be treated as audience for All India Radio. Similarly, Doordarshan can claim more than 80 percent of the population as its audience because its signals can reach that many people. For a newspaper, audience would be defined in terms of all individuals who are within the distribution range of the papers. For a cable TV system the audience reach will include all residents within the wired area.

Mass media may be available but the capacity or willingness to us the media may not be there. A large section of the population does not have the radio receivers or television sets. Thus, only those who own the radio sets may be treated as audiences of All India Radio. But access may not overlap ownership. In fact, there are many people who watch television programmes at the houses of neighbours or friends or in community centre. Groups watching a popular television at television shop is a common sight.

Many families do not buy newspapers but their members may read newspapers at various places like teashop, barbershop, library or even at neighbours' or friends' house. This, those who have direct access by virtue of ownership along with those who are non-owners but get exposed in other ways accessible audience. Who are non-owners but get exposed in other ways constitute the accessible audience.

Everyone who has access to radio or television does not necessarily use them. In a family that subscribes to a actually expose themselves to the media audiences. Again, no one is exposed to the total content of any medium. No one listens to all the programmes broadcast by All India Radio. Similarly, it is impossible to watch all the programmes of Doordarshan. Many people do not even glace at the commerce page of the newspapers. There are many young people, specially students, who read only the sports page. So audiences can also be seen as programme specific or content specific, that is, populations actually exposed to specific media contents.

Another important aspect of media behaviour is that all users of media content are not uniformly exposed. There are people who listen to news everyday without fail. Others may listen to news, says on an average of five days a week. Still others may be people whose exposure to news or radio is nil.

The Effect

Another way to think about audiences is in terms of individuals who have been exposed to mass communication products and have undergone a change in their knowledge, opinions, attitude or behaviour. A person may not recall anything of the person, after watching an advertisement, may immediately rush to buy the advertised products. Voters generally do not change their voting preference after listening to election broadcasts by the representatives of political parties.

Value of Audience : The most interesting feature of a mass communication audience is its dual nature. At one level media audience is a collectivity formed in response to media content and defined by attention to that content. When a new newspaper is launched, people gradually start reading it. MTV, STAR TV, and ZEE TV have created their own audiences.

Alternatively, audience may be conceived as collectivity that exists already in the systems and mass media may begin to cater to its information and entertainment needs. Krishi Darshan may aim to cater to the needs of the farmers. Yuvvani attempts to cater to needs of the youth. Femina is meant for the women whereas seminar is meant for the intellectuals.

In the first case, media or its content is the cause of the creation of the audience, but in the second case, the audience become the cause of the creation of the media content.

In many case, it is very difficult to determine whether audience is responsible for creation of the media content or the media content has created the audience. The fact is that the audiences are both, the cause as well as the response to the mass communication process. A new newspaper creates its own readership but at the same time it tries to the needs of the targeted readers.

The original audiences were the sets of spectators for games, stage plays or dispension of justice by the king. Such pre-media audiences existed in all cultures in one form or another. Audience for religious discourses have played a very significant role in the spread of social and political ethos.

Invention of printing revolutionised the whole character of audience. This was the beginning of mass audience. The most important change that the took place was that the audience participation as a private act became possible. People could now take the printed materials to secluded places and undergo a totally private experience. This led to another important change. The audiences become delocalised. It was no more necessary for all members of the audience to be present at one place. A book had readers spread all over the world.

The advent of newspapers created mass audiences in the real sense. Newspapers also converted mass audiences into potential receivers of commercial message or advertising. The advent of electronic media further delocalised the audiences. The information carried by electro-magnetic waves could cross the national boundaries. The audiences were now spread over the whole world. The members were separated from each other and their distance, physical and social, from the communicators also increased.

The audiences now not only took the form and character of masses but they also acquired the features of a mass society. The satellite communication, coupled with cable network on the ground, has brought a situation where the whole world population can be treated as one audience.

The types of audiences can be distinguished based on their demographics characteristics and mental make up.

Elite audience are composed of the people who are decision-makers and trend-setters in the society. They are economically well to do and are highly educated. They have high status in the society. Their numbers is very small but their influence is very strong. They may also be the owners or controllers of the mass media institutions. The members of the elite audience are the early adopters of communication technologies. Their actual media consumption is generally low.

General Audience—They are very large and highly divers groups that represent the broad cross-section of the society. Majority of the people to this category. The media content is generally targeted at them. Their participation determines the success or failure of content or medium.

Specialised Audiences—These audience are composed of individuals who possess similar characteristic. They are relatively small in number. Mass media generate special contents for these audience groups. Programmes for tribals, for housewives, for college students, etc. are example of programmes for specialised audiences. Similarly, journals like Mainstream, Femina and Economic and Political Weekly have limited but known readership.

Market Value : Rise of consumerism has led to a situation where audiences are treated as markets. The media products is a commodity or service offered for sale to a given body of potential consumers, in competition with other media products. Their potential or actual consumers can be referred to as markets.

With the commercialisation of broadcasting and telecasting in our country, the audience are being treated more as markets. There is competition between Doordarshan, STAR TV, ZEE TV, MTV to capture as big an audience as possible. Drastic changes in the programme content of Doordarshan main and Metro channels is an indication of the fact that even the state controlled medium is forced to view audiences as markets. Audience, according to the market concept, can be defined as an aggregate of potential consumers with a known socio-economic profile at which medium or message is directed.

Audience has a dual significance for the media. Firstly, as set of potential or actual consumers of media content and secondly, as the audience for advertising message. Thus a market for media content is simultaneously a market for other products; media serve as advertising vehicles for delivering messages to the potential customers of other products. Advertising is the largest source of revenue for all media. In fact, no medium can survive if not supported by advertising or some other sources. Till the time AIR and Doordarshan were not commercial, the government used to subsidies their services. The most popular programmes of radio and television attract the maximum advertising. Not only that, advertising rates are the highest for prime time programmes. The treatment of audiences as markets has social and moral implication as well. First, when the relationship between the media and audience is that of producer and consumer, the character if relationship become manipulative. The aim is torn sell as much as possible.

Secondly, the members of the audiences are markets and are treated as passive receivers. The audience are lured by cleverly designed message, Thirdly, the success of the media is measured not in terms of needs fulfilled but in terms of sales of the products. Lastly, the market view is that of the media owners and media producers. Audiences never see themselves as markets.

Response of Users : Audience is the single most important element in any conception of mass communication. The development of the relationship between the mass media and the audience can be seen in two contrasting ways. We may consider the availability of a large number of media units as media explosion.

In this conception, the media occupy the central position and information from the various media is seen as acting upon the audience.

But if we observe the media audience relationship carefully, we find that the audiences actually exercise their choice as to which medium is to be used and also which content they would like to be exposed to. Marshall McLuhan saw the audiences at the centre of the numerous attacks by different media. He referred to this as media implosion as against the media explosion.

The efforts required for attending to mass communication may be considered in terms of the availability of the media and the ease with which we may use the media.

Expense involved and the time required are also important factors in "the effort required." Watching a film on television is less expensive, less time consuming and little efforts is required for it as compared to watching a film in a cinema hall.

The uses and gratification theory of the media effects proposes that basic human needs motivate individuals to attend to particular forms of mass media and to select and use messages in ways they find personally gratifying. Thus, audience members make a conscious and motivated selection amongst the various mass media and also amongst the various item of content.

The producers of mass communication keep a hand on the pulse of their audiences in order to make their products more and more acceptable. Audience feedback systems are the mechanisms through which information regarding audience reaction is taken back to the owners, controllers and producers of the media. There are two distinct feedback system; market-based feedback system and research based feed-back system. Mass Communicators receive the following information through the market-based feedback system: (a) audience access to the media; (b) audience exposure to the media.

The above mentioned information is received by the communicators by three methods:

Audiences decision to subscribe to newspapers or magazines is a direct feedback about the popularity of the publication. Rise and fall of circulation is a very important feedback that the market provides. More and more houses paying for cable TV connections indicate the increased popularity of the. satellite channels. At the same time, it may also indicate that the audiences are not very happy with the Doordarshan programmes. Increased circulation of a news paper implies endorsement of the style and editorial policies of the new paper. Sales at box-office is a good feedback about the popularity of a film.

Sometimes, audience reactions to, mass communication are very actively solicited. Coupons, rebate offers, bring-this-and-get-a-discount and similar practices are used to measure the impact of particular promotional efforts.

For books, magazines, papers, video and audio cassettes, film and cable TV connections, the audience behavior has a direct bearing. More consumers mean more revenues. In case of radio and television and even news papers and magazines, the largest share of revenue comes from advertising. But again the advertising rates are determined by audience size, and thereby audiences exert their influence, through indirectly.

Direct Feedback—Mechanisms of direct feedback are provided in each media system. Newspapers and magazines have columns reserved for letters to the editor sent by the readers. Similarly, radio and television networks have programmes reserved for comments, reaction suggestion from the audiences. Unsolicited letters and telephones also provide important feedback. In some cases, casual conversation between employees of mass media and members of audience may provide important feedback.

A careful observation of the media in our country over the last two decades would reveal the felt needs for direct feedback from the audiences increasing. Space devoted to the letters to the editor column in newspapers and magazines has increased. Similarly, more and more air time is being given on radio and television for programmes where representative of the audience are allowed to give their reaction and suggestion.

Media Reviews—Media give the greatest importance to the feedback through the reviews. Every news paper and magazine has media review column written by a media critic. In these columns, the media critics examine the mass communication of radio and television. Similarly, there are regular review of films, audio and video cassettes published in newspapers and magazines.

The role these media reviews is two fold. One, the owners, controllers and specially the producers of radio and television programmes take the comments very seriously. Secondly, these reviews provide information to the audiences. They, in fact, provide expert opinion and influence audience to notice and use particular mass media content. A radio or television programmes or a film or book or a song sequence commented favourably becomes acceptable to the audiences. Many people buy or read a book after reading its review.

In our country, there were no reviews of the print media except in academic journals till recently. Now, some newspapers have introduced these. For example, The Pioneer has a weekly column Blue Pencil by G S Bhargava. It appears on very Sunday and critically comments on the coverage in different newspapers.

Firstly, the critic acts as a link between the producers and the audience. At this point, the critic performs the role of calling attention to the availability of information and recommending responses. Secondly, the critic may provide his expert comments to the producers. At this point, the act is an interpretation of how and why the audiences reacted positively or negatively to the content. Various functions performed by the reviewers can be listed as follows:

(a) Informing audience what is new and interesting.
(b) Raising the cultural level of the community.
(c) Advising the audiences on how to use their time and money.
(d) Helping artists and performers to understand how their efforts are being received by the audiences.
(e) Recording the history of mass communication.
(f) Entertaining audiences with their articles and reports.

The market-based feed back and the reviews are more or less passive systems. Feedback information gets generated without the producers making efforts for it. They leave many questions unanswered. A newspaper will get information that its circulation is decreasing but it is not known as to who are the people who have stopped subscribing and why have they done so. Similarly, media critics may not comments at all on a programme or their comments may be considered subjective. Research based feedback systems are created to provide systematic information about audience response to a particular mass communication products of services.

Many media organisations have their own audience systems. For example, there are Audience Research in All Radio and Doordarshan. These units keep on collecting audiences responses to various programmes. Based on the research finding, the producers may improve their programme; some programmes may be discontinued or their timings may be changed.

Reliable and systematic information collected about the listenership or viewership leads to ratings of different programmes. The use of the media by advertisers and made to reach the desired audiences in a more cost effective manner. In our country, programmes regularly. It is hoped that soon it will evolve into an authentic and reliable system.

Various Types of Patrons : Mass communication does not mean communication for everyone. The media and their audiences come together through a process or natural selection. Media tend to select their audiences by means of content. The audiences also tend to select among and within the media primarily on the basis of content.

Different media may different audiences but there is a considerable overlap between the audiences of one medium with those of the other. Researchers have shown that persons who are above average in exposure to one medium to other media as well. A person who reads a news paper is likely also to read magazines, listen to radio and watch television. Lazarsfeld and Merton called this phenomenon as all-or-non principle. A person interested in escapist entertainment will find it in books, magazines, films and televisions. Anyone who has little opportunity to use one medium because of poverty, illiteracy, ignorance or lack of time or interest-will probably have little opportunity to use any medium.

Newspapers attract very heterogeneous audiences. Children and young people generally do not read newspapers. Most of the readers read only the headlines or at the most read the introductory paragraphs. The finance page has a special readership composed of businessmen and those involved in economic and commercial activities. Sports page has an audience of predominantly young people. Editorial and edit page contents have a very small readership.

Magazines are generally read by people with more education and those belonging to higher economic strata, in general, young people are likely to use newspapers and magazines for entertainment, older people for information and views on matters of public life. Adults do more news reading than young people; the latter pay more attention to photographs and visuals like cartoons and comic strips.

More males read newspaper and also at greater length than females. Higher economic status is generally accompanied by increase in the reading of public news, sports news and society news. People belongs to low and very low socio-economic strata generally read local newspapers or they more attention to local news in regional or national news papers. Middle-class readers to read national news papers. Highly educated and rich people tend to read international newspapers and magazines or the newspapers and publications of other countries.

Before the advent of television, radio was the medium for all classes. However, many people neither owned radio sets nor did they have access to radio in any other way. Transistor revolution spread the ownership of radio receiving sets very widely. But in our country at no time more than 60 percent of the families owned radio sets.

Not-so-poor people and belonging to lower middle classes generally owned single band or two band radio sets. As a consequence, their exposure was mostly confined to local radio station or medium wave stations. People with efficient receiving systems listened not only to AIR but also to foreign systems like BBC, Voice of America, Radio, Moscow.

After the advent of television, radio listening in television owning households has fallen drastically. Many television owning households do not use the radio sets at all. The predominant use of radio today is for music in the background while people are engaged in other works. Many people use radio as an announcer or time. Unlike in U.S and other western countries, radio is not much used in motor vehicles in our country. Audio-tape players have become more popular in cars, buses and trucks.

Young persons use radio to listen to film and non-film music. Adults also listen to music but they tend to use radio as a source of news and information. Housewives may use radio as a companion during the day when they are alone. Young men and women appearing in competitive tests use radio as an important source of information, specially news and current affairs programme. Spotlight and Samayaki are very popular among those sitting in civil services examinations.

The tremendous popularity of television is at the expense of radio. With the advent of television, total time devoted to the media has increased. All sections of the population wish to watch television. Many have their own sets. Others watch television at neighbours or friends houses or at community centres.

News and current affairs programmes of Doordarshan are seen by more educated section of the society. Common people tend to watch entertaining serials. Ramayana on Doordarshan had the largest ever largest ever audience. DD Metro is more popular than the main channel of Doordarshan. Generally, people now subscribe to cable network systems. ZEE TV has a wide audience in Hindi-speaking middle and lower classes. The audience of STAR TV is restricted to middle and upper middle classes. MTV has an audience of young and rich who are relatively more exposed to western culture and values. Research has shown that programmes like Krishi Darshan have very small audiences even among the farmers. It is important to note that the viewers of television also become the audience of the films. A number of films are shown on various channels of television. Besides there are many programmes that the based on films. The television and films industries have become closely related and there are films now produced only for television.

Till television spread its networks, films were the most widely used mass media. All sections of the population, very poor to very rich, went to cinema theatres to watch films.

With the advent of television, VCR, VCP, satellite transmission and cable networks, the films watching in cinema halls has decreased considerably. But the total exposure to films has perhaps increased.

Different types of films have different audiences. Common people generally like to watch masala-films that have an adequate mixture of emotions, comedy, violence, dance, music, sex etc. The new-wave films, the art films and low cost films have an audience that is composed of more educated, socially conscious and intellectual section. Religious films based on epics have an audience composed mainly of rural people, women, illiterate poor etc. Similarly, informative films or films with social messages have different audiences.

Books attract people who are above average in education and also in their use of the serious contents of other media. Books are more likely to attract young adults than older ones, people living in urban rather than in rural areas, people or high income rather than low income. Readers of English books attract audiences more from highly educated, well-off people. Books in Hindi languages are read mostly by the people belonging to these language groups. Generally, book-readers have a high exposure to other media.

Communication is one of those human activities that everyone recognise but few can define satisfactorily. Communication is talking to one another, it is television, it is spreading information, it is our hair style, it is literary criticism: the list is endless. This is one of problems facing academics: can we properly apply the term 'a subject of study' to something as diverse and multi-faceted as human communication actually is? Is there any hope of linking the study of, say, facial expression with literary criticism? Is it even an exercise worth attempting?

The doubts that lie behind questions like these may give rise to the view that communication is not a subject, in the normal academic sense of the world, but is a multi-disciplinary area of study. This view would propose that what the psychologists have to tell us about human communicative behaviour has very little to do with what the literary critic has.

This lack of agreement about the nature of communication studies is necessarily reflected in this book. What we have tried to do is to give some coherence to the confusion by basing the book upon the following assumptions.

— assume that communication is amenable to study, but that we need a number of disciplinary approaches to be able to study it comprehensively.

— assume that all communication involves signs and codes. Signs are artefacts or acts that refer to something other than themselves, that is they are signifying constructs. Codes are the systems into which signs are organised and which determines how signs may be related to each other.

— assume, too, that these signs and codes are transmitted or made available to others: and that transmitting or receiving signs/codes/communication is the practice of social relationships.

— assume that communication is central to the life of our culture: without it culture of any kind must die. Consequently the study of communication involves the study of the culture with which it is integrated.

Underlying these assumptions is a general definition of communication as 'social interaction through messages.'

The structure of this book reflects the fact that there are two main schools in the study of communication. The first sees communication as the transmission of messages. It is concerned with how senders and receivers encode and decode, with how transmitters use the channels and media of communication. It is concerned with matters like efficiency and accuracy. It sees communication as a process by which one person affects the behaviour or state of mind of another. If the effect is different from or smaller than that which was intended, this school tends to talk in terms of communication failure, and to look to the stages in the process to find out where the failure occurred. For the sake of convenience we shall refer to this as the 'process' school.

The second school sees communication as the production and exchange of meanings. It is concerned with how messages, or texts, interact with people in order to produce meanings; that is, it is concerned with the role of texts in our culture. It uses terms like signification, and does not consider misunderstandings to be necessarily evidence of communication failure—they may result from cultural differences between sender and receiver. For this school, the study of communication is the study of text and culture. The main method of study is semiotics (the science of signs and meanings), and that is the label we shall use to identify this approach.

The process school tends to draw upon the social sciences, psychology and sociology in particular, and tends to address itself to acts of communication. The semiotic school tends to draw upon linguistics and the arts subjects, and tends to address itself to work of communication.

Each school interprets our definition of communication as social interaction through messages in its own way. The first defines social interaction as the process by which one person relates himself to others, or affects the behaviour, state of mind or emotional response of another, and, of course, vice versa. This is close to the common-sense, everyday use of the phrase. Sometimes, however, defines social interaction as that which constitutes the individual as a member of his culture or society.

The two schools also differ in their understanding of what constitutes a message. The process school sees a message as that which is transmitted by the communication process. Many of its followers believe that intention is a crucial factor in deciding what constitutes a message. The sender's intention may be stated or unstated, conscious or unconscious, but must be retrievable by analysis. The message is what the sender puts into it by whatever means.

For sometimes, on the other hand, the message is a construction of signs which, defined as transmitter of the message, declines in importance. The emphasis shifts to the text and how it is 'read.' And reading is the process of discovering meanings that occurs when the reader interacts or negotiates with the text.

This negotiation takes place as the reader, brings aspects of his cultural experience to bear upon the codes and signs which make up the text. It also involves some shared understanding of what the next the text is about. We have only to see how different papers report the same event differently to realise how important is this understanding, this view of the world, which each paper shares with its readers. So readers with different social experiences or from different cultures may find different meanings in the same text. This is not, as we have said, necessarily of communication failure.

The message, then, is not something sent from A to B, but an element in a structured relationships whose other elements include external reality and the producer/reader. Processes is that they occupy the same place in this structured relationship. We might model this structure as a triangle in which the arrows represent constant interaction, the structure is not but a dynamic practice.

At one time or another almost everyone has responded to the question "How did this [disaster] happen?" with a statement like "Don't ask me. I just work here." In some cases the excuses is a legitimate one. Someone other than the person making the statement made a decision or took a step which created a problem, but far too often it is a decision, action, or lack of action by the person offering the excuse that led to the inefficiency or failure. Although the performance of every member of an organisation is in many ways influenced by the activities of other members, in the final analysis it is the individuals' choices which decide their destiny in the organisation. It concentrates on communication in organisations because it is through communication that individual employees gain the information on which they base choices and exercise the influence which translates their choices into action. The goal of this book is to give readers a sense of how organisational communication is used strategically, that is, how individual employees analyse the situations thy face at work and choose the appropriate communication strategies to use in those situations. The book assumes that all employees are goal-oriented in some important ways and that if they understand how communication functions in their organisation they will be better able to use their communication skills to achieve their objectives and those of their organisations. The book explains when it is appropriate to use a variety of communication strategies, including the denial or responsibility and the claim of ignorance ("I don't know. I just work here"), and more important, when not to use them.

One of the most important recent developments in the way people look at organisations has been the increasing amount of attention paid to different aspects of communication. Managers and researchers alike have recognised that businesses must maintain at least an adequate level of communication in order to survive, that increasing the effectiveness of communication within a firm contributes to the efficiency of its operation, and that in some cases highly effective communication can increase productivity and eventually profitability. Perhaps more important has been the realisation that people who understand how communication functions in a business, who have developed a wide repertory of written and oral communicative skills, and who have learned when and how to use those skills seem to advance more rapidly and contribute more fully to their organisations than people who have not done so. As a result the number of college courses and professional training programs concerned with organisational communication has mushroomed. Of course employees cannot function effectively unless they possess the technical skills that their positions require. But more and more it appears that being also able to recognise, diagnose, and solve communication-related problems is vital to the success of people in even the most technical occupations. Accountants must be able to gain complete, accurate, and sometimes sensitive information from their clients, supervisors of production lines must be able to obtain adequate and timely information on which to base their decisions, managers of different divisions must be able to give their subordinates clear instructions, make sure those instructions are understood, create conditions in which their commands will be carried out, and obtain reliable feedback about the completion of the tasks that they have assigned. In a recent survey of 700 middle managers, almost 85 percent of the respondents reported that it was their subordinates' communication skills (or lack or them) which determined their success or failure in critical situations. Although these managers also noted that factors like their subordinates' job-related expertise and loyalty to their supervisor and organisation also had an important impact on their effectiveness, it was their ability to communicate effectively that was crucial in most cases.

However, being able to communicate effectively at work requires two kinds of knowledge. First, it requires an understanding of the relationships that exit between communication and the operation of organisations. Since communication processes influence the way an organisation operates and are simultaneously influenced by key characteristics of the organisation, neither organisations nor organisational communication can be understood adequately if they are examined in isolation of each other. Second, effective communication depends on employees' understanding how to choose appropriate communication strategies in different situations. This book intends to provide readers with an understanding of strategic communication skills, the ability to analyse a situation, select an appropriate communication strategy from a number of available options, and employ that strategy in an optimal way. However understanding strategic communication demands that an individual understand how communication functions in organisations, how it creates and solves problems, how it makes some situations occur and how it prevents others, how it makes some outcomes more probable and others improbable. This chapter will introduce these two most important concepts: the role of communication in organisations and the characteristics of strategic organisational communication. Subsequent chapters will expand each of these concepts and explain how they contribute to the success of complex organisations and their members.

Historically, formal organisations have been examined from two very different perspectives. One view has depicted them as the combination of a number of different components, each of which is linked to each other on the basis of some carefully planned and clearly articulated design. People who accept this perspective believe that organisations are designed in three distinct steps. Designing an organisation begins with an analysis of a potential market and a decision about what products-goods or services the organisation should produce. Designers then decide which tasks must be performed in order to produce the desired output and determine how each of these tasks can be completed most efficiently. Finally, designers organise the various tasks into structures and sequences which are intended to maximise the efficiency of the total operation. Since many of the components of the organisation are people, someone must be assigned the job of seeing that all who are involved in each part of the production process understand the tasks they are to perform, how they are to accomplish those tasks, the fact that they must accomplish them in a timely and efficient manner if the organisation is to function properly. In this perspective, communication is important for instrumental reasons. It functions in ways which allow members to share the information necessary for the successful completion of a complex array of interdependent tasks. Although the end products, task requirements, employee skills, or relationships among these components may change when market conditions or technologies change, this perspective assumes that the rational design of an organisation will stay relatively constant. At least, the organisation will stay stable enough so that the designers can draw a picture, usually in the form of an "organisational chart," which accurately reflects its operation.

Another viewpoint describes organisations as complex, interdependent matrices of ongoing process, not as a rational, carefully planned combination of interrelated static components. This distinction is important for two reasons. First, it leads to a view of the members of an organisation as actors, not as relatively inert components of the organisation. Employees constantly are making choices about how they will act in the variety of situations they face. Second, organisations are networks of interdependent human actors whose actions both create situations they face allow them to respond to those situations. Although organisations can be designed by objective, outside planners, their designs constantly are in a state of change. Businesses are composed of large numbers of people who constantly are monitoring their own actions and the actions of others, processing that information, and choosing those courses of action that they think are appropriate.

This description of organisations does not imply that their members are either manipulative or Machiavellian although it would admit that some of them are. Instead, it suggests that people are active agents who have their own reasons for acting as they do. They are not mechanical components of the production process, doing only what they are designed to do in precisely that way in which they are designed to do it. They are choice-making members whose actions are part of a complicated array of ongoing processes.

Within this perspective, communication is important to an organisation for two reasons. First, communication is the means through which people acquire the information and develop the criteria by which they decide how to act. Second, communication is the process through which they put their choices into practice. That is, through communication members of organisations learn that there are precedents in their organisation which constrain their choices, and they learn what those precedents are. Through communication with others, they develop and express the purposes which guide their actions. They are able to consider the potential effects of different actions only because they are capable of communicating. In addition, it is through communication that members of an organisation are able to coordinate their actions with other members of the organisation. Because the complex array of tasks that must be performed in an organisation are independent, each member of the organisation can perform only if other members do also. In almost situations, only a small proportion of the activities of any one employees will be necessary preconditions for the successful action of other employees. However, for each member of the organisation, there are some actions that must be taken if the organisation is to operate. And, because all members must depend on the actions of some other member(s) in order to do their jobs, they must be able to predict accurately what those other people will do in different situations. Being able to do so requires employees to understand why they act as they do and to recognise that they regularly respond to certain situations in predictable ways. Communications is the process through which people make sense out of the actions of other people, it is the means by which they are able to understand how they can coordinate their actions with the actions of others.

Human action is contextual, it is the result of the choices people make within the situations they perceive themselves to be.

Unfortunately, these two views of organisations and communication often are seen as being mutually exclusive. Scholars who focus their attention on the design or structure of organisations and the functions of communication in organisation that have been described in this chapter often overlook the complex processes through which people decide how to act at work. Conversely, when scholars concentrates on understanding the relationships between processes of communication and processes of organising, they often deemphasise the tasks people perform at work and the function communication plays in the completion of those tasks. Understanding strategic organisational communication requires an analysis of both the functions of communication in organisations and the processes through which communication guides the actions of members.

Practical Side

In some important ways communication functions as a tool for members of organisations: It allows them to issue, receive, interpret, and act on commands; it allows them to create and maintain productive business and personal relationships with other members of the organisations; and it allows them to manage ambiguity and uncertainty.

Two types of communication make up the "command" function: direction and feedback. People perform necessary task effectively only when they choose both to initiate action and to limit their actions in clearly prescribed ways. Some members of organisations, usually those given the formal titles of supervisor or manager, issue messages which tell othei members to take action and to limit that action to a particular series to be taken at a specified time and at a specified place. If the person to whom the message is directed does not act, or if the person acts inappropriately, the command function will not be wholly successful. It is inevitable that people will resist commands to some degree. In order to function, organisations must influence people to act in ways in which they otherwise would not act. For instance, few humans would choose on their own to perform seemingly minor, repetitive tasks hour after hour, day after day. But a large proportion of production-oriented organisations could not exist if it was not possible for some people to persuade other people to perform these tasks at a predetermined rate for a predetermined period of time with a minimal amount of creativity. Assembly lines operate successfully only because a complex array of very specific commands are communicated to a large number of people in a way that somehow persuade them to follow those commands exactly. If any worker a does a job in a new, varied, unanticipated or creative way, the productivity of the assembly line is reduced. When automobile workers respond to the boredom of their jobs by choosing to install parts backward, upside down, or not at all, the quality of the final product usually us reduced. When they respond by celebrating the end of monotonous week with a Thursday afternoon or Thursday through Sunday visit to a local bar, their ability to follow commands exactly on subsequent days usually is reduced. Although these deviations from expected behaviour often do little damage, they create enough problems that most Americans learn at an early age "not to buy a car which was built on Friday." Other types of organisations involve even larger numbers of people whose actions must be initiated and controlled if the organisation is to function. Consequently, the command function of communication relies on process of persuasion and influence. Its effectiveness depends on the availability of some form of influence and some communication strategies through which some members organisations can persuade other members to act in specific and unnatural ways.

The command function also involves the production of adequate feedback about the actions that actually are taken by people who have been issued commands. Supervisors often assume that their subordinates will carry out their commands. This assumption is especially strong when the supervisor has issued a set of routine instructions. Comfortable in the knowledge that their commands will be carried out, supervisors instruct other people to take actions which, when completed, will allow the task that the unit has taken on to be accomplished. If any of the people who are involved in the command process fail to carry out the commands they were given properly or promptly, the supervisors will need to modify the commands that were given to the other people and accurate feedback about the extent to which each of their commands has been carried out.

Almost all people who have worked in organisations which produce tangible products can remember instances in which they found themselves surrounded by piles and piles of partially finished products because some person or group of people failed to receive, understand, or carry out commands. These situations usually strike the workers who are gazing at the piles as being terribly funny, both because they know that the error is someone else's headache and because they have been allowed to take a lengthy break while waiting for the bottleneck to be eliminated and the unfinished products to reach their stations. Rarely does the supervisor who issued the commands find the situation quite as humorous. The piles of unfinished products do, however, give this supervisor feedback about the effects of the commands. Organisations do seem to function more efficiently when supervisors have access to more timely and less tangible command-related feedback.

Command-related communication typically comes in one of two forms: publications and instructions. The differences between the two forms are important because employees' reactions to a command are related in part to the form in which it is issued. Organisations produce a variety of formal written policies and procedures. The published communications have three important characteristics. First, they create the impression that the commands is directed to a general audience. No one has been picked out as the recipient; the message seems to be addressed to anyone. Second, they create the impression that the command is official; that is, it is written by the organisation or by someone who represents the organisation rather than by any one individual. Finally, They suggest, both that the command is a relatively permanent injunction and, indirectly, that the problem it addresses is important and recurring.

In contrast, instructions are oral commands, generally given in a face-to-face encounter and addressed to a single person or clearly defined group of persons. Instructions are highly flexible commands which seem to be transient rather than permanent.

They are viewed as being linked to a specific problem which is relatively new, rare, or unprecedented and are from an individual rather than from the "organisation." Because publications and instructions are different forms of commands, they are appropriate to different kinds of situations. The success of any command depends on part being issued in the proper form.

One function of communication in formal organisations is the command function. Because organisations are composed of large numbers of people who play interdependent roles, their actions must be coordinated effectively. Successful coordination is achieved when members initiate the actions they have been directed to undertake. It occurs when some members of the organisation communicate in ways that create the kind of situations in which other members of the organisation will choose to take the precise actions that are envisioned in the commands. Both the process of creating a appropriate situation and the creation of clear and influential command messages depend on the strategic competence and communication skills of the participants. The command function of organisational communication relies totally on complex processes of constructing, interpreting, and choosing actions in response to a particular type of communication.

Organisational communication also fulfils a relational function, businesses are composed of human beings who are involved in interpersonal relationships with other human beings. Unlike non-work relationships, in which people have a relatively wide degree of freedom in deciding who to form relationships with, the structure of formal organisations dictates that each employee must form relationships with a clearly defined group of people. Sometimes, perhaps most of the time, members of organisations are required to form effective "working relationships" with people with whom they never would choose to form personal relationships. For a number of reasons, imposed relationships are less stable and more prone to friction than are "natural" ones.

Like natural relationships, working relationships can succeed only if the parties involved can achieve at least a minimal degree of understanding and cooperation. To do so they must be able to comprehend the meaning of the messages they exchanges with each other, assess each others' motivations with some degree of accuracy, and negotiate some agreements about how they will act toward one another. Unless these minimal requirements are met, the development of effective working relationships is impossible. Like all relationships, working relationships inevitably will involve some friction, misunderstanding, and conflict about the proper nature of the relationship. However, in non-working relationships the parties usually develop a degree of commitment to each other and to the continuation of the relationship. Typically they will have voluntary started relationship and will made a number of decisions to continue it in spite of conflicts and frictions because they continue to receive benefits from it. To some degree at least, their commitment is mutual and intrinsic to the relationship. In working relationships, the parties may have very little commitment to the relationship itself. Someone or something else, a supervisor of the organisation-initiated the relationship, the parties stay in it because their roles in the organisation seem to demand that they continue to work together, and the benefits they receive from it are derived from their place in the organisation rather than from the relationship itself.

When people lack an intrinsic commitment to a relationship, it is more difficult to resolve their differences and the degree of communication skills necessary to maintain it is greater. Minor irritations are not overlooked, minor conflicts are not easily resolved, and major disagreements erupt into open confrontation because neither party is as concerned that an open conflict might threaten the continuation of the relationship. Fortunately, and almost inevitably, people do form close personal relationships with some of those with whom they have effective working relationships. Although this means that their work situations will be more pleasant than otherwise would be the case, it also adds a number of complicating factors to the relationship. They must negotiate boundaries the two dimensions of their relationship, arriving at some mutual agreement that they will communicate differently with each other while at work than they will while in other contexts. In addition, they must cope with the fact that their personal relationship is being observed by a large number of people with whom they have working relationships and that the existence of the personal relationship may further complicate some of their working relationships. "Don't have an affair with your boss, or at least don't let anyone know you are" really is very good advice.

Through processes of communication, working 'relationships are formed, maintained, and in some cases, transformed into personal relationships. As these relationships begin and develop, the participants in them begin to perceive their jobs, their organisation, and their roles in that organisation differently. These perceptions combine to define the situations that each individual believes one faces at work. Perceptions provide the parameters and guidelines within which each individual makes decisions about how to act. These choices influence the character of the relationships with other members of the organisation, and these changed relationships influence other members' perceptions of their organisation and thus influence their actions. Other members' actions in turn alter the character of their relationship and consequently influence the parameters and guidelines within which other members make their choices. In a complex matrix of processes, communication, relationships, perceptions, and choices, the "situations" in which people find themselves at work are created.

In addition, the relationships that people form at work influence their performance in complicated and important ways. Employees' perceptions of and satisfaction with the tasks they are asked to perform are affected by the quality of the relationships they form with the people around them. Similarly, their satisfaction with their jobs will influence their ability to form valued and stable relationships with their co-workers. The quality of employees' relationships with their co-workers influences their ability to gain the information and support they need in order to perform their job and influences their willingness to provide the information and support their co-workers need. The nature of supervisors' relationships with subordinates influences their ability to understand the messages they exchange and the probability that any particular command will be carried out. For all these reasons, the relational and command functions of organisational communication are interdependent and interactive. The success of one depends largely on the success of the other.

The third major function of communication in organisations is the management of ambiguity. Humans are essentially choice-making beings, and their activities at work are essentially choice-making activities. Each day they face a series of decision-making situations. In some of these situations they make choices for the organisation; in others their decisions are more personal. Their choice making is complicated by two factors. The first involves the multitude of motivations an individual generally incorporates into decision making. In each organisational choice-making situation, a person simultaneously must consider the effects selecting one of a number of available options will have on one, one's co-workers, and one's organisation. In some situations the personal concern will be more important than the relational or organisational ones; in others, the decision maker will be concerned primarily with the interests of the organisation and only indirectly concerned with one's own interests. Some different situations will involve different combinations of self, relationship, and organisational interest, organisational choice-making is a complex and potentially confusing process. If the individual faces a situation which provides clear and explicit guidelines for determining how these interests should be balanced, it is relatively easy to make effective choices. However, choice making typically takes place in situations in which the guidelines for action are either unclear or contradictory. Communication then becomes the process through which an actor manages an ambiguous situation.

Second, organisational choice making is complicated by the ambiguity of the organisations themselves. The objectives of an organisation at a particular time often are not clear to its members. In addition, the objectives of a particular unit in the organisation or of particular members also may be ambiguous. In organisations which are undergoing rapid change or which exist in rapidly changing environments, these objectives may be particularly confused.

Also, the complex histories of modern organisations complicate the choice making of their individual members. Most situations are not completely unprecedented. The people involved have faced similar situations in the past and can draw on those experiences to help them make effective choices in the new situation. But precedents sometimes hurt choice making more than they help it. Individuals will recall that in similar situations in the past they made a certain choice. They also remember that their choice was followed by a certain good or bad result. They will tend to believe that it was their decision that led to the result. If the outcome was favourable, they will tend to repeat the decision. If the outcome was negative, they will tend to avoid taking any similar course of action. But in most cases, choices made by a single individual are only one part of a complicated series of events and decisions which lead to an observed outcome. Not realising this, individual tend to make subsequent choices based on the mistaken belief that it was their choice that cause a particular outcome to occur in the past. In this way the availability of precedents can reduce the quality of the choices that are made.

Precedents complicate choice making in another way. When faced with a decision people tend to search their memories for similar situations. When they discover a precedent they feel a great sense of relief because the new situation suddenly becomes clearer and easier to manage. However, people often discover precedents which really are not precedents at all. They recall past situations that they were able to manage and then define the new situation in a way which makes it seems similar to the past, comfortable situation. Through this process they often overlook important differences between the two.

Organisational choice-making situations are inherently complex and almost always ambiguous. They are simplified and sometimes distorted by characteristically human thought processes. They also are simplified and sometimes distorted by typical communication process. Members of organisations use communication in two primary ways in their attempts to manage ambiguity. First, they communicate to each other in order to structure, to make sense out of, new situations. They seek out information which will help them gain a perspective on the problem, and they seek out support from others which will confirm their interpretation, of the problem and strengthen their commitment to a particular course. In addition, they use communication in favour of a particular way of looking at the problem and in support of a preferred option. Through communication with other members of the organisation they are able to create a shared mutual understanding of what a problem is and how it should be addressed. If the information they gain through communication has been sufficient, relevant, and accurate, and if the shared perspective that they have created has been appropriate to the problem, communication will have improved their decision making.

But if the information gained has been inadequate in any significant way, or if the perspective that has been adopted by the people who were involved in the communication is flawed in any important respect, the availability of communication will have reduced the quality of the decision and further complicated choice making in the future. In the latter case, organisational communication has been used to reduce ambiguity artificially; it has not been used to manage ambiguity successfully. Sometimes processes of communication allow members of organisations to make foolish decisions and become comfortable with and strongly committed to them. In other instances communication allows members to make choices which satisfy their needs and the needs of their organisations. In some cases organisational communication even may provide the basis for making the best possible decisions. A variety of processes inevitably influences the potential effectiveness of the ambiguity-management function of organisational communication.

Communication fulfils three major functions in formal organisations—a command function, a relational function, and an ambiguity—management function. For any organisation to succeed, each of these functions must operate at or above some minimal level of effectiveness. For any individual members of an organisation to perform their roles successfully, they must be capable of using a variety of communication skills to issue effective commands and respond adequately to commands issued by others, to develop and sustain efficient working relationships, and to manage ambiguity strategically. However, some kinds of organisations are designed in ways which lead their members to rely most heavily on one of these three communication functions. Some organisations rely most heavily on the command function, others on the role of communication in the management of relationships, and others on the effective management of ambiguity.

Every organisation must have adequate command, relational and ambiguity managing communication. However, the relative importance of these three functions varies in the three different types of organisations. "Traditional" organisations, rely most heavily on the command function of communication and less heavily on the other two. Human relations and resources organisations depend on effective relational communication. Some versions of this type also rely heavily on the command function. In most versions the ambiguity-managing function has a limited role.

The final type, "systems-contingency" organisations, relies heavily on ambiguity-managing communication. In this type, relational and command functions, are important in some situations and less important to others. In fact, it is the assumption that command and relational communication must be combined in different proportions in different situations that distinguishes the systems-contingency type from the traditional and human relations and resources type.

The ideas of the German sociologist Max Weber have been an important part of the study of organisations for decades. In America Weber is best known for his analysis of bureaucracy and bureaucratic organisations and for his discussion of the relationships between the characteristics of a culture and the uses of three different types of leadership-traditional, rational-legal, and charismatic authority. An equally important but less well-known component of Weber's work is the overall perspective that he took in studying organisations, the theory of "ideal types." This perspective rests on a particular set of assumptions about the nature of organisations and the appropriate means of studying them. His ideas provide a method through which employees can understand their organisations and make effective decisions about how to act on them. Weber's primary assumption was that organisations are composed of human actors who are enmeshed in independent activities and who continually are making decisions about how to act. Their choices are based on the meanings they attribute to the actions of others and on their interpretations of the organisational situations in which they are involved. When people enter formal organisations they bring with them a long history of monitoring their actions and the actions of others, of processing the information they obtain, and of choosing from among a number of options. People from a particular culture develop ways of monitoring perceiving, and acting which are very much like another.

These perceptual "filters" are not identical, of course, because every individual has had unique experiences and has been part of a particular group of relationships with others. To some extent all members of a culture will have developed their own beliefs about what actions are "normal" and proper and about what meanings can be attached to different messages. However, within all this diversity and individuality lies a common core, a culture-bound framework for making sense out of people's actions and of deciding how to act in response. It is this common interpretive schema that defines a culture and distinguishes it from other cultures.

When employees from a particular culture come together within a formal organisation they bring with them a common way of interpreting and responding to one another. But once they come together, their interpretive frameworks begin to change in subtle but important ways. Human develop their interpretive frameworks through their experiences with other people. Relationships formed with people at work provide us with additional experience communicating with and making sense out of the communication of others. As a result, people drawn together in a formal organisation begin to form new "mini-cultures" at work. These new ways of interpreting and acting both retain the basic frame-work of the employees' general culture and reflect the more specific frameworks that develop through working relationships. The complicated interrelationship that exists between the broad patterns of action that characterise a society and the patterns that develop within an organisational "culture" was the basis of Weber's theory of ideal types.

Weber argued that researchers can understand organisations if they can understand how actors (employees) in them interpret their surroundings and choose among the wide variety of different courses of action that are available to them. The study of organisations should begin with careful observations of the choices that employees make. Eventually these observations will reveal that different groups of employees use different sense-making schemes. Researchers will begin to recognise that members of some organisations typically interpret and act in ways which are different from those in which people act in other organisations. At some point these observers will begin to construct mental images of organisations whose employees share the same basic interpretive frameworks.

For example, employees may perceive that their organisation is like an army—a formal structure with a clearly defined administrative staff which, for some as yet unexplained reasons, is obedient to commands issues by superiors. This type of organisation would function properly if it exhibited a number of necessary characteristics: each member of the staff occupies a specific position in the organisation which has been clearly defined, written duties and a clear place in the hierarchy of the organisation: each person knows who the supervisor is? who the subordinates are? and how each of them fits into the hierarchy of the organisation: each employee is selected on the basis of qualifications for the job, determined by some "objective" measure like educational background or a score on an examination; works under a contract which can be terminated if performance is inadequate; and can be promoted to a more responsible or higher paying position only on the basis of performance or seniority.

Of course, there may be no "real" organisation anywhere which has all these characteristics. Because this type of organisation is an abstraction, which represents the perceptions of a number of different groups of employees, it exists only in the mind of the observer; it is an "idealised" example of a particular "type" of organisation. It is an image of how a certain type of organisation should be designed and how it ought to operate, note a summary of the characteristics and operations of a group of real organisations. But these mental conceptions of ideal types can be useful for researchers. If researchers or managers or any other members of a real organisation understand how different types of organisations should be designed and operated, they can use that knowledge to detect and solve problems in their own organisation. To do so, they would examine their organisation, looking for features of its design or operation which do not correspond to the necessary features of the most relevant ideal type. Armed with perceptions of the essential features of a number of different types, the researcher or manager can discover cases in which the members of the organisation do not choose to act in the ways that are necessary for the organisation to function efficiently. Once these discrepancies are discovered the observer can make careful decisions about how to alter the organisation or change the conditions under which the members make decisions about how to act. When these changes are implemented, the real organisation will begin to operate more like the ideal type to which it is most closely related.

Unfortunately, these are very abstract ideas. A summary of them might increase their clarity. Weber's approach to the study of organisations rests on his theory of ideal types. It suggest that an observer can begin to understand how an organisation operates by attempting to understand how its members interpret and respond to the situations they face in the organisation. The observer then can design the organisation to increase the probability that its members will choose to act in precisely those ways that are in its best interests. Employees always will make their own decisions about how to act. They are human, and consequently they will continually be involved in observing, processing, and responding to their surroundings. But they make their choices based on their interpretations of the situations they face. Both their perceptions and many of the key characteristics of the situations they face can be created strategically through communication. However, appropriate situations can be created only if the people who design organisations know the elements that must be included. The search for these necessary features begins with the construction of a group of ideal types of organisations. Observers ask "What kinds of organisations do employees' interpretive frameworks suggest are possible?" and construct a list of features necessary for each of these "mythical" organisations to operate most efficiently. The most important features will involve the conditions under which employees will choose to initiate and limit their actions in desired ways. Among these necessary features will be certain characteristics of organisational communication. After observers have delineated the features of each ideal type of organisation, they can begin to examine existing organisations, searching for points at which the real organisations differ from the ideal type. If they can detect important differences and determine the reasons for them, they can begin to isolate problems in the real organisation and develop strategies for reducing them.

Of course, Weber assumed that most of the "observers" would be scholars involved in academic research. But his perspective can just as readily be used by employees. The social psychologist Fritz Heider once argued that human beings think like researchers think, that the same analytical tools that theorists use to understand the world around them can be used by other people to understand their environment and to decide how to act in the situations they face. Heider's notion that people are "naive theorists" suggest that all theoretical perspectives, of which Weber's of ideal types is one, are based on our interpretations of reality and can be used by us to understand the realities that surround us. This assumption underlies the ideas that will be presented throughout the book. If readers can understand how communication functions in different types of organisations, they can examine their own organisations, determine how communication functions there, and choose the best communicative strategies for responding to the situations they face. Equipped with an understanding of how communication functions in different types of organisations and explanations of why communication functions differently in real organisations, readers can intelligently observe their own organisations and ask themselves these questions: how does communication operate in any organisation? How must people, including myself, act in order for this organisation to operate successfully? Why do they sometimes act in those ways and sometimes act differently? How can I act in order to make the organisation work more effectively and to make the greatest contribution to its success and to my advancement?

These are the kinds of questions. Weber suggested that researchers must ask; the questions provide the kind of information from organisational theory has made. More important, they are the kinds of questions that members of organisations must ask themselves before they can choose the best communication strategies to use in different organisational situations. Through understanding how different types of organisations operate and why a particular organisation functions differently, the "naive theorists" who make up an organisation can adopt the best available communication strategies.

Organised Effort : For more than two thousand years

communication scholars have argued that people communicate most effectively if they adopt the communication strategies that are most appropriate to the situations they face. Plato's intellectual rival, Gorgias, argued that knowing how to adapt to different situations was the only kind of knowledge that was available to human beings and, consequently, should be the focus of education. Some equivalent to Gorgias' concept of adaptation, an idea he labelled Kairos, has been important to the study of human communication since his time. Historically, training students in the art of adapting their communication to different situations has involved two steps: (1) teaching them to analyse the situations they face and choose the best strategies for those situations, and (2) equipping them with the repertoire of communication skills needed to implement those strategies. This book will concentrate on providing readers with the first kind of knowledge. It will examine the myriad of features which make up organisational situations, plan the kinds of communication in which employees must be competent, they and their organisations are to function effectively, describe the strategic through which they can gain the information necessary for them to adapt intelligently to the situation they face at work, and provide guidelines for choosing the optional communication strategies to use in those situation. Although it will discuss a variety of communication skills and suggest when and how those skills might be used by members of organisations, it will make no attempt to provide detailed training in the skills themselves.

Bibliography

Angharad, N. Valdivia : *A Companion to Media Studies,* Blackwell, New Delhi, 2004.

Arya, Umesh : *News Vocabulary's,* Anmol Publications Pvt. Ltd. New Delhi, 2000.

Awasthy, G.C. : *Broadcasting in India*, Allied Publishers Private Ltd., Bombay, 1965.

Balsara, Rati : *Advanced Dictionary of Journalism,* Dominant Books, New Delhi, 2004.

—— : *The Working Journalist's Guide to Substance and Style,* Dominant Books, New Delhi, 2003.

Barnett, Marvin : *Survey of Broadcast Journalism 1970-71 : A State of Siege,* Grosset and Dunlap, New York, 1971.

Bernard, H. W. : *Principles of Journalism : A Basic Text*, Allied Publishers Private Ltd., New Delhi, 1998.

Bhatnagar, V. : *Role of Press in Women's Development Issues,* Printwell, Jaipur, 1996.

—— : *The Role of Press in National Resurgence,* Printwell, Jaipur, 1996.

Boyce, George, James Currant and Paul Wingate : *Newspaper History : From the 17th Century to the Present Day,* Constable, London,1978.

Budd, R., Thorp, K.R., and Donohew L. : *Content Analysis of Communications,* MacMillan, New York, 1967.

Cameron, James : *Point of Departure,* Oriel Press, London, 1978.

Carey, James W. : *Communication as Culture : Essays on Media and Society,* Routledge, New York, 1992.

Chakravarty, Suhas : *Press and Pliant Governors,* Kanishka Publishers, New Delhi, 1997.

Chaturvedi, J.F. : *The Indian Press at Crossroads,* Media Research Foundation, New Delhi, 1992.

Chauhan, S.S. : *Principles and Techniques of Journalism,* Vikas Publishing House, New Delhi, 1982.

Chauhan, Swati and Navin Chandra : *Hand Book of Journalism Style and Substance,* Kanishka Publishers, New Delhi, 1999.

Cohen, S. and Young, J. : *The Manufacture of News,* Constable, London, 1973.

Critchfield, Richard : *The Indian Reporter's Guide,* Allied Pacific Pvt. Ltd., Bombay, 1962.

Curran, J., Gurevitch, M. and Woollacott, J. : *Mass Communication and Society,* Edward Arnold, London, 1977.

Czitrom, Daniel J. : *Media and the American Mind* : *From Morse to McLuhan,* University of North Corolina Press, Chapel Hill, 1998.

Davis, Howard and Walton, Paul : *Language, Image, Media,* Basil Blackwell, Oxford, 1983.

Davison, W. Phillips : *Mass Communication Research* : *Major Issues and Future Directions,* Praeger, New York, 1974.

Defleur, M. L. and Others : *Fundamentals of Human Communication,* Mayfield, London, 1993.

Desai, Amit : *Journalism and Mass Communication,* Vikas Publishing House, New Delhi, 2002.

Dwarakadas, Jamnadas : *Political Memoirs,* United Asia Publications, Bombay, 1991.

Eaman, Ross A. : *The Media Society* : *Basic Issues and Controversies,* Butterworths, Toronto and Vancouver, 1987.

Eisenstein, E. : *The Printing Press as an Agent of Change,* Cambridge University Press, New York, 1978.

Emery, Edwin : *The Press and America,* Prentice-Hall, New Jersey, 1997.

Emest, C. Hynds : *American Newspaper in* 1980s, Hastings House, New York, 1980.

Gandhi, M.K. : *Young India* (1919-27), Tagore & Co., Madras, 1922.

Gunning, Robert : *The Technique of Clear Writing,* McGraw Hill Book Co., New York, 1999.

Gupta, Hemendranath Das : *Desabandu Chittaranjan Das,* Publications Division, Government of India, New Delhi, 1960.

Gupta, Om : *Media aur Samaj,* Manohar Publishers, Delhi, 2002.

Gupta, Om, Ajay S Jasra : *Information Technology in Journalism,* A.&M. Publishers, Delhi, 2002.

Gupta, V.S. : *Media and Development,* Har-Anand, New Delhi, 1994.

Hachten, W.A. : *The World News Prism : Changing Media of Inter-national Communication,* Iowa State University Press, Iowa, 1996.

Hall, S., Clarke, J., Critcher, C.Jefferson, T. and Roberts, B. : *Policing the Crisis,* Macmillan, London, 1978.

Hernandez, Ramos, P.F. and Schramm, W. : *Development Communication—History and Theories,* in *International Encyclopedia of Communications,* Oxford University Press, New York, 1989.

Hohenberg, John : *The Professional Journalist,* Holt, Rinehort and Winston, New York, 1969.

Jhingan, M.L. : *The Economics of Development and Planning,* Konark Publishers, New Delhi, 1994.

John,· R. Zaller : *The Nature and Origins of Mass Opinion,* Cambridge, New York, 2001.

Johnson, Stanley and Julian Harriss : *The Complete Reporter,* The MacMillan Co., New York, 1942.

Joseph, M. K. : *Outline of Editing,* Anmol Publications Pvt. Ltd., New Delhi, 2000.

Khemchand, Rabin : *Journalism and Human Development : Making of the Global Newsperson,* Dominant Books, New Delhi, 2001.

Kichar, R. S. : *Electronic Media and the Library Services,* Discovery Publishing House, New Delhi, 1999.

Krippendorff, K. : *Content Analysis : An Introduction to its Methodology,* Sage, California, 1980.

Kumar, K. J. : *Media Education, Communication and Public Policy,* Himalaya Publishing House, Delhi, 1990.

MacDougall, Curfis D. : *Interpretotive Reporting*, MacMillan Co., New York, 1957.

Madhavan, P. K. : *Careers in Publishing,* Vikas Publishing House, New Delhi, 1997.

Mark, C. Jaylor & Esa : *Imagologies Media Philosophy,* Routledge, UK, 1996.

McClelland, D.C. : *The Achieving Society,* Princeton, New York, 1961.

Mujuni, J.P. : *Studies in Media Education*, Deep & Deep Publications, New Delhi, 1995.

Mumtaz, N. : *Journalism Guidance, Measurement & Statistics,* Takshashila, 1996.

Panickkar, K.M. *: The Foundation of New India,* George Allen & Unwin, London,1963.

Rau, M. Chalapati : *The Romance of the Newspaper,* National Council Educational Research and Training, Delhi, 1975.

Rau, M.C. : *Social Change and the Unchanging Press*, Government of India Publication, New Delhi, 1982.

Sampath, K. : *Introduction to Educational Technology*, Sterling, New Delhi, 1981.

Schwarz, P.A. and Krug, R.E. : *Ability Testing in Developing Countries : A Handbook of Principles and Techniques*, Praeger, New York, 1972.

Sethi, Patanjali *: Professional Journalism,* Orient Longman, Bombay, 1974.

Tahmankar, D.V. : *Lokmanya Tilak,* John Murray, London, 1956.

Verma, J.S. : *Media and Cultural Environment*, Methuen, London, 1969

Vernon, P.E. : *Personality Assessment*, Methuen Co. Ltd., London, 1964.

Vilanilam, J.V. : *Reporting a Revolution,* Sage, New Delhi, 1989.

Vittal, N. : *Information Technology,* A.& M. Publishers, Delhi, 2001.

Zaina, A. Michael : *Codes for Media,* Rashmi Publications, Chennai, 2002.